Dorset at War

Dorset at War

John Murphy

Dorset Publishing Company

Knock-na-cre, Milborne Port,
Sherborne, Dorset DT9 5HJ

*First published 1979 in Great Britain by Dorset Publishing Company,
Knock-na-cre, Milborne Port, Sherborne, Dorset DT9 5HJ. Copyright
© Dorset Publishing Company, 1979. Main text by John Murphy
with additional material and picture research by Rodney Legg. No
part of this publication may be reproduced, stored in a retrieval
system, or transmitted in any form or by any means, electronic,
mechanical, photocopying, recording or otherwise, without prior
permission of Dorset Publishing Company.
ISBN 0 902129 33 3*

---

*Picture coverage substantially due to the Department of Photography
at the Imperial War Museum, with special thanks to Jeff Pavey, Alan
Williams and Mike Willis.
Typesetting by Sue Robins, with presentation by Jonathan S. Hebert,
at Photo-grahics, Lower Lye Farmhouse, Yarcombe, Honiton,
Devon.
Technical assistance with the reproduction of plates from
contemporary British and German documents provided by Jack and
Rosemary Denner at Charlton Reproductions, 26 Charlton Road,
Shepton Mallet, Somerset.
Printing by Redwood Burn Limited at Yeoman Way, Trowbridge,
Wiltshire.
Cased in buckram by the Binding Division of Redwood Burn Limited
at Royal Mills, Esher, Surrey.*

Contents

Foreword

NO PERSON who was alive during the traumatic years of World War Two could write an account of that era without nostalgia seducing the pen from fact into myth. I found my first attempts at recording Dorset's war smacked more of a Vera Lynn song lyric than an authentic story of those years. So I scrapped the pages and started again, to produce, hopefully, a factual history book. In doing this I have had to include the good and the bad, and consequently will upset a few people. To avoid the truths would be to please a minority and mislead the majority.

War, generally, brings out the best and the worst in people. 1939-45 in Dorset was no exception to this. Many mayors shed the inane, silly grins of fete openings and became real leaders of their towns, often stirring the people with Churchillian-style speeches. Public-spirited men and women volunteered in force for important tasks, but this admirable rush to serve was tarnished by an accompanying undignified stampede to secure reserved occupations.

Even worse were the people of the county who saw the American 'invasion' as compensation for years without a tourist trade. Like vultures, they pounced on the young foreign soldiers, a large percentage of them already labelled for death, to treat them like several summer seasons of moneymaking rolled into one.

To put the remainder of the book in the right perspective it is necessary here to go back to the mid-1930s. This was a time of no hope — unemployment was high and those lucky enough to be in work were constantly in fear of losing their jobs. Wages were low, class distinction rampant. Britain's leaders, muddled and ineffective in peacetime, were soon to be found even more wanting in war.

Tory Dorset was confused. Incredibly, the politics of Hitler were less abhorrent than the biggest fear of all — communist Russia. Viscount Cranborne, the Parliamentary member for South Dorset, tore away more Dorset security by turning on his own government when the semi-ghost Chamberlain turned the other cheek at Munich. Cranborne resigned as Under Secretary for Foreign Affairs, and let rip with vehement speeches that condemned his own party as much as the Nazis.

Such unprecedented behaviour soon had him hauled before the South Dorset Conservative Party, but it was more of a token inquiry to appease the 'true-blues' of the county than a Spanish inquisition. Deep down inside themselves, everyone knew that Cranborne spoke the truth. A member of the Government, Duff Cooper, had resigned at the time of the Munich Nazi's laugh-in, and Winston Churchill, bloodshed yet to float him from insignificance, had found some thirty stealthy allies to join his opposition to his own government. Cranborne came out fighting again as the staggering British approach to war took on a semblance of sense in 1939. This time, ostensibly at least, he had his party in his corner.

Apprehensive and bewildered, Dorset slid into six years of war that was to see it in the front line for danger, and playing many a vital role. When the fighting was over, the county was never the same again. Whether the change was for better or worse is for the reader to decide, and this book should assist in the making of such a decision.

If I have given older folk a pleasant sojourn into the past, and showed the young what life was like then, this writing will have been worthwhile. I pray that it does credit to those who lived through it, and, above all, those who died.

This book has been part of my life for more than three decades. It goes back to when I was 12-years-old, and cycled excitedly to meet the first giant US Army road convoy threading its way to Portland. Trying to stifle the fear slammed into me by the roaring of many motors and the nerve-jangling crash of tank tracks against the tarmac, I met the young men who, as olive-drab clad ghosts, have plagued me ever since.

Perhaps this is my penance for having enjoyed those terrible years of war with the ignorance of a schoolboy. A merciful ignorance that, in 1944, spared me the awesome knowledge that the boys I laughed and joked with were rehearsing for their own violent deaths. I saw them leave, filing aboard landing craft — still grinning, but all wondering what lay in wait for them across the English Channel. No conjecture could have stretched to the horror of the Normandy landings, particularly Omaha Beach — where my briefly-known friends went ashore.

Armed with my own sparse memories I moved among the past-middle-aged of Dorset, doing my research among those who remember. The reaction of the majority shocked me. The German is forgiven, the wartime Italian has become a joke, but dislike of the American GI has survived through the years.

The pages that follow are unlikely to chip away at this long-established acrimony, but I feel I will have achieved something if they bring a better understanding of the period and the men who lived, and died, during it. Which raises the question: "Why bother, after all these years?".

We all have to bother — for we meet our yesterdays again tomorrow.

Let slip
the dogs of War

January 1939 — September 1939

Be strong and of good courage: That way and that way alone will calamity be averted.
— *Viscount Cranborne, Member of Parliament for South Dorset.*   January, 1939

DORSET GRABBED at 1939 as if it was to be the best year ever. Train whistles shrieked at midnight. Hands were joined throughout the county while *Auld Lang Syne* was sung with as much fervour as *Deutschland Uber Alles* was being rendered in Europe. War belonged to some other world, some other time. This was a new year.

Motorists, still a novel and privileged breed, filled the two hundred tables at Askers Roadhouse, and danced to Dorchester's Novelty Aces seven-piece band. In Weymouth, Maurice Moores and his Boys, at the Regent Dance Hall, cashed in on the cinema's influence, and had four hundred dancers prancing to *Heigh Ho,* the dwarfs marching song from Disney's *Snow White.* An additional treat was two plays by the 'J Juveniles,' though presenter Mrs Jarvis must have whispered a prayer when she chose the titles — *Peace* and *Goodwill.*

If military men were not praying, Colonel R.M. Dawes must still have had his fingers crossed behind his back when he wished revellers at Bincleaves Hall — the home of the Dorset Regiment RA(T) — a 'Happy new year.'

With the doors of the Gloucester Hotel tightly closed against the cold winds sweeping Weymouth's Esplanade, and any thoughts of war, Mr and Mrs Gordon Cummings delighted guests with the right kind of food from a buffet, the right kind of music from Harry Crocker and his band, and an elaborate welcoming of the new year.

For a while, the fears of the county were lost in this silly season. But it ended, and Cranborne was there like a returning toothache. All listened to him. The docile accepted his intentions as good, the thinkers wondered if he, like other politicians in the country, was not just making personal publicity out of the crisis. Neither side have been effectively answered since.

Hero or charlatan, Cranborne dowsed the cigars at the annual smoking concert in Portland's Conservative Club, when he advised: "Be strong and of good courage. That way and that way alone will calamity be averted."

While Portlanders were stubbing butt ends on this glum warning, it was the turn of the South Dorset Victuallers to hear the bad tidings. At the Clinton Hotel, the mayor of Weymouth, Councillor J.T. Goddard, introduced the president of the association, Philip Pope, who kept things nice and light with a talk on the assessment of licensed premises and malting barley problems. The second speaker, Alexander Pengilly, did not spoil any digestions with his breezy account of the qualities needed by a member of Parliament. Then it was as if a Panzer division had knocked a wall of the building out. A cold chill swept the room as Cranborne got to his feet.

First praising Parliament as "that great British institution", he went on to speak of peoples in Europe who had been unable to stand the "heady wines of Democracy". Freedom had slipped into licence, licence into anarchy, leaving democracies to crumble and be replaced by dictatorships.

A few days later, speaking at the Grand Cinema, Swanage, he raised hopes by saying that he did not believe in the inevitability of war. Then he made a seaside winter even more drear, by adding that neither did he believe in the inevitability of peace.

Asking Cranborne to a party had the effect of Dr Marie Stopes asking the Pope in for a chat, but it became the gimmick of the day, and the ladies of Wyke Regis Women's Institute felt that he must be their guest. Firing words like bullets, he shot down talk of twin-sets and tweed skirts. Hitting hard at Neville Chamberlain, and the little result his approaches to Hitler and Mussolini had brought, he said: "These dictators have tasted blood and have applied a policy of force and had considerable effect with it. We must make England an impregnable fortress."

This war-on-war-off confusion had the people of Dorset shattered. Though it was pleasant to believe in Chamberlain's peace, it was more realistic to accept Cranborne's views. Most compromised by ignoring both, and the dithering went on.

Proving that party time was not yet over, six hundred old folk gathered at Weymouth's Sidney Hall for the 63rd annual dinner under the bequest of Sir Henry Edwards. Served by two hundred voluntary waiters and waitresses, among whom were several prominent local personalities, each oldster was given a party hat and a pound of tea apiece. Each of the men had a bonus of a quarter ounce of tobacco.

The Dorset Heavy Brigade, at their Weymouth headquarters, had two celebrations in one at their annual get-together, for the commanding officer, Colonel G.G.H. Symes, had been awarded the Order of the British Empire in the new year honours list. Such a gathering of soldiers could not avoid a mention of war, and it came from Brigadier Boger. Referring to the previous September's test mobilisation, he displayed the incredible naivety of those dangerous times, saying "the fact that the Territorials are ready is, no doubt, one of the causes of preventing war". Brave and willing as the Dorset lads were, their presence would hardly make one change of plan necessary where Hitler's mighty army was concerned.

January ended in a bad week, with gales sending the sea crashing over Chesil Beach to flood part of Portland. Then Tuesday brought spring-like weather that lured people out of doors, to catch them in a blizzard on Wednesday. But this nasty bit of weather didn't prevent guests coming from as far afield as Ilminster to the Corn Exchange, Dorchester, for the annual dinner of Dorset agricultural workers.

The big draw was the star guest — Clement Attlee, the leader of the opposition. Never before had a Labour leader had such a chance in the Tory fortress of Dorset. Hitler had pulled down the Conservative banner, and the clumsy Chamberlain had trampled on it as he meekly moved away from Munich. All wanted to know what Labour would have done if Munich had been their responsibility. This was Attlee's big chance — and he muffed it.

For the first part of his hour-long speech he touched on many political subjects, and agriculture, naturally. He advocated nationalisation as the only answer to the industry's current difficulties. At last, he got around to the big question, and answered it with a parable. Unfortunately, Attlee's reply belonged more to the obscurity of political speeches than it did the beautiful simplicity of Jesus Christ.

"People may ask what I would have done at Munich," he began, to be interrupted by a member of the audience advising "I wouldn't go there if I were you." - -

"Exactly," commented the unruffled politician. "Suppose you had a man who was driving a heavy lorry. He drove it mile after mile on the wrong side of the road, and after narrowly missing other vehicles, came to a position where a collision seemed inevitable, swerved and ran over a child. You might ask me what I might have done had I been driving. I would not have driven on the wrong side of the road. The trouble is that the government has been driving on the wrong side. I would remind you that the right side for an Englishman to drive on is the left."

This bit of double-talk left the audience with just one mystery — what would Attlee have done at Munich?

Another event causing consternation at this time, though not of the political variety, was the Dorset press ball, to be held on Shrove Tuesday at the Sidney Hall, Weymouth. The prediction was that the ticket price (6s. 6d.) was exorbitant for the area, and the hall would be empty. Somehow, possibly motivated by the promise of two stage and screen stars being there, eight hundred people found the necessary money, which, incidentally, included a meal.

Just after midnight, Colonel Hansen, VC DSO MC — commanding officer of the Verne Citadel's 2nd Lincolnshire Regiment at Portland — stepped on to the stage that was ablaze with lights, and introduced film star Leslie Howard to the huge crowd. Suave and sophisticated, every inch a star, Howard said how he loved Dorset, and had been stationed at Bovington Camp during the Great War, spending every off-duty moment exploring the countryside.

Thrilled by this articulate display by an idol of the silver screen, the crowd was now hungry for glamour. On stage came the lovely Ann Todd, the star who had New York raving about her performance in *South Riding*, but she was scriptless in Weymouth, and too shy to utter a single word. The crowd fell into a disappointed silence, then gave the star loud applause as she managed a charming "Thank you" when presented with a bouquet.

Weymouth in February appointed an air raid warden, who had to have a car, and they paid him a yearly sum of £75 to run it. Added to his salary of £250 per annum, this gave him a gross weekly income of £6. 5s. 0d. For those in work, a new Ford Prefect was £145, and a three bedroom house £500. But there were 4,229 unemployed, 1,106 of them in Weymouth.

February brought a distraction for the romantics of the county, when a fashionable London wedding linked two well-known Dorset families. The bride was Joyce Harcourt-Slade, younger daughter of Mr and Mrs James Harcourt-Slade, of Bradford Peverell, and the groom was Philip Rolph Pope, second son of Major and Mrs Rolph Pope, of Dorchester. The wedding took place at St Mark's church, North Audley Street. It wasn't likely that the reception was a dry one, for the groom was a director of Dorchester brewers, Eldridge Pope.

But it was not all frivolity. One government department decided to do something constructive in case war came, and all local authorities were asked to do a survey to see how they could house children who might be evacuated from the large towns and cities. Weymouth's mayor Goddard liked words — and he sent every householder in the borough a long letter which explained, how, why, where, when and for what reason evacuees might come from the cities to the area. He could probably have cut his letter down to the bit that interested most people: they would be paid 10s. 6d. a week for the first child billeted, and 8s. 6d. for each additional child.

This move by one section of the government seemed to spark off action that was remarkable in those days. The Prime Minister made a stirring call to service in a Monday evening wireless broadcast. This was followed up with a national service guide popping through every letterbox. Inquiry bureaux opened in most towns. At 10 St Thomas Street, Weymouth, W.A. Russell was in charge, and together with his assistant, A.E. Jones, and a band of clerks, was able to supplement the bald information given in the guide.

The aim of national service was twofold. Firstly, to fill vacancies that existed in various branches of defence, both civil and military. Secondly, to safeguard the essential industries and services in wartime, therefore avoiding recruitment of those who in the public interest had to be retained in their occupations. Volunteers came thick and fast for Air Raid Precautions (ARP), the regular police, police auxiliaries, regular fire service, auxiliary fire service, and, in lesser numbers, the regular fighting services.

Dorset got involved in another child refugee scheme at this time — with the Germans. A committee was set up to supervise the settling of German children in the county. H.A. Natan, of Clayesmore, a school at Iwerne Minster, was secretary, and among the prominent people on his committee were the Bishop of Salisbury, the Bishop of Sherborne, and the mayor of Blandford, C.S. Tripp.

There was a massive response to Natan's public appeal for homes for the children, who were aged five to seventeen. Most offers came from lower income families, and many from the poor. Several parents wanted a companion for an only child, and the demand for girls exceeded by far that for boys. Plans for the older children included training in handicrafts and agriculture. An appeal was made to farmers to take boys over the age of fourteen, for training on the land.

Thinking of war provoked a fear of poison gas. It had been used on the battlefields in the previous war, and Mussolini had already employed it in the horn of Africa. Protection against this hideous form of warfare was given priority, and Weymouth was ahead of the rest of the county. Councillor Jackson, a busy man, had been around all the schools instructing children on the fitting of masks. Warehouses were commandeered as main depots, while distribution centres were set up at schools. These were often unnerving places, with women fainting and even having hysterics while the Martian-like masks were fitted.

When he'd fitted the kids out with masks, Jackson was looking around for another problem to tackle, and he asked the town clerk, Percy Smallman, if evacuees would be coming to Weymouth. The clerk replied that he had interviewed a representative of the government department responsible, and had been told that if an emergency arose, and if

Weymouth was considered a safe place, refugees from the big towns and cities would be sent there.

Dorchester councillors were getting an equal number of 'ifs' when they inquired. Rumours about evacuees were getting a lot of people into a state. Councillor Guppy said he'd heard that six thousand evacuee children were being sent to Dorchester, and he was concerned about housing this number. Perhaps the most urgent question asked by councillors, obviously under pressure from the people, was if billeting would be compulsory. This query was motivated by the fact that those most able to accommodate evacuees were those least likely to want to.

One 'if' that had completely disappeared was the one prefixing the sentence "if there is a war". Everyone now knew there was going to be a war, the big question was when. Dorset was not alone in being unprepared, for the whole country had been misled and confused. Far from being ready for war, Dorset was unprepared even to get ready.

But a slice of social conscience — a rarity in this period — had the county anticipate the welfare state. Until then, doctors had not been for ill people generally, but for those who could afford them. But Dorset introduced a scheme whereby for 10d a week, families, in conjunction with national insurance, could register with the doctor of their choice and have free medical advice and treatment. Headquarters of the scheme was at 22 High East Street, Dorchester.

A fear can always be replaced by a bigger one, and those employed in the offices of local authorities found that a threat to their job caused them more worry than the promised war. This was a proposed reorganisation of local government, referred to as "a dangerous spirit abroad" by E.P. Everest, chairman of the Parliamentary committee of the Dorset branch of the Rural District Council Association.

When the local council boys had left the hall, wondering if they were to be left in a good job, another group moved in to inaugurate a national service register. Lord Shaftesbury, Lord Lieutenant of Dorset, suggested that the boy scout motto 'Be prepared,' was one that should be impressed on the community at large. The point missed by Lord Shaftesbury, and by all other speakers at that time, was that the community was willing to be prepared, if one of the speakers could advise them on what to prepare for.

Like now, housing then was used as a weapon to control the population. Even in our modern times, no student remains an anarchist when he has married, got responsibilities, and needs a house. It has gone on so long that it is accepted. Everyone knows there is a housing shortage, nobody asks why. But, in 1939, the scandal of Cerne Abbas did hit the headlines. No house had been built there in living memory and many villagers lived in condemned property. It caused a public outcry when a family just managed to escape outside as their house collapsed.

But the publicity did not last long enough to help the villagers. The Cerne story was pushed from the headlines by the shock resignation of L.H. Scott, second officer of Dorchester's fire brigade governors. After having put in nine years and five months valuable service, Scott packed it all in just when it looked as if he'd be needed. Dorchester council met to consider his reasons for resigning, but could not do so because he had not told them. Reluctantly, they accepted his notice.

Back at Weymouth, the council was getting its priorities muddled. Parents wanted to know what shelter would be given children at school in the event of air raids. The council's first idea was to close the schools. But this wasn't practical. To close them each time there was an air attack would require some agreement with Hitler on warnings being given. To close them indefinitely could mean that at least one generation would grow up without education. This idea was dropped in favour of digging shallow trenches close to each school. These pithy efforts afforded no protection, and brought protests from all quarters because the majority of the trenches had inches of water at the bottom.

Brushing this problem aside, the council got down to what they considered real business — building a new road from Redlands to Westham embankment bridge. The war was to stop this, but there was no dissent in the chamber at the time. But a new bit of stupidity did cause a split in the council, when a proposal was brought forward from the beach and entertainment committee to build a new golf pavilion at the cost of £2,700. This was seen by several councillors as a project for the "chosen few".

Alderman F.W. Peaty called it wicked, and Alderman Moggeridge said the links would make a valuable building site, suggesting that the council take them over for this more community-minded venture. In support of the new pavilion, Councillor Wheeler said the money spent on the building, which would have accommodation for a steward, would be a good investment as the links were a valuable attraction for the town.

With flooded trenches for children, no air raid shelters for adults, and no thought being given to coastal defences, the borough treasurer was asked what Weymouth was worth on a commercial basis. With Hitler the only possible customer, and he wouldn't have to pay, it is surprising the question was taken seriously. The council officer estimated £2,233,000, proudly adding that the town was in a strong financial position. Among seaside towns with a population of 20,000 to 30,000, Weymouth was the second lowest rated in the country, and only two towns had a better rate collection.

More danger conscious than most towns, Dorchester proved it by setting up a Police War Department, which cost £1,105 for the first year.

With an air of defeat already over England — and the war had not yet started — there were many competitions for the dreaming up of slogans that would convince everyone that the truth was lies. This may have had some psychological effect generally, but it did L.H. Douch of Broadmayne a bit of good. He won £1,000 in a national contest.

Weymouth's luck was still out, and one of the few men doing something constructive in the threat of war, Air Raid Precautions officer, Captain Lyndon Moore, was leaving town. He had applied for a post in Newport, Monmouthshire, and got it despite stiff competition. Weymouth Debating Society tossed around the question of compulsory call-up. The society was evenly split — fifteen votes each way — but the government solved the problem shortly afterwards by introducing conscription, for the first time ever in a Britain at peace.

No one seemed certain about civil defence. L. Ribbings, joint secretary of the Dorset National Service committee, tried to clear things up by making a statement saying that those in reserved occupations could enrol for civil defence, but were precluded from registering for full-time service.

Trouble seemed a bit closer when A.W. Street, of the Air Ministry, in London's King Charles Street, announced that bombers were coming to Dorset, though they would be on our side. A section of Lyme Bay, four miles square and with its inner edge six miles from Lyme Regis, had been designated as a bombing range. It was to be used in daylight hours only, and not at weekends. Bombs dropped there would not exceed 120 lb in weight, unless sand filled.

On directions from the government, and under the presidency of Trevor Morgan KC, the Western Traffic Area was preparing for war by dividing transport into divisions made up of smaller groups, to allow for more efficient possible use of goods vehicles in an emergency. In London (14s. 0d. return on a cheap ticket) there was a chance to join crowds on pavements watching a parade that was aimed at boosting the flagging morale of Britain. Trying hard to do that were one tank, a machine-gun carrier, and a lorry.

Surrounded by military, air, and naval stations, Weymouth was in a position to do far better than the big city, but Poole did a bit of one-upmanship. On a Sunday afternoon, three thousand participants lined up close to Poole's shopping centre. In a procession one-mile long, which represented every department under the heading of national service, they wound along a two-mile journey through the streets, watched by forty thousand people.

The Territorial Army was there, in full regalia and with mechanised units and modern arms mounted for inspection on trucks, followed by air raid wardens, fire service members, auxiliary fire service, ex-service organisations, special constables, St John Ambulance, Red Cross, an Air Force lorry carrying monster bombs, a mobile first aid station, and even contingents of the scouts and guides. Three bands provided marching music — from the Royal Tank Regiment at Bovington, the 4th Battalion Dorset Regiment, and Dr Barnado's Nautical School.

The vehicles encircled the cycle track at the far end of Poole Park, while the marchers formed up in front of a platform from which Colonel J.J. Llewellin and representatives of various political parties, briefly but effectively put over the needs of the country. What went down best with Poole's seventy thousand residents was the news that the whole grand display had cost them just £25. The corporation paid only for some roping and timbering in the park, and teas for the organisations involved. Each unit had been responsible for its own transport costs.

Faces were red in Weymouth. Perhaps wishing he had thought of the idea, Goddard, the mayor, drummed up his own bit of patriotism by slamming those who dashed from cinema and theatre seats while the national anthem was being played. This failed to come up to Poole's splendid effort, but it did show that Weymouth's first citizen was on the right side.

Every day was bringing something new — like blackout rehearsals, news that the 4th Battalion Dorset Regiment's establishment total of 633 men had recently topped the thousand mark, and the less inspiring information that Billy Cotton would be appearing in Weymouth on Sunday 6 August, with Elsie and Doris Waters following him the next week.

The animosity most felt toward the Germans, the local authorities, government, or even each other, was channelled into another direction when that good old target for hate, the Irish Republican Army (IRA), was blamed for the cutting of telephone lines on the Dorchester to West Stafford road, severing communications with Warmwell aerodrome.

At least there were no distractions in despising the IRA. Taking a real dislike to the Nazis was difficult, for no one seemed to know if they were really baddies. It all became more muddled when the Wessex Tea Rooms, Dorchester, was used by Ralph Jebb, prospective British Union of Fascists candidate for West Dorset. Jebb lived at Downton Manor, near Salisbury, and was a close friend of Mosley. He was the only person who received the movement's highest badge of honour, the 'Gold Distinction'.

If a second opinion was needed, it could be had at the Corn Exchange, Dorchester, where Sir Oswald Mosley was giving an address. The fascist view was arguably not a great distance further to the right of Dorset's Tory politics of the day. This made a difficult and uncertain situation even more confused.

A friendlier exercise in public relations came at Warmwell Royal Air

Force Station, when pressmen were invited to a preview of the coming air day. Reporters with the stomach for it could take a trip into the air. It paid off, for ten thousand people packed in the following Saturday to be thrilled by a spectacular put on by Warmwell Armament Training Squadron (ATS). There was a low-level fly past in the afternoon, and some astounding aerobatics by Flight Lieutenant Finny, an RAF instructor from the Air Service Training School at Hamble, Southampton.

The highlight of the show came at teatime when most of the people were in the refreshment tents. The siren sounded and the crowd tumbled out into the open air. But they did not head for the specially constructed shelters. Instead they stood excitedly watching five Ansons sweep in to attack a factory building far out on the airfield. Three Hurricanes came roaring in on the Ansons, one of which was brought down while the other four flew off. Within minutes, the Ansons were back, closely followed by the Hurricanes. A thrilling battle ensued until a whistling bomb did its work and the factory blew up in smoke and flames.

Few in the crowd could have realised they were watching a sample of the future in Dorset skies, although death not publicity was soon to be the end product.

Altogether some forty aircraft took part in this display — Wallaces,

Dorset Territorials have a 'pull through' time at Corfe, where they were in camp during the remaining days of peace in 1939. The part-time soldiers did not have a good time, being washed out during torrential rain.

Ansons, Harts, Fairey Battles, Hawker Hurricanes, as well as a squadron of reconnaissance craft — Singapore flying boats with four Rolls Royce engines apiece and a speed of 136 mph, from Calshot on Southampton Water.

To learn a bit more about fighting wars, the Dorset Territorial Regiment went off to camp at Corfe, were washed out in a cloudburst and sat in a sea of mud singing *Pack up your troubles.* A real circus came to Dorchester. Three special trains brought the gigantic Bertram Mills Circus after its nineteenth and most successful season at Olympia.

August bank holiday weekend was a crazy one. A kind of last fling had 100,000 people flock into Weymouth. The police were besieged by trippers looking for lodgings, they slept in cars along the Preston beach road, and the sands looked like an open-air doss house. All records were broken at the railway station on Saturday, with the Great Western Railway bringing 25,342 visitors, and 10,823 coming by the Southern Railway. Post offices were crowded, and 100,000 "Wish you were here" cards were sent off over the weekend. Even a cloudburst on the Saturday afternoon failed to spoil things, although five thousand tons of water dropped on the town in five minutes.

It was still raining during the next week, when King George VI arrived at the railway station for a review of the Home Fleet — euphemism for a

The beauty queen of Weymouth, Anne Morgan, shakes hands with her counterpart from Swindon, Olive Browning, on Weymouth sands on a Wednesday afternoon in the late summer of 1939.

mobilisation. Most of the reserve sailors recalled that after that review they did not get home for another six years. Many never returned at all.

Crowds lined the street as the royal car drove to Bincleaves, though the Fleet was hidden from shore by a thick mist. "Don't worry, Mr Mayor, it's raining everywhere," the King cryptically replied when he received an apology for the weather. It was Weymouth's big day, but it was paid for in discomfort that night. The King's departure had delayed trains, leaving 45,000 people milling about at the station. With all platform space taken, the outside yard was packed solid. Restaurants and cafes throughout the town had been filled to capacity all day. Many trippers were unable even to get a cup of tea, which led to an outbreak of fainting at the station.

The local St John Ambulance Brigade, soon to start stirling years of war work, moved in swiftly to deal with the casualties. Two doctors worked unceasingly. The waiting room was an improvised casualty station, and when this was full the parcels office was taken over. The crowd at the station that memorable day was more than double the previous record.

The last outing of peacetime for Weymouth's butchers, on the Thames in 1939. In the picture are Mr and Mrs R C Andrews, Mr and Mrs Lewington, Mr and Mrs Shiers, Mr and Mrs Lawson Jones, Mr and Mrs Ferguson, Mr and Mrs House (Maiden Newton), Mr and Mrs Avant, Mr and Mrs Gould, Mr and Mrs Dan Lawrence, Mr Davis (Portland), Mr and Mrs Cox, Mrs Arscott senior, Mr and Mrs Arscott junior, Mr and Mrs Howell, Mr and Mrs Blackburn, Mr and Mrs Habgood, Mr and Mrs Whittle and Harry Virgin (Yeovil).

A toast by tank crews and fitters in the dining hall of the Royal Armoured Corps at Bovington. They drink to success in a new war, but their faces are hesitant and apprehensive.   Photograph: Imperial War Museum.

A 'dummy' war took place in Weymouth the following Saturday. It began at 6 pm, with zero hour from 11.30 until half past midnight, when complete blackout was enforced over a thirty mile area. Air raid sirens were sounded, aircraft droned overhead, destroyers tried to enter Portland Harbour, and the ships of the Home Fleet were blacked out.

The lessons learned were never fully known, but it was clear that if Hitler attacked when a north-north east wind was blowing, as it had been on the night of the practice, few people would have heard the warning. Not that the residents of Abbotsbury were left in any doubt. The death bell was tolled, and people tumbled out into the blackened streets, wondering what was happening.

Some things were coming together well, though. Like the light anti-aircraft battalion of six officers and 76 men, divided into headquarters and two troops, that Captain C.J.L. Sheppard MC of High House, Lynch View Avenue, was instructed to form. Each troop was to have a Swedish design light ack-ack gun of the type much publicised in the press and cinemas at that time. Leslie Hore-Belisha, the War Minister, said that similar guns would soon be manufactured in Britain, and until then those of foreign make would immediately be available.

The first evacuees arrived. Tired from a long journey, bewildered looking, but still managing a wan smile, the pathetic line of them paraded out of the station. Reception and administration was remarkably good. They were taken to centres in buses, sorted and documented, then dispersed to various billets. This initial organising, which had been anticipated as the most difficult part of all, was actually the easiest. The mass evacuation had no facilities or time for social or religious selection. Dorset ladies cringed as their carpets were used as if they were London playgrounds. Sparkling white sheets were by morning soaked with urine, often by the mothers as well as children.

No criticism can be levied on either side. Lodgers and hostesses eyed each other, both sides close to tears. Both had led entirely different lives until then. Both had expected something better and were disillusioned.

Now Mrs Trott's got a mother and child;
As polite and kind as could be.
They don't give her any trouble at all,
And the mother helps with tea.

Cumberland Clark,
the Bournemouth poet,
in a contemporary verse
entitled 'Evacuation'.

September 1939 — December 1939

My message to the people must be what is, I feel, an echo of their own thoughts. It is that victory and long lasting peace will soon be ours.

— Councillor A.T. Moss, Mayor of Wareham &
Purbeck Council. Christmas, 1939

SUNDAY MORNING, 3 September 1939, divided the intentions of Dorset folk. Some sat at wireless sets to hear the declaration of war direct from the Prime Minister, whilst others heard the message from clergymen in pulpits. Such an announcement was profoundly dramatic at St. Peter's Dorchester, when the rector, Rev. A. Wilkinson Markby, told a congregation packed with military personnel that the country was at war.

Most people found the realisation a relief after the anticipation. Words had been spoken, we were at war at last, but what did that mean? Neville Chamberlain could not say what it meant. It was not so long before that he had said there would not be a war. Would the Germans attack Britain today, tomorrow, next week, or never? As the days passed without anything disturbing occurring, the war game did not seem to be a bad one. A new life began to take shape in the county. Neighbours who had ignored each other for years, were now gossiping over the garden wall. Humour was to the fore, with householders putting crudely written posters in their windows, saying "Wanted for Murder — Adolf Hitler".

But among this fun there was still an underlying anxiety, shown by notices in the windows of ARP headquarters, such as "Aircraft passing overhead this afternoon — don't be alarmed, they are British". It was apparent that when the people weren't laughing together, they were worried. Something was sure to happen soon. Not knowing where, or what it would be, was a secret nightmare for most.

In Weymouth, a straggle of late holidaymakers found a different kind of fun on the sands, helping corporation workmen fill the small sacks that were placed around the town as a protection against bomb blast. In response to Dorchester's borough surveyor, H.G. Strange, 24 volunteers turned up at the depot in Poundbury Road, to fill five thousand sandbags before the day was through.

Dorchester council set up a War Cabinet with facilities for dealing with matters at twelve hours notice. Weymouth followed, finally shelving the go-ahead plans that had made it infamous in peacetime. Alderman Moggeridge showed signs of being a prophet when he suggested that the council be put into cold storage for five years, then brought out to "carry on with the job". But members adopted the plan of the clerk, Percy Smallman, that the council be put into recess indefinitely. The war cabinet comprised the mayor, Goddard, deputy mayor Bert Biles, and the town clerk as sub-controller.

Top priority in the county now was the assembly and distribution of gas masks. The clergymen of Dorset, recently under heavy fire for preaching war and peace at the same time, put in a lot of time at this work. At Charminster, the Rev. D.B. Eperson was in charge, assisted by Captain Bennett of Wolfeton House, who had returned to the village as its controller of the ARP.

Dorchester's 14,000 masks were handled by willing volunteers. There was great praise for Miss Ruegg, headmistress of Dorset County School for Girls. Her staff and pupils cycled considerable distances to take charge of assembly and distribution. Thanks also went to Major R.G. Bridgeman, governor of Dorchester prison. His unlikely helpers, the inmates, had forfeited their recreation period to assemble gas masks. Praise for the convicts was a bit muted, as no-one was sure whether it had been voluntary work or if they had been given no choice.

ARP wardens distributed the three hundred masks at West Stafford's Institute, where anyone in difficulties putting on the sweaty rubber-smelling things received help from Mrs Slade, of Bradford Peverell. Blackout had come into force two days before war was declared. All street lighting and illuminated advertisements were switched off. All premises had to be effectively screened, car headlights fitted with regulation masks, and sidelight glasses packed with two thicknesses of paper. Pedestrians were disoriented. After dark there were regular splashes caused by bodies falling into Weymouth Harbour. Any humour in this situation was dispelled by more than one of these accidents being fatal.

It was not long before blackout infringements led to court hearings. Few could take the lighting restrictions seriously, and there was sympathy with one Weymouth man. Called from his bed by a warden, in the early hours of the morning, a slit of candlelight at the side of his window was pointed out to him. With great patience he turned the warden's head

The country starts a war in 1939, and Weymouth starts a new football season with a team comprising R. V. Clarke, Ashmead, R. Symes, J. Wales, Condliffe, N. Clarke, Rodd, Parsons, Lovell and Hellier.

A defiantly happy group pictured on Weymouth sands shortly after the outbreak of war. Soon, the roundabout in the background was dismantled and replaced by desperate defences against the expected German invasion.

seaward, where searchlights from the ships of the Royal Navy were lighting the town brighter than noon on an August Monday.

On the fateful day of 3 September there were already four thousand evacuees in the county. This number increased weekly, with adherent problems growing even faster. Some evacuees were complaining that the area was too quiet for them. They expressed a desire to be home, where they could dance *The Lambeth Walk* in the streets on a Saturday night. By that time, even lots of the do-gooders were wishing that the refugees were doing their dance — anywhere but in Dorset.

Wareham's time was just beginning, on a Saturday afternoon when the arrival of evacuees coincided with a thunderstorm, soaking everyone to the skin. There was also an immediate problem of few, if any, householders being prepared to billet expectant mothers or those with babies. But under the efficient chief billeting officer, A.T. Selvey, who was also Wareham's additional sanitary inspector, arrangements worked better than had been anticipated. Apart from the customary style of billeting, the council had furnished empty houses at Worth Matravers, Morden, Lytchett and Wool for the evacuees.

All but one of the problems were handled by billeting officers. Some of the children were uncontrollable, upsetting their hosts by wrecking furniture and bedding. Evacuee women complained their early morning tea was cold, while Wareham hostesses were moaning about guests who refused to help with the housework. The odd case, that had to go to the tribunal, concerned a local man who found it difficult to adjust to having an attractive young London mother around the house, and assaulted her.

Within weeks, more than a fifth of the town's refugees had gone home, which was good news for most of the townspeople. But the fleeing guests had left a mountain of debts behind them, and Selvey was asking the council what could be done about it. There was nothing that would help the traders already caught, but the future was prepared for by adopting the system of a particularly keen billeting officer, who had the home addresses of all evacuees in his village.

More good news for the locals came with the announcement that an original figure of 1,642 evacuees in the area had now dropped to 767, but the bad news came from Selvey again, who said that most of those who had returned home had written to him saying they hadn't realised how good it was in Dorset until they had returned home — now they were asking to be allowed back. The council magnanimously directed him to take back all those wanting to come.

Things went much easier at Charminster, where just 34 children settled in quickly and happily. In Dorchester, evacuees and householders had begun a swap market, changing billets and boarders in an attempt to reach a happy medium in relationships. But the already strained administration couldn't have coped with the resultant chaos, and the chief billeting officer, J. Adrian Hands, put a stop to it with firm action.

Most evacuee children were needy, and local people donated clothing for their use. Schools were hopelessly overcrowded and worked a shift system, with evacuees attending for one half of each day and the local children the other half.

Just as virtually every town and village was groaning about their boarding evacuees, Abbotsbury was complaining about not having any. For a reason that has never been explained, neighbouring Chickerell had done a pied piper and lured all of Abbotsbury's evacuee children away.

An inaudible cheer vibrated through Weymouth one Sunday morning. The expected bombing of London had not happened, and fathers from West Ham and Poplar hired coaches, at 10s. 0d. return, and came to Weymouth to take their families back home. There was little time for packing, and startled but happy hosts watched their departing guests

With the war still young, some Weymouth boys take a walk along the new road beside Radipole Lake. With gas masks at the ready, are F. Hull, R. Livingstone, R. Warwick and D. Dowle.

drag suitcases that looked like clothes explosions.

It had become a case of 'us' and 'them', but an alliance between both sides was formed to get more paid in allowance. The 8s. 6d. had been increased to 10s. 6d. for children over sixteen, but it was pointed out that those a bit younger ate just as much. B. Giles, head of Acton Schools Evacuation committee, said that foster parents were approaching parents for financial help in keeping the children, and this was ruining the scheme.

So the Weymouth Householders Association and the Evacuee Teachers committee made a joint approach, and the subject of a raise in allowance was broached at a council meeting, accelerating an already stormy set of discussions into a row. Councillor Vickery asked members how they felt about a soldier's wife with four children, who had just 11s. 0d. to keep herself and them on. He said he knew of one such woman who had gone on to the poor law at Weymouth the previous day. This brought cries of 'Shame' echoing around the chamber, and the plea for more evacuee money was turned into a non-starter.

But Councillor Martyn did not want the subject of evacuees to drift away. It was a very sore point in Dorset, and he asked the town clerk if there had been any correspondence between the council and the London authorities before Weymouth received seven thousand refugees from one of the city's worst slums. The clerk's reply was like an epitaph for council officials before and since: "There wasn't, but we did complain afterwards".

Martyn went on to relate how a woman carrying a baby and accompanied by other children, arrived at his door one night. They were in a terrible state, and his two daughters had to strip the clothing from the evacuee children, and burn it. He said it was a deplorable state of affairs, and enquired of the clerk if London had been told that Weymouth was a safe place. Smallman told him that, on the contrary, ten reasons for not accepting evacuees had been given, but they had arrived nevertheless.

Caught up in this phase of story telling, Councillor Smith related to the meeting how two small evacuee boys, obviously lost, had turned up on his doorstep in the dark. He wanted to know who was responsible for the changing of billets. The ARP was a scapegoat for all problems at that time, and Smith ended his tale by asking: "What is the ARP for?".

The mayor asked him: "Do you want us to reprimand the ARP?"

There was no time for this to be answered, as Moggeridge asked Smith what had happened to the two boys. When told that Smith did not know,

Even in its early months, the war had stretched beyond Europe. One imperial achievement, the Suez Canal, was a lifeline of Empire. Its patrol planes, Lysanders, were made in the Westland aircraft factory at Yeovil, on the Dorset-Somerset boundary.

Moggeridge made some pointed remarks about shutting the door on children on such a bad night, which set off a heated exchange between him and the other councillor.

When a semblance of peace had returned, Alderman Peaty wanted to know if it was true that the evacuation scheme had cost Weymouth £30,000 to date. Alderman Oliver said that the comfortable Greenhill residence of Captain Hamblin had been requisitioned as a home for a hundred evacuee expectant mothers. No issue seemed to promote such anger as an enjoyed conception in London leading to an expensive confinement in Dorset, and Oliver wanted to know if the medical officer would take charge of arrangements at Greenhill, adding that the cost would be over £1,300 a year, excluding rent and rates. He wanted to know if this expense would be met by the Ministry of Health, and the town clerk assured him that it would.

Away from the council offices, publicans were learning what they would be paid for boarding soldiers. For soldiers, when meals were provided, 10d. a night was paid, with 8d. for each additional soldier. Breakfast was 8d. each, dinner 11d, tea 3d, supper 1s. 0d. Payment for a horse was 2s. 3d. — for a stable room with 10lb oats, 12lb hay, and 8lb of straw a day. The allowance paid for an officer, who would buy his own food, was 3s. 0d, for the first officer, and 2s. 0d. for each additional one.

With the shortage of food uppermost in minds, Dorset's shopkeepers introduced their own unofficial rationing. One section of the government put a standstill on retail prices, while a different department made insurance of shop stocks compulsory. The kindest thing that could be said about insurance companies is that they like the odds on their side. With the Luftwaffe likely to be soon flattening most of the shops in Britain, premiums for this cover were high. This was discussed at the first wartime meeting of the Weymouth Chamber of Commerce, the largest gathering ever, and it was predicted that the insurance would push up the price of many commodities by fifty per cent. At this meeting, members were advised to close their shops at 6 pm on Mondays, Tuesdays, Thursdays and Fridays, 1 pm on Wednesday, and 7 pm on Saturday.

Weymouth had become a contraband port at the outbreak of war, with headquarters in the Edward Hotel. In the first four weeks of hostilities, out of a total cargo of 513,000 tons, a thousand tons were seized as contraband from 74 ships bound for neutral and enemy ports. One Danish ship pulled in for cargo examination had ten bags of coffee beans in the hold, marked simply 'Adolf Hitler'. The first blow was struck at the teetotal dictator and the ten bags were confiscated.

On 16 September, this half-joke of a war lost some of its comedy as the sound of explosions thudded across the sea from the Shambles. En route from New York to Antwerp, the 5,965 ton Belgian steamer *Alex Van*

Opstal blew up and sank. The 49 officers and crew, plus eight passengers, were safe, although six were detained in hospital after a Greek steamer had brought the survivors into Weymouth.

Examination vessels, which a short time before had been pleasure steamers selling happiness around the Dorset coast, puffed out to discover the cause of the explosion. A torpedo was suspected, but the captain's view that his ship had struck a mine was later accepted. This meant that Germany was violating the international laws of the sea.

Within three weeks, more explosions were shaking the Dorset coast. This time it was the Dutch steamer *Binnendyk*, on a voyage from New York to Rotterdam, when ordered to change course for Weymouth and a cargo inspection. That was the last turn of the ship's wheel. On 7 October, 14 officers and 28 men turned their heads while on a rescue vessel, to watch their ship, ablaze from stem to stern, sink by the bows.

Again no definite reason for the sinking could be given. But this taste of war had the Weymouth St John Ambulance team up with the Royal Navy to form a naval first aid scheme for such emergencies. And the town got its first glimpse of what would shortly be a common sight — shocked, bedraggled displaced persons, owning only what they stood up in.

Soon there were more sea survivors in Weymouth, but not from action

Following bren-gun training at Chickerell Camp in 1939, men of the 4th Battalion Dorset Regiment queue at an underground cookhouse. Some are wearing the forage caps that were replacing the conventional stiff army caps. Eventually, these forage caps were succeeded by berets.

Northumberland Fusiliers heave a Norton across a sample of the sort of obstacle that war would bring. A chalky trench near Blandford was included in their training programme.
Photograph: Imperial War Museum.

in local waters. With a cargo of coal for the Argentine, the 3,677 ton Whitby steamer *Sneaton* had been three days out into the Atlantic from Cardiff when she was sunk by a German submarine. Prominent in this incident was an odd early-war chivalry. The U-boat commander spoke good English, and came up beside the *Sneaton* to apologise for sinking the vessel. He advised the crew to take ample food with them in the boats, and forecast that they would soon be picked up by a British warship.

This was a small comfort to the crew, who had to leave a dead stoker aboard and move off in shark infested waters. As they pulled away, the quaint manner of the submarine captain shone through again as he called out: "So long, boys. Sorry I had to do it, but it was my duty." Within an hour and a half a Belgian oil tanker, the *Alex Andrea,* picked up the crew and brought them to Weymouth, where they were housed in the Salvation Army Hostel, School Street, and the Sailor's Rest.

Grim as it was, this was war by proxy for Dorset people. The survivors, the injured, the dead, all came from somewhere else. Saturday 14 October changed this. The random selections of death in wartime stopped with its pointer at the county. For the first time in this war, Dorset men lost their lives.

There was a joke that the new war was to be fought with the weapons of the old. This was not fully true. HMS *Royal Oak* lay at Scapa Flow without any protection. Through stupidity or negligence, the great ship was hit, to roll over, taking eight hundred men to their deaths.

Among them was a Wareham boy, John William Bellas Savage (popularly known as Billy), the son of Mr and Mrs H. Savage of 14 Holton Heath Road. This lad was just seventeen. At West Stafford, a little girl of four tore at her mother's heart each time she asked when her daddy would be coming home, bringing the big doll he had promised her. Her father, Chief Petty Officer Frederick Steele, would not be coming home again. Having served for 22 years in the Royal Navy, being in the Great War together with his six brothers, he had come out on pension but had been recalled when the war began.

Widowed in Weymouth was Mrs Helmore, of 17 Hillcrest Road. Her husband, Petty Officer William Helmore, perished in the *Royal Oak*. In the Navy for nineteen years, he was the father of three children. The

From Blandford, reconnaissance units of the Northumberland Fusiliers set out in convoys through the chalkland villages of Cranborne Chase. For many inhabitants of the dusty inland countryside, away from the siege mentality of the coast, it was their first experience of the rumblings of war.   *Photograph: Imperial War Museum.*

youngest one, born the previous August, he had never seen.

Plush, the little mid-Dorset village, was saddened to learn of the death of Petty Officer Frederick Charles Beeling, whose parents lived in the village. He was married, with his wife living at Gosport, and had one child. His mother said she had last seen her son, who was aged 38, in May, soon after he had been transferred from the aircraft carrier *Courageous.* When the *Courageous* had been sunk she had sighed with relief. "He was a good son," she said with great emotion, "but there are hundreds of parents like us who have suffered loss". Mrs Beeling had another son in the navy and a third who was a cripple.

Martinstown lost a young member of its community — 20 years-old John Hocking, who had been raised by his grandfather, Thomas Everden of Old Brewery Buildings. The dead boy's aunt, Mrs Bartlett, received a letter from him written the day before his death, saying that he was alive and well.

There were luckier relatives, although they went through hours of hell between the radio announcement of the *Royal Oak* sinking and notification that their men were safe. A policeman made a Saturday evening call at Stottingway Cottage, Upwey, to tell Mr and Mrs Alfred Ayles that their son, Able Seaman Victor Ayles had survived the sinking. At 11 pm the same night a similar message was delivered to Mr and Mrs George Lucking, of Gould's Hill, Weymouth, telling them their son, Stoker Cecil Lucking was safe.

Mrs Barrett, of Broadwey, Weymouth, heard news of the sinking while shopping at Dorchester, and spent a sleepless night at 16, St Helens Road — the home of her father-in-law — until the police called at 5.55 am, to say that her husband, Petty Officer W. Barrett, had survived.

Mrs Kenny, of 10 Ackerman Road, Dorchester, was reading a letter from her son, Ronald, when she heard the news on the wireless. She had been worried for two weeks, since receiving a letter from him in which he had instructed her what to do if his ship went down. It was as if he had a premonition. But, at 2 am Sunday morning, the police brought her thankful evidence that he was right about the ship, but wrong that he was to perish in it.

Another Dorset tragedy came close on the heels of the sinking of the *Royal Oak.* Sympathy went to Captain A.F. Jolly, chairman of Weymouth British Legion, and Mrs Angell, of Thornlow School, the brother and sister of Captain Richard Jolly RN, commanding officer of the destroyer *Mohawk,* who was killed during an air attack on the Firth of Forth.

Censorship was now adding to the general confusion, and relatives often had no idea where serving men were. At Frampton, Mrs Gray was idly flicking through the pages of an illustrated magazine when she came across a photograph of her brother embarking for France. She knew he had been conscripted, but it gave her a shock to learn that he was then serving in France.

Call-up was the cause of countless headaches, not only for those who went, but even more so for the ones dodging it. Sickened by the actions of some men, a group of Dorset women were threatening to form a "White Feather Brigade" to shame the cowards. But it was debatable whether it was braver to meekly be conscripted, or to say you were not going to be, and stay home. The county's first conscientious objector, a Dorchester man, was placed on the list by the South-west Conscientious Objectors tribunal at Bristol, with a proviso that he spent the duration of the war in ambulance, agricultural or humanitarian work.

Not so fortunate was a young Portesham man, whose case had been put back by the tribunal so that he could produce letters supporting his claim. He had told the chairman that he could not break the commandment that man "shalt not kill". Back in front of the board a second time, he had a letter from his mother and one from his vicar. Mother obviously meant well, but she shot a hole in his case by saying she was certain he would "kill himself" if called up. It was not disclosed what the vicar said, but it obviously did not amount to what the lad wanted to hear, for the tribunal ordered that he be ready for immediate service in the armed forces.

Another man tried to get away from it all in a different manner. A 27 years-old Taunton man, serving a two year prison sentence at Dorchester, swept the governor's chimney, and walked away from the establishment carrying a bag of soot. A ladder had him over the wall. Then he stole a cycle and rode it until reaching the Frome Weir, where a flock of sheep from Poundbury Fair blocked his way. Discarding the bike, he ran off across the fields.

The ARP hadn't yet been needed, and was causing more rows than a Trotskyist in the Young Conservatives. The organisation was said to be costing Weymouth £600 a week, a disgrace which turned into angry outbursts when it was learned Dorchester's ARP was costing the town nothing. There were also accusations that, with unemployment still high, businessmen and their wives were drawing a substantial second income from positions in the ARP.

Hitler had not started action in our direction at that time, which was just as well because Weymouth's council chamber was an arena that saw arguments come close to violence. Councillor Williams opened one meeting by wanting to know if, with a population of 33,000, and 325 ARP volunteers, Weymouth needed 54 paid wardens. Behind him, Councillor Martyn was ready to fire a salvo and let go the first shot by asking the town clerk if any member of the council was a paid warden. Mr

Smallman replied that there was one.

"I have heard of people with pensions, and with jobs of £3 to £5 a week, grovelling to get into the ARP," growled Martyn.

Councillor Medlam, whose response indicates he was the one councillor mentioned, asked Martyn if he was referring to him.

"If the cap fits, wear it," retorted Martyn, and they went on to tougher stuff. "Is it true," he asked, "that a lot of men have joined the ARP at an age when it would have been right for them to join the Armed Services?"

The mayor agreed that this was true.

"The same thing is happening now as happened in 1914-18," Martyn complained. "Young men who should have gone overseas were joining the police at Weymouth. Some are conscientious objectors, another name for damned cowards. Others have something the matter with them, like a floating kidney or a floating heart which got down into the seat of their trousers. There were hundreds of such men then, getting double and treble what a soldier was. They call themselves Englishmen. They would crawl in under anything rather than go into the army."

After the acrimony had eased a little, the town clerk gave out the good news — Weymouth had been declared a vulnerable area and no further evacuees would be sent there. Then he balanced things out with a little bad news — the cost of policing the town for the King's visit the previous August, when officers had been brought in from all neighbouring counties, had been £549.

Despite the bad feeling, one of the first men to get a warden's badge caused a lot of interest. He was ARP Munroe, manager of the Clinton Restaurant. Neither did he get his badge for little reason. He and his staff were fully qualified in first aid and the fighting of incendiary bombs. The basement of the restaurant (the Clinton is now a Debenham store at the King's Statue end of St Thomas Street), had been converted into a bomb-proof shelter where diners could finish their meals in comfort and safety if there was an air raid.

But the rumour-mongers were eager for stories, and these alterations had the Clinton subject to speculation of becoming six separate things: it was to be a hospital; converted into a gas mask store; commandeered as a barracks; reinforced into a Maginot Line; reconstructed as a barrage balloon depot; or rebuilt as a secret store for submarines, with an underground canal to the sea. None of these things came to pass and the most attractive thing about the Clinton was its three-course meal, costing just 1s. 9d.

Lives had been lost in the war, but there was still an uncertainty about it all. An alliance between Russia and Germany began to make the old suggested contract with Hitler seem more tempting. An unofficial survey was held in Dorset, and the answers averaged out at a determination to

Reconnaissance troops and dispatch riders of the 1st Battalion of the Northumberland Fusiliers trained for the new war from Blandford Camp.

Photograph: Imperial War Museum.

fight Germany. In fact, Mr Mowlem, a porter at Dorchester station, expressed his willingness to have a go personally, even though he was aged 52. Mr Pearce, a Portland newsagent, said Hitler ought to be thoroughly thrashed before any thought was given to peace, but he added, with an insight not invoked by many in those days: "Of course, it's easy to say that if you're not one of those who has to do the fighting."

An opinion that must have made most people envious, when few of them could wait to see the next set of headlines, came from Miss J. Richards, an Upwey girl who worked as a shorthand typist in Dorchester. "I haven't read a newspaper for weeks," she declared. "It's out of our hands anyway, so why bother?"

Maybe nobody trusted Hitler, but Dorset people, with the enjoyment the underprivileged got, and often still get, from watching the activities of the privileged, got lost in the ultra-glamour of a society wedding. Big crowds milled around outside of St John's church, Smith Square,

Westminster, when the Hon. Pamela Digby, daughter of Lord and Lady Digby, Minterne House, Cerne Abbas, married Randolph Churchill, son of the First Lord of the Admiralty. The bride's father, the best man, and the groom himself were all in uniform. After the ceremony, family and a few close friends returned to Admiralty House, where they were received by Lady Digby.

This fleck of pleasant froth did not last on the bloody waters of war, and HMS *Kittiwake* came limping into Portland Harbour after striking a mine in the Channel. Five of her crew were missing believed killed.

Then came the day of the big check-up, possibly the beginning of the modern 'Big Brother' system that has each and every one of us detailed and filed. Like a census with teeth, every householder was asked to give complete details of each person in the house on a chosen night. This was for the issue of identity cards and, eventually, ration books.

No buildings had yet been knocked down by bombs, and the authorities felt safe when E.G. Savage opened the county's most expensive educational building — the South Dorset Technical College had cost £46,000 to build.

At the time, the Sabbath still belonged to God, and was controlled by those who say they are his earthly agents. The clergy would not allow the cinema to filch any churchgoers, and opening time on Sunday was very late in the evening. Life in the armed forces is, always has been and always will be, infinitely boring, and servicemen were looking for entertainment on Sundays. The County Council's general purposes committee agreed to bring the 8.15 pm cinema opening time forward to 7 pm, but rejected a plea for a 5 pm opening. Weekday matinees were arranged for soldiers, sailors and airmen, but then their girlfriends were working. As they didn't go alone, the scheme fell through.

Instead of a noisy war, Dorset had become remarkably quiet. The roads were practically deserted, and garages began to look like furniture shops — with the hulks of sheet-covered laid-up cars stored for the duration. Taxi drivers, who had been struggling along on a ration of twenty gallons of petrol a month, were relieved when this was raised to sixty gallons. Changing train services had altered mail deliveries. Instead of the usual morning and afternoon delivery (usually around 4 pm), there was only one delivery made — in mid-afternoon.

News coming across from Europe showed the British that they were not the only ones complaining about conscription. German men between the ages of 41 and 55 were moaning because they had been drafted into the Army (because of first war experience) while younger men were still left at

The dust of war rose from the dry downlands of Cranborne Chase as the Northumberland Fusiliers learnt to recce in the field.　　　　　*Photograph: Imperial War Museum.*

home. Crime, particularly drunkenness, was on the increase in Dorset, and the Chief Constable, Major A.W. Peel Yates, blamed influx of labour building military establishments as the reason.

Things were looking up fractionally for the county's farmworkers. Men over the age of twentyone had a raise of a shilling a week, bringing the rate for a 48-hour week up to £2. Those under 21 got sixpence. Miss Marsden, chairman of the Women's Land Army in Dorset, announced that the Ministry of Agriculture and Fisheries had laid down a condition of employment that all Land Army girls over the age of eighteen were to be paid £1. 8s. 0d. for a 48-hour week, while the younger ones picked up £1. 2s. 6d.

Home-grown food was vital and local authorities were asked by the government to make land available for allotments. Portland Council was quick to comply, but couldn't find one person prepared to take on an allotment. Dorchester was very fair, making land available in several parts of the town, but again found few to take the offer.

War chipped away at Portland's stone trade, and F.J. Barnes's Slidcroft works put its eighty men on a three day week, just seven days after the Bath and Portland Company had introduced the shorter week for its workers.

Tiny Cerne Abbas had its population swollen by three hundred soldiers, but troops and locals got on well together and there was complete harmony in the village. West Stafford had a large number of people enter its ARP course, but only three stayed the distance. Mrs Baggs, Mrs Higgins, and Mrs Sadler were the few, and they passed with flying colours.

Dorchester decided to try out its air raid siren, but few could hear it. In fact, Councillor F.C. James lived just two hundred yards from it, but his wife and son did not hear it either. This caused something of a panic — needlessly, for the German aircraft usually managed to pass overhead before the warning was sounded. It was agreed that four sirens would be placed in strategic positions around the town.

With Christmas coming, the South-west divisional food officer helped housewives by stating that the maximum retail price of sugar would be 4½ d. There was also a smattering of the festive spirit about, in words if not deeds, and somebody suggested that cinema seats be reduced in price for men in the armed forces. But the cinema managers were tuned to the message from the bank manager rather than the one from the manger. They replied that they had not noticed other commodities, such as butter, being cut in price for servicemen, so failed to see why cinema seat prices should be viewed differently.

For the first time in seventeen years there was no Dorchester mayoral fund for the unemployed. Councillor C. Stroud gave the reasons as a staff already overworked, and less unemployed persons in the town. But he did make a patriotic speech to make up for it, in keeping with all other mayors in the county. Their voices, hoarse from giving directions, offering advice, and giving hope, were toned down for the Christmas messages.

No one anticipated a lively Christmas in towns darkened by blackout, and houses saddened by bereavements, but a surprise awaited all. A small concession for shopkeepers was to have a dimly-lit 'open' sign, as it was a good omen. People shopped early in the day, but they spent as if this was to be the last Christmas of all — which was a distinct possibility.

So, sorrowing for the dead, bruised by inconvenience, addled by propaganda (from both sides), the people of the county of Dorset ended the traumatic year of 1939. During that make-believe, pathetic Christmastide, they were mercifully spared the awesome knowledge of the years of hell that lay ahead.

We're ready, aye ready, for war-time in Piddlecombe-under-the-Hill.
We'll all do our duty as Britons true, and our positions fill.
We're digging trenches and dug-outs too,
Blacking out windows and painting them blue,
There's plenty for everybody to do in Piddlecombe-under-the-Hill.

Cumberland Clark,
the Bournemouth poet,
with lines about 'Our Village in
Wartime'.

January 1940 —
June 1940

Don't worry, everything is going to be all right.
I am coming out of this safely. I can feel it
within me.

— a passage from a letter from her husband, received by a
Dorset wife two days before he lost his life in action.

TRAGEDY AND worry belonged to members of the Royal Navy and
their families at this stage of the war. On the increase were the number of
telegrams delivered to Dorset doors for the wives or mothers of sailors.
When the submarine *Undine* was sunk, Mrs Cryer, of 21 Newberry
Terrace, Weymouth, was told that her husband, Petty Officer Lawrence
Cryer, was missing believed drowned. She was not that unlucky however.
A second notice announced that he had been captured by the Germans
and was in good health.

In many cases, the Germans had a tortuous way of releasing news
about men they had captured. This system caused a lot of anxiety for Mrs
A. Yates, of 88 Portland Road, Wyke Regis. Her two sons, Edwin (22)
and Albert (20), both stokers, were reported missing in the sinking of the
Glow-worm, a 1,340 ton *Hero* class destroyer. A neighbour called Mrs
Yates from her bed one night, to say she'd been listening to the German
radio and heard Albert's name given as a prisoner of war. It was
authentic, for his date of birth (25 December 1919) had been given. This
information relieved Mrs Yates of one worry but put her into a state of
anxiety waiting for news of her other son. Another telegram concerning a
crew member of the *Glow-worm* was delivered to Mrs J.W. Townsley at
15 St George's Road, Portland. This shock was followed by better news —
that Mr Townsley was in German captivity, but had been wounded.

West Dorset was not doing badly at this time, with Alderman W.J.
Emmett, mayor of Lyme Regis, announcing that the ambulance fund he
started had reached the stage where the vehicle could be ordered.

A little way down the road, at Bridport, there was sorrow at news of the death of Chief Petty Officer Frank Legg, a cook on HMS *Exeter*. He had died from injuries received in the *Graf Spee* battle of the River Plate.

While the men were fighting and dying, the women of Dorset were busy with the needles, knitting comforts for the servicemen. Shaftesbury's British Legion Women's section had sent off ninety parcels of woollies to Shastonians in the armed forces. Swanage and district comforts committee had passed items to all serving men from the area, while the tiny village of East Stoke, with eighteen men in the services, had schoolchildren knitting as well as 25 village women. Wool was wound with gusto at the Woodsford Castle Tuesday evening sessions organised by Mrs Stephens.

Some of that warm clothing would have been welcomed in Dorset that January. In the exceptional cold icy roads kept motorists down to a crawl — good practice for the twenty mile-per-hour speed limit in the blackout. There was a chill in the Weymouth treasurer's department, too, but it had nothing to do with the weather. The well-paying beach had not let the council down the previous season, but many of the traders using it had, by not paying their rent. A lot of money was outstanding, and the town clerk was authorised to recover it, through legal action if necessary.

Even in the cold, Dorchester's Chamber of Trade was getting steamed up over a proposal of the town's five banks — that they change early closing day from Thursday to Saturday — and felt it would harm trade.

Still no German aircraft had attacked Dorset, but it was decided to exercise the sirens by sounding a warning each Monday afternoon at 2 pm, beginning on the first Monday in February. Showing it was no respecter of vocations, conscription caught up with the vicar of St George's at Oakdale in Poole, the Rev. S.B. Wingfield-Digby, as well as Rev. J.B. Collins, vicar of Canford. Both clergymen had volunteered some time before their call-up.

By now, the irksome, dreary blackout was being moaned about. The government had authorised that street lights could be used, providing they were masked to conform with a new legislation. It was discovered that modifying Dorchester's 360 street lamps alone would cost £350, so the idea of brighter streets was set back until firm quotes and guarantees of delivery could be obtained from the firm manufacturing the modifications.

There was a growing demand for the blackout to be lifted — as no bombing had occurred — but it was shot down by the Home Secretary, who said that the Germans had developed new high-speed bombers. The lighting restrictions must stay.

Rationing, on the other hand, was introduced with little fuss. The housewife had conditioned herself for it, and most saw rationing as preferable to the alternative of first-come first-served. Most had already selected the grocer they wished to be registered with.

The evacuee game was still being played, and a winner was a Dorchester man paid compensation because his wartime guests had completely wrecked his home and possessions. The family responsible had returned home to London, reported inspector L. Sayers, of the National Society for the Prevention of Cruelty to Children, who added that the case had been followed up. The London officer reported that the condition of both the children and the home was appalling. The parents had no control over the children, five of whom slept in one filthy bed. All suffered from rickets and defective eyesight, and lived an animal existence.

New laws imposed by war resulted in two men appearing at Bournemouth court, charged with keeping pigeons without a permit. This was contrary to defence regulations, for the feathered pets in peacetime could be valuable message carriers in time of war. No conviction was recorded against either of the men, but it served as a reminder to other pigeon fanciers who had not registered with the police.

Finnish ships had long been frequent and welcome visitors to Dorset waters, and now that the country was having trouble with Russia, the Finnish vice-consul in Weymouth, George Cox, was receiving donations to help the Finnish Red Cross. Other problems were caused by the defence of the tiny country against the communists. Perhaps the real truth of who was actually on the side of whom in World War Two will never be known, but this incident — with gifts of money being made to fight the Russians — is an example of the complexity of it all. Not long afterwards, British sailors were going through the hell of Russian convoys, to bring help to the communist country.

Not only those receiving sad telegrams were upset by the system of notifying the bereaved. The complete disregard of those actually fighting the war was in evidence in the way women were passed yellow envelopes at their doorstep, opening them to find a cryptic message that said, in effect, "He's dead."

Such messages, using the minimum of effort to achieve the maximum in tragic effect, popped into many Dorset homes when HMS *Grenville* and HMS *Exmouth* were sunk in the same week. The fearful knock came to 26 Glyde Path Road, Dorchester, and 10 Marie Road in the same town. The first address was the home of telegraphist Hubert Medcraft, who, with 23 years service in the Royal Navy, had been home on ten days leave the previous November. The Marie Road address was the home of a native of Taunton, Petty Officer Reginald Priddle. In the navy for twenty years, he left a widow, two sons and a daughter.

A survivor of the *Grenville* sinking, Petty Officer C.E. Croft, got the hero's welcome he deserved when returning home to Frampton. In the navy for sixteen years, and serving on the *Grenville* since she was commissioned, he had been in the boiler room when the torpedo struck. Though he got out safely, he went back in and rescued two of his three colleagues.

There were no survivors from the *Exmouth,* and among those who perished were Lieutenant John Oliver, son of Weymouth's chief ARP officer, Captain W.R. Oliver R.N. of Preston, commissioned Gunner A.H. Budden, 39 Southlands Road, Electrical Artificer W. Uphill, whose wife lived in Abbotsbury Road, and Leading Telegraphist Albert Ambrose Palmer, son of Mr and Mrs S.W. Palmer, of Sutton Rise, Preston. All were from Weymouth.

Missing believed drowned was Able Seaman William Leslie Ewart Collins, a native of Charlestown. Within eight months of getting his pension, he had a brother also serving in the navy. His parents, Mr and Mrs William Collins, lived at 19 Alexandra Terrace, Charlestown, Weymouth, while his wife and two children were at Newport.

Two days after reading a letter from her husband — "Don't worry, everything is going to be all right. I am coming out of this safely. I can feel it within me" — Mrs Bick, of 112 Norfolk Road, Weymouth, was officially informed that her husband, Leading Seaman Ernest Bick had lost his life on the *Grenville.*

The sad case of Mrs Miller, 14 Nothe Parade, Weymouth, sparked off a protest that reached as far as Winston Churchill. She had been expecting her husband home on leave, and was particularly happy because their son celebrated his tenth birthday that coming Thursday. Just before midnight on Monday evening, she dashed to answer a knock at the door, thinking it was her husband, Yeoman of Signals George Miller arriving home. Instead, she was handed a telegram saying that he had lost his life. Until his luck had run out then, Mr Miller had lived a charmed life. Ninety minutes before the 1918 Armistice, he had been torpedoed, but he survived and enjoyed 21 years of peace.

Upset by this cruel system of informing relatives, Weymouth's Methodist minister, the Rev. Ralph Allport, was loud in protest: "I think the present system is, quite literally, shocking," he protested, "and if it is continued people might just as well learn of their bereavements by reading the newspapers."

Adding his voice to this, and citing the case of another local woman, a Weymouth magistrate said: "This poor woman was alone in her house when a knock raised her from her bed. She was handed a telegram. There was no-one there to console her at that time of night. She might very well have dropped down in a dead faint at receiving the news in such circumstances. Think of her anguish and complete helplessness. Surely some better time could have been chosen for the delivery of the telegram."

Not a believer in localised moaning, Rev. Allport wrote off to Churchill, then First Lord of the Admiralty. The minister was wise enough to know that, in war or peace, the individual has no effective method of complaint, but writing probably made him feel better:

My Lord — In my capacity as officiating Methodist Chaplain to the Royal Navy at Weymouth, my attention has been drawn to the case of Mrs Miller, of 14 Nothe Parade, Weymouth, whose husband, George W.H. Miller, Yeoman of Signals, has been lost in HMS *Exmouth*.

The telegram informing her that he is missing is enclosed. It will be observed that it is written in pencil and difficult to read in poor light. Apparently, it was despatched from Portsmouth at 10 pm, but the telegram was, in fact, delivered to the woman's address at 11.31 pm, when she was called from her bed to answer the door to receive it.

The case is not an isolated one but typical of several brought to my notice in Weymouth, where on the same day three other next-of-kin received similar telegrams at a very late hour.

I have no doubt that the system of notifying the bereaved by telegram regardless of the hour and private circumstances and state of health of the recipients is the least troublesome to the authorities responsible for this duty. There is a widespread feeling among ordinary people, however, that the method is at all times unduly curt and on occasion extremely callous in operation. News of this kind, always acutely distressing, might well be more fittingly conveyed.

May I suggest, with the deepest respect, that you would earn the gratitude of people in all parts of the country if steps were taken to supercede this unhappy system.

Would it not be possible for the heads of departments concerned to avail themselves of the services of many excellent men and women, now belonging to voluntary organisations, whose tact and experience fit them admirably for this sad task of breaking the news prior to official notification through the post.

Did this letter ever come before Churchill? It is very unlikely. The telegrams went on arriving, with one going to 35 Easton, Portland, telling Mrs G. Bowen that her husband, Warrant Engineer Bowen, with thirteen years in submarines, had lost his life in the sinking of the *Thistle*. A few days earlier his wife had posted him a photograph of their ten months-old son.

Changes were then constantly taking place in the county ARP. Leaving for active service was Chief Officer Quilton, of Broadmayne. His post was filled by Major Sheppard, of Owermoigne, who took over the district covering Owermoigne, Broadmayne, Tincleton, Monkton and Came.

The workers of Dorset were agreeing to a penny a week being taken from their wages and donated to the Red Cross. Dorchester was declared a 'safe' area, and it was declared that no public shelters would be erected there. Who made this strange decision, and why, remained obscure. The Chief Constable, Major Peel Yates, issued a directive that no German or Austrian male between the ages of sixteen and sixty would be allowed to enter the county without his permission. Any such alien found here would be interned.

Those in charge of security were embarrassed by the convict who had escaped from Dorchester jail some three months previously. In prison garb, carrying a hay fork, he had travelled across the county, living on berries. He reached Exeter without incident and walked into a tailor's shop where, unchallenged, he bought a suit and changed into it. He was later arrested at Ealing and charged with breaking into a house at Corringway. His exploits made it obvious that any undesirable, German, Austrian or otherwise, would be safe in Dorset providing a pitchfork was carried.

April brought praise for the finance department of the county council. The first wartime budget began with a proposal that the rate be dropped to nine shillings per £1 of rateable value. Then the chairman of the finance committee, G.M. Damers, (the son of a former 'Chancellor') showed he had inherited something from dad by making an eloquent and

Southern Command had a school of camouflage based at Poole in 1940. One of its creations was a labyrinth of pillboxes in the soft sandy cliff edge at Canford Cliffs. Behind them lay the lifestyle that needed defending.   Photograph: Imperial War Museum.

informative speech that had the committee take his advice. The rate was dropped to 8s. 9d.

At Dorchester, the chief evacuee billeting officer, J. Adrian Hands, was handing out bouquets for the way the town had handled the touchy situation of enforced guests. Fewer evacuees had returned home from Dorchester than anywhere else, and the authorities were so pleased that they were not going to send any more to the town. The planned figure had been 1,600, but only 1,200 were actually sent. Of these evacuees, 800 still resided in Dorchester. The rural district had been threatened with 1,900, but had got only 800. Only 145 of these had not returned home. Beaminster had received 550 of a planned 1,300, but less than eighty stayed behind to enjoy the Dorset way of life.

Meat now joined other rationed foods, with each adult allowed 1s. 10d. worth, and each child 11d. worth a week. For many families it was now death at sea that was a regular county visitor, and Dorchester lost another seaman. This time it was in the first Narvik action on a fjord in Norway. Frank Ramsdale lost his life in action at the age of twenty-one. That coming September he was to have become engaged to Eileen Laming, daughter of Mrs Laming of the George Hotel, on Eileen's eighteenth birthday.

On a sunny afternoon, the British fascists tried their luck in Dorset again. But the public was wiser now — aware that it was the 'Right' of politics that caused wars, but those who could afford to only be on the 'Left' that fought in them — and they had a rough reception. The meeting was an open-air one, at Maumbury Rings. Speakers were R. Saunders and Temple Cosson, prospective British Unionist candidate for Exeter, both of whom advocated support of Mosley's peace policy.

Angry servicemen fought skirmishes with fascist heavies and the police, trying to overturn the loudspeaker equipment, which was mounted on a trailer. As things got more violent, the trailer was hastily hitched up and towed away, followed by shouted abuse. This new awareness settled the social question of 'conchies' (conscientious objectors), and no one wanted anything to do with them. The tribunals ordered successful objectors to work on the land or in Civil Defence, which had both sections screaming: "Why us?"

Wareham ARP's Major Holland Swann found it "derogatory that a man refusing to serve his country in the ordinary way is placed in a voluntary organisation as if it were a shelter from duty." The attitude was understandable, but it needed far more courage to refuse to fight than to line up and go with the rest, and those who refused were usually of above average intelligence, and an asset to their units, who were denied younger help by conscription. Two thousand public-spirited Dorset people queued to give blood for wounded soldiers, when an army transfusion unit held a three-day campaign in the county. Then all were queueing to collect new ration books that would come into force on 1 July. Not only did these new books give housewives the chance to change grocers if dissatisfied, but also made a good job of confusing them. These fresh coupons had a change of colour — with green for meat; orange for bacon and ham; yellow for butter and margarine; pink for cooking fat.

But this dormant war was now erupting in violent action across the Channel, and fears were gripping Dorset. Uncertain that 'safe' really meant safe, councillors at Dorchester were pressing for public air raid shelters, but were told that the county council had jurisdiction over this. News from Europe was getting grimmer each day, but was still remote enough not to greatly upset the people of the county. Then, on 21 May, this changed, and the war brought its horrors to Dorset. Two grey steamers edged to the quay at Weymouth. Shocked onlookers watched as, where a year ago laughing holidaymakers would have filed down to the jetty, shuffling lines of Belgian refugees made their slow way to the quay; bedraggled, dirty and unsmiling, the men unshaven, all dressed in rags, feet in carpet slippers. Some carried babies, all looked tired and shattered. Some were on stretchers and the watchers gasped in horror as they saw a girl of sixteen with a gruesome bullet wound in her forehead. Others had heads wrapped in bandages, the orange stain of iodine like war paint smeared on their faces.

They had been industrialists a few weeks before, working in the factories of Brussells, Liege and Antwerp. Then a peaceful way of life had ended as terror dived out of the skies. They had fled on a terrible two hundred mile trek to a French port. On the way, under orders from Hitler, pilots of the Luftwaffe machine-gunned them. Eight days the journey had taken, with the old staggering and the arms of young mothers aching from the weight of their babies. But they had made it and the sea journey across the Channel had been uneventful.

Though not forewarned, resilient Weymouth was ready. The Alexandra Gardens Theatre was turned into a reception centre and dining hall. Refugees arriving too late to leave on the special trains that day were billeted in the Regent Dance Hall and local schools, guarded by sentries with fixed bayonets.

Added to all the other problems of receiving such a large number of displaced persons, was the difficulty of language. Two Catholic priests, Father Wilfred Carter and Father Jules Ketele, assisted by Harold Hollaway and a French sailor, worked untiringly as interpreters.

They heard awesome tales first-hand. One family of sixteen Belgians had left home — only three of them arrived in Dorset. Some lucky ones had managed to catch a train into France. One young man related how the train had been moving for about two hours when his mother had spotted a plane with swastika markings high in the sky. It quickly dived, flying low along the length of the train, again and again, shattering every window with machine-gun fire. The refugees had lain on the floor and, miraculously, none had been hurt.

A middle-aged man named Geebald told how he had left home together with his brother, the brother's wife and their small child. They had found a train, but the baby was crying from hunger and the mother took it to find milk. She had not returned when the train pulled out. The man was left wondering if she was dead or a prisoner of the Germans, and at a loss to know which of the two answers was the best to pray for.

One woman, her face and eyes disturbingly vacant, moved like a dummy clutching a battered old steel helmet that had belonged to her husband who had been killed. In an attempt to cheer-up a sad looking woman who was accompanied by three children, Father Ketele joked: "Are they all yours?" To his consternation, the woman broke into heavy sobs, blurting out that she had seven children when leaving home eight days before, and the three were all she had left.

Propaganda, British this time, had people afraid to believe anything. There were stories that German paratroopers had dropped in Belgium, wearing all kinds of civilian clothing, and that poisoned chocolates were made available to the people. This question made the interpreters particularly interested in one Belgian man, who seemed to have experienced more action than the others. He was asked if he'd seen any bombing. "Bombing!" he almost shouted the reply. "Yes, bang bang all round. My wife. My children — I have lost them. I think they were killed."

This Belgian had actually seen German paratroopers descend in civilian dress, but he knew nothing of poisoned chocolates. Further confirmation came from a local army sergeant home on leave from the British Expeditionary Force. Enjoying a short rest at his home, he said: "We were the advance guard, and they called us the 'Murderers'. Our job was to meet Hitler's gang and hold them up. Then, when the main British force had retreated, we became the rear guard. Our engineers did some good demolition work. We had orders not to shoot prisoners, but we were near an airfield when about fifty German parachutists came floating down. There were too many of them for us to capture, so I had no alternative but to order open fire. We opened up with brenguns, and they were as dead as mutton when they hit the ground. My boys went over to

The pride of Southern Command, at a time when it was hard pressed to find that much to boast about — a 9.2 inch defence gun is installed at East Weare battery, 400 feet above the south-eastern approaches to Portland Harbour. Said the caption writer: "More and still more guns are being mounted around our coasts to give an invader a warm reception should he attempt a landing."   Photograph: Imperial War Museum.

make sure they were all dead. They were in all kinds of dress — padres, peasant women, and nuns, but each had a tommy-gun under his clothes."

War, bringing the threat of air attacks, was getting closer. A new evacuation scheme was set up, with Dorchester people being told that the earlier promise of no evacuees had changed to a further 2,300 who would be sent there. But the bombing jitters brought some good results. The construction of air raid shelters commenced at Dorchester.

In Europe, the list of Dorset heroes was beginning, and on it was Lieutenant Colonel Eric Lechmere Stephenson MC of the Dorset Regiment, who was awarded the Distinguished Service Order for skilfully withdrawing his battalion with a complete disregard for his own safety. But a dose of heroics does not ease the pain of defeat. All over the country people were hearing about the British army fleeing before the might of Germany.

In Dorset, it could be seen happening. The small boats went back and forth across the Channel. Britain had put an army on to the continent without making any provisions for possible defeat. Soldiers who had lost every battle were subjected to the further indignity of the country they served not even being able to rescue them in military vessels. Bravely the civilian seamen, some elderly, others just boys, brought their weary passengers back, passengers who had fought bravely a fight their government had lost for them in advance. Those soldiers landing locally crowded out the post offices on the coast of Dorset, as each man was allowed one free telegram to inform relatives that he was safe.

Now accustomed to handling civilian refugees, Weymouth suddenly had a foreign military displaced persons emergency thrust upon it. The mayor and town clerk had a telephone call on 31 May, telling them that 6,000 French troops were being withdrawn from Flanders, to be brought back to this country for recuperation and reassembly before returning to France to continue the fight against the Nazis. Dorset had been chosen for this temporary visit of foreign troops, and Weymouth as the reception centre. The town clerk, Percy Smallman, asked how long the town had to prepare, and was told that the Frenchmen were already on the way.

A loudspeaker was sent out to tour the town announcing that the troops were coming. In those days, in any crisis, all thoughts seemed to go to the use of schools, and all those in Weymouth were closed so the buildings could be used to house French soldiers. If there is a way of measuring standards of education it would be interesting to compare the wartime days to our modern schooling. Though closed for weeks at a time, with a long period of half-day tuition, and with the pupils leaving at

Evacuation — the British Expeditionary Force comes home from Dunkirk.

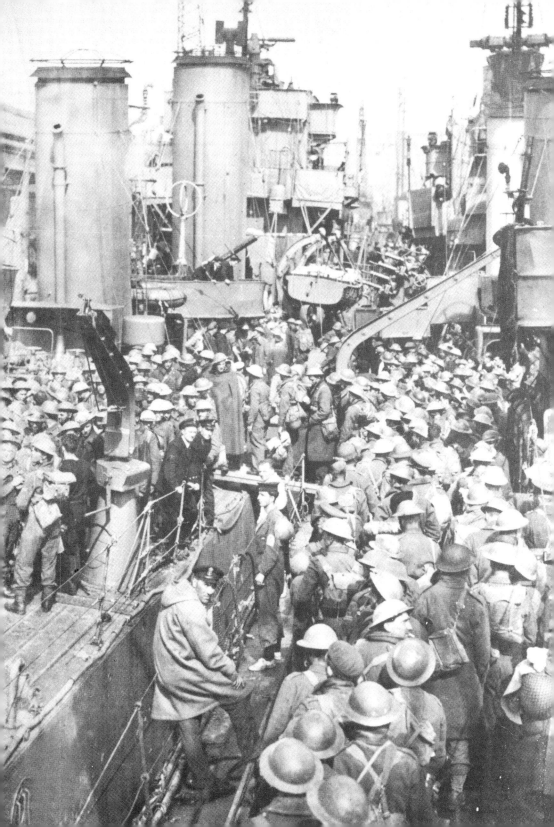

England alone: the new Premier, Winston Churchill, visits shore defences in the sand dunes "somewhere on the south coast".

fourteen, it could well be that most children of 1940 were better equipped educationally than some of today's are.

At five o'clock the following morning, Weymouth station once more set the scene for an unusual happening, as the first train carrying the French soldiers arrived. Right opposite the station, the former Christ church, then converted into a 'Welcome club' for evacuees, was the reception centre. Among those helping with administration work were the teachers from the forcibly closed schools. Each Frenchman, and there were coloured Moroccan soldiers among them, was issued with a tin of 'bully' and half a loaf, then taken by bus to schools at Broadwey, Preston, Wyke Regis, Radipole, Holy Trinity, Cromwell Road, St John's, St Paul's, Melcombe Regis and St Augustine's, as well as to the Sidney Hall and private billets in surrounding villages.

There was an instant rapport between local people and the strangers. Hospitality, unprecedented in the area, was shown them. Despite language barriers, friendships of depth were formed. By 20 June, lessons were taking place in the schools again, and sad farewells had been waved to the French troops as they left to fight a war already lost.

On this day, the feet of more strangers were treading the Weymouth harbour side. This time it was British subjects — 23,743 of them — fleeing their homes in the Channel Islands. Many of the men from the islands, angry at being driven away by the German threat, rushed to get into uniform and fight back. Others, more reluctant to become soldiers, were rounded up by the ever-searching departments responsible for conscription.

Some idea of how proficient Weymouth had become in dealing with such emergencies comes with the knowledge that in one week, in addition to the Channel Island refugees, 3,531 people fleeing from other war zones were also landed in the town. This brought the weekly total to a staggering 27,400 refugees.

So, as the halfway mark in 1940 arrived, Dorset had coped well with a war affecting other people in other countries. Within days, the Luftwaffe was to deliver regular supplies of terror to the county. No longer able to play a supporting role on the sidelines, Dorset was really at war.

Oh! See him walk in battle-dress,
Private Sir Digby-Gray,
Eat bull·-beef in the Privates' Mess
In his aristocratic way!
Heir to a noble line indeed,
He does not scorn with the men to feed,
He's answered the call of his country's need,
Private Sir Digby-Gray!

Cumberland Clark,
the Bournemouth poet, penned this
tribute to the spirit of self-defence
shown by the Dorset aristocracy.

July 1940 —
December 1940

*We owe a tribute of gratitude and affection to
the one who has departed. He has given his life
for his King and country, and those things for
which we Englishmen stand.*

— Clergyman's words at the funeral of a Portland air-raid victim

WITH THE enemy just across the Channel, having got there with
amazing speed and ease, there was no reason to think he was to allow a
narrow stretch of water to stop further advances. Most of Dorset was
proclaimed a defence area, with all civilians in the control of the
Commissioner for the South-west Region, Sir Geoffrey Peto. Ironically,
the inhabitants of the county prepared to defend their freedom by totally
surrendering it to their own masters.

*OPPOSITE: "One of Britain's teeth.........the big gun ready for action. Among the many
big guns waiting to deal death and destruction to the enemy should he attempt an
invasion, are huge 12-inch howitzers on railway mountings. They fire a shell weighing a
third of a ton." The picture was taken by a Mr Malindine on 26 February 1941, and shows
the 14th Super Heavy Battery of the 5th Corps at Furzebrook near Wareham. Camouflage
netting is draped overhead. Two of these guns were sent into Purbeck, and concealed
under 3,456 feet of steel scaffolding, 4,200 yards of Cullacort netting and 10,400 yards of
steel wire.*

*NEXT PAGES: The 12-inch howitzers that provided some of the most comforting
propaganda photographs of the winter of 1940 were a handful that someone had
forgotten to scrap after the First World War, and they had survived in store at Chilwell
Ordnance Depot, Nottingham. Two were shipped to France in 1940, in time to be lost in
the Dunkirk evacuation, and it may be one of these that is shown firing in the final picture
of the sequence. The other action shot, of a shell in midair, was taken "somewhere in
England". The one photographed, rather effectively, at an angle was in the process of
being positioned so that it could look out from underneath a rail tunnel. As for the shot of
the three together, it was probably taken in Hampshire before the guns were moved to
Dorset, and it may interest railway enthusiasts to know that another picture in the series
shows they were being pulled by Southern Railways engine No. 2342. In July 1941, the
two guns from Furzebrook were hauled to Bulford on Salisbury Plain for firing tests. Bits
of metal flew off one of the mountings with the recoil. The big guns never made it back
into service.*

This control stretched all along the coast and for twenty miles inland, taking in the towns of Bournemouth, Poole, Weymouth, Portland, Dorchester, Blandford, Sturminster, Wareham and Swanage. Movement within the zone was not restricted, but anyone wishing to enter it had to have good reason, plus a permit from the police or military authorities. Part of Chesil Beach and the Nothe Gardens Beach, Weymouth, was put out of bounds to civilians.

Identity cards had to be carried, and produced on request of a police officer or serviceman on duty. Not all accepted this strict regime easily, and when Pc. Gentle stopped a bus at Martinstown one morning, asking to see the identity cards of the passengers, one man refused to comply. Taken to court, he wasn't punished for failing to produce his card, but was fined 5s. 0d. for using the wrong kind of language in his protest on the crowded bus.

This was a case of individual rebellion against authority, not a display of disloyalty to Britain. But there was a contingent in this country whose sympathies lay with the fascists. It appeared at the time that they were so active the Germans often knew what was happening before our side did, but the reason for this awareness is now known to have been German radar.

A glaring example of this efficient long-range spy service came on 4 July 1940. The anti-aircraft defence in south Dorset was in keeping with most other British efforts at the time — pathetic. There were a few World War One guns, widely dispersed. Not that the position with heavy guns was much better. For example two batteries of 12-inch railway-mounted howitzers were all that Southern Command had for the entire coast west of Chichester. Later in the year they were to come to Dorset. With a range of nine miles, they were positioned at Furzebrook at the heart of the Purbeck heaths. A 750 lb shell is a lot of explosive but it might not have overly worried an invader at a rate of fire of one round every three minutes. Dorset needed usable guns.

To rectify this situation, a Royal Navy anti-aircraft gunship HMS *Foylebank* was moved into Portland Harbour on 4 July. On that morning, twenty Nazi aircraft came roaring out of a glaring morning sun — diving straight on the *Foylebank*. It would be ludicrous to call this attack coincidence, and later that month British scientific intelligence were to discover the reason.

In the Portland attack, direct hits left the *Foylebank* with only one gun firing. This was operated by hand by Leading Seaman Jack Mantle, as the ship's electric power was out of action. Even then he was terribly injured, and the story of his courage, which resulted in the posthumous award of the Victoria Cross, is well known. It is a sad reflection on us all to consider that the sun lounge built in memory of Jack Mantle in the

Portland's Home Guard pictured outside the Drill Hall at Easton.

grounds of Portland Hospital, now stands derelict and neglected.

Hitting the *Foylebank,* where the first ever VC in territorial waters was awarded, provided the Luftwaffe with a neat equation in casualties inflicted on the crew — 60 unhurt, 60 injured, 60 killed. The raid, early in a long season of air attacks, also brought a new concept to this war, with a number of Portland civilians, both men and boys, killed. Two German planes were brought down and the remainder flew off, mission accomplished. The 'all clear' was sounded. In the naval base, where contractors McAlpine were digging an underground tunnel, employees who had sheltered during the raid, came out to stand in the morning sunshine and look at the destruction below them.

Out over the sea, one German flyer discovered he had a bomb left. In later months, when ideals had begun to slip, it would probably have been jettisoned into the sea. Not that morning. The pilot turned and came back over Portland Harbour, to release his bomb and catch the men

OVER, LEFT: German air reconnaissance survey of Portland Harbour, with Weymouth quay towards the top right. Ships are identified by numbers, and gun sites by letters. The one obstacle that is neither (figure 9, centre right) is an anti-submarine net that can be seen in greater detail on the facing page.   *Photograph: German High Command.*

OVER, RIGHT: German air reconnaissance photograph, taken in 1940, of the centre breakwater of Portland Harbour (seen from the north-west) showing the East Ship Channel (top) blocked by anti-submarine nets, with another line (bottom) that could be moved in place across the North Ship Channel as well. Photograph: German High Command.

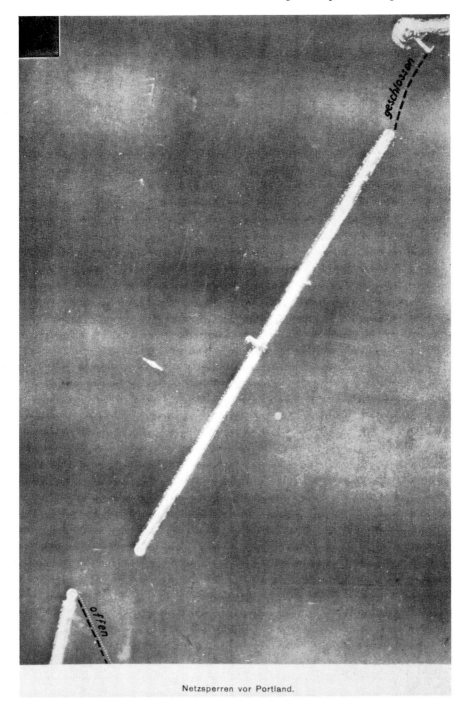

Netzsperren vor Portland.

standing outside of the tunnel. Nine of them were killed.

Even the funerals of these five men and four boys were affected by war. Fear of further air attacks catching large gatherings in the open, restricted the mourners to families only. The words at the beginning of this chapter were spoken over one of the men, Robert Collins Dryer, aged 39, at the Fortuneswell Methodist Church, by Rev F. Jowett.

HMS *Delight,* a 1,375 ton 'Defender' class destroyer, was dive-bombed by Stukas and sank twenty miles south of Portland Bill on 29 July 1940. Sixty miles from the French coast, she was no chance victim for the Luftwaffe. The reason for her fate was not generally known until the history of Britain's wartime scientific intelligence was published in 1978 and Rodney Legg, editor of the Dorset County Magazine, added a detailed note about the *Delight* to a feature his magazine carried on Dorset's war at sea. The next twelve paragraphs are his sequel to the loss of the *Delight.*

Shortly after she went down, a German operational radio message, monitored and decoded by the British Code and Cipher School at Bletchley Park, reported that the ship "had been sunk with the aid of Freya reports".

'Freya' was the codename for some device. Her name was plucked from Norse mythology and Dr Ronald Jones, head of scientific intelligence at the Air Ministry, had already heard of "Freya Gerat" (Freya apparatus).

Following a mention of "Freya-Meldung" on 5 July (Freya reporting) he had bought a book on myths from Foyle's and found that "Freya was the Nordic Venus who had not merely sacrificed, but massacred her honour to gain possession of a magic necklace, Brisinga-men. The necklace was guarded by Heimdall, the watchman of the Gods, who could see a hundred miles by day or night".

The last phrase is the crucial one — making Heimdall a wholly appropriate code for radar, though rather too obvious. Freya was chosen, by association, in its place.

Twelve days before the loss of *Delight,* Jones had used this reasoning to predict the existence "of a coastal chain and detecting system with a range of a hundred miles". The sinking of the destroyer removed any possibility that Freya was detecting associated objects in the sky — for *Delight* had neither balloon protection nor a fighter escort.

"The apparatus must have been able to detect her directly," Jones concluded. "It appeared to be sited near the village of Auderville on the Hague peninsula north-west of Cherbourg, but it had to be very different from our own coastal chain stations, since it was completely undetectable

Britain behind barbed wire — soldiers kept their invasion vigil all along the vulnerable South Coast.

on the best air photographs that we possessed of the area.

"This confirmed the idea that Freya was a fairly small apparatus, which had already been suggested by the fact that it had been set up so quickly after the Germans had occupied the Channel coast."

Aerial photography improved by January 1941 to produce the first indistinct shot of a Freya turntable, about 20 feet across, at the edge of a field near Auderville. The shadows were different widths in successive photographs. It was thought that the difference "might be due to whatever it was rotating between exposures, so that at one instant it had been more or less end-on to the direction of the sun, and at a subsequent incident more nearly broadside-on. In fact the difference in breadth was only about a tenth of a millimetre on the print, and it was a very fine observation; but it was quite positive".

R.V. Jones explains the outcome in his book *Most Secret War* (Hamish Hamilton). On 22 February Flying Officer W.K. Manifould brought back a clear photograph of two square-mesh aerials.

Derek Garrard, seconded to Jones from the Telecommunications Research Establishment at Worth Matravers, drove back to Dorset and — after being arrested as a Fifth Columnist in a 'Defended Area' — succeeded in picking up Freya transmissions on a VHF receiver at the 2.5 metre wavelength.

Air Marshal Joubert called a meeting in Whitehall with only one item on the agenda: "To discuss the existence of German radar".

July 1940 saw the start of continuous air raids over Southern England, and Dorset was the western front line for the Battle of Britain. The first German aircraft to crashland on Dorset soil was a Dornier 17 m, which came down in a field close to Fleet church, after being hit while attacking shipping in West Bay. The only survivor was the pilot. Taken to the farm of J. Nobbs, he nonchalantly passed a packet of Players cigarettes around his captors, proving that men and military equipment had not been the only things captured by the Germans in Europe.

The civilians who serviced Dorset's front-line Battle of Britain airfield at Warmwell near Dorchester at this time have emerged from Len Deighton's best-seller *Fighter* as some of the minor villains of the Second World War. Rodney Legg has looked into the role of this wartime base, opened in 1937 but now once more a landscape of fields and gravel pits, and contributes this summary of its history.

The accommodation provided for the pilots of 609 Squadron "was so

Dorset's war, in the middle of 1940, was on the frontline — the Channel. Whatever the cause of the end of this ship, its epitaph was in English: "Ablaze from stem to stern, an enemy tanker sinks in the English Channel while the pilot of an RAF plane looks down on the victim of his bombing attack. Day and night our machines maintain a ceaseless watch on land and sea."

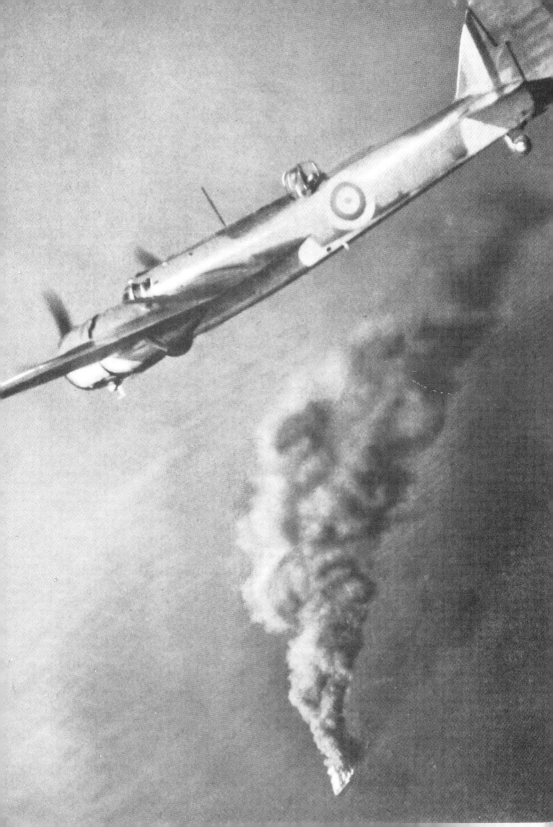

bad that many preferred to sleep under filthy blankets in the dispersal tent. The Station Commander, who showed no urgent desire to remedy this situation, complained that the pilots were not getting to the Officers' Mess promptly for meals and ordered the dining room to be locked except at prescribed meal times".

Because the Luftwaffe kept different hours, the British pilots were often going hungry. The position deteriorated to the extent that the Warmwell cooks even refused to get up early to make breakfast for the squadron.

Squadron Leader George Darley remembers going into the Warmwell kitchen and himself preparing eggs, bacon and tea for his men. The cooks were angry when they turned up for work and found a heap of dirty dishes. They complained to the Station Commander and he in turn sent for Darley and told him never to use the kitchen again.

Later that day, Darley led 609 Squadron against a formation of Ju-87 German bombers heading for Warmwell airfield. The attack was successfully fought off, with only two or three bombs landing on the airfield. When Darley returned, he says, he could not resist the temptation to ring the Station Commander — and told him he did not expect any thanks "for saving the hangars, personnel, and planes, not to mention the Officers' Mess and kitchen".

Perhaps the philosophy was that the more uncomfortable the men were made to feel on the ground, the more prepared they would be to escape into the sky and fight for Britain.

In July 1940 three of the Spitfires of 609 Squadron were lost in action off Portland. Not until 18 July did it claim two enemy aircraft in return. The squadron on the base, number 152, shot down two Messerschmitt 109s over the Isle of Wight on 16 August and claimed ten kills over Portsmouth on the 18th. Hurricanes of 87 Squadron from Exeter defended south Dorset from an attack by 120 German aircraft on 15 August. Their commander, 27-years-old Squadron Leader T.C. Lovell-Gregg, was killed in the action and is buried in the airman's plot at Warmwell churchyard.

The bombing of Warmwell airfield happened on 25 August 1940, with only a little real damage and no casualties. In the sky, four enemy kills were claimed, and two British pilots died. "You must bring the RAF up to battle," Goering had ordered. The following month 609 Squadron claimed nineteen German aircraft for the loss of two of its pilots. They fought over London on 15 September, which at the time was regarded as the peak day of the Battle of Britain (with total claims of 186 enemy planes shot down) but within days the Air Ministry was warned by its own intelligence department that no more than 76 planes could have been accounted for — and German records examined after the war showed the actual figure was 62.

Overclaiming was almost always unintentional, but inevitable as faced with swift action on all sides, pilots were unable to follow their supposed victims down to the ground. Sometimes more than one fighter accounted for the same bomber. No station commander was going to disallow a claim that one of his men was genuinely convinced he had scored.

One of the raids that crossed Warmwell was thought to be directed at Yeovil, a town with the Westland aircraft factory, but instead the scholastic abbey town of Sherborne was hit with three hundred bombs. Pilot Officer Eric Marrs DFC of 152 Squadron returned to Warmwell with his undercarriage jammed. Only one wheel was down, and it refused to retract, leaving him no option but to land a perilously unbalanced Spitfire. A fighter touching down in this condition is extremely tricky to keep level, and liable to lose a wing and explode. Marrs' skill was such that the plane was only slightly damaged and he himself unhurt.

Tragedy, however, often came when it was least expected. Pilot Officer John Allen had arrived at Warmwell on 8 November 1940. Three days later he had an engine failure and made an immaculate forced landing near Broadmayne. His luck did not last out the month, though, and on 29 November his Spitfire, R 6907, plunged from an empty sky into a wood at Durweston near Blandford. Investigation of the wreckage showed no apparent reason for the crash. He was only nineteen.

At the height of the Battle of Britain, Weymouth Hospital had a special patient. He was Pilot Officer Robert Francis Doe, from Surrey, who had fifteen destroyed Nazi planes to his credit. Injured in a dog-fight over Dorset, he brought his turbulent war with him — an incendiary bomb dropping outside the door of his ward and another outside the window by his bed.

Just twenty years old, he was the new kind of hero, in sharp contrast to the rugged characters of Hollywood Western films. Shot in the left arm, hand and foot he told his story, interspersing it with RAF expressions like "simply wizard" and "awful prang".

"I was taking part in an attack on fifty German aircraft over Dorset," he said. "Suddenly, I found myself in the middle of them. I felt a blow on

OVER, LEFT: The sea is to burn! One of the ideas for defending vulnerable sandy beaches was project 'Fougasse'. It was tested on the southern shore of Poole Harbour, where optimum conditions were presented by a shallow and usually calm expanse of tidal water. Shoreline pipes projected out into the harbour, and when released the oil surfaced as a series of slicks. Photograph: Imperial War Museum.

OVER, RIGHT: Poole Harbour ablaze for project 'Fougasse'. Oil released through pipes enlarged into a continuous strip, and was ignited. The idea had practical possibilities in the early part of the war, when any aid to coast defence was welcome, but it relied on the enemy arriving in good weather. Waves would disperse the slick. Photograph: Imperial War Museum.

my shoulder and the plane went into a hell of a dive and started smoking. Fortunately it didn't burst into flames, but I lost control completely, and I stepped out."

He made "stepping out" sound like alighting from a bus rather than parachuting, badly wounded, through a sky of darting planes and bullets. Blacking out on the way down, he was unconscious when picked up by soldiers.

In this one battle he had accounted for nine enemy aircraft, and was awarded the Distinguished Flying Medal while in hospital. The same day he became engaged. Still bandaged and limping, he was fretting for the day when he could get back into action.

Meanwhile, back at the hotels and guest houses along the Dorset coast, there were moans about "financial distress" caused by the prohibition of visitors. Meetings were held, where there were complaints of paying rates for businesses that could not operate. Bournemouth and Poole hoteliers collared their member of Parliament and asked him to urge the Government to relax the controls.

At last, the war seemed to become the great leveller it was expected to be, and the touching of forelocks to the squire looked like being a thing of the past. It was still a shock, though, when the Lord of the Manor of

The other symbol from the summer of 1940 — rows of neat graves in the RAF plot beside Warmwell church.   *Photograph: Ivan Mason.*

OPPOSITE: To the defenders, the Spitfire was the plane of 1940. By the end of the year, as the pressure eased, its reputation would begin to spread abroad.

Hinton St Mary, Captain George Henry Mane Fox Pitt-Rivers, was held by the authorities under *Defence Regulation 18b*. At the time of the evacuation of children from the big cities, he had strongly opposed the billeting of children in the rural areas of Dorset. He was on the right of the far right, and consequently joined 1,600 British subjects who were held in prison without trial, though as a proportion of the population the number was insignificant, and later to be exceeded in peacetime by internment in Northern Ireland in the 1970s.

An all-out drive to collect salvage began — aluminium for aircraft construction was launched in Dorset — with women's organisations playing a main role. A special group was formed at Dorchester, with Miss Chadwick, of 22 Queens Avenue, as chairman. Mrs Hallett, of 14 St George's Road, was secretary, together with members Miss Marsden, Mrs Pitfield, Mrs Bush, Mrs K. Abbott, Mrs Cornick, Mrs H. Lock, Mrs Hunt, Mrs Sheppard, Mrs Voss, Miss Tilley, Miss Howard and Miss Ferrett. This scheme was entered into with the right spirit. At Wareham, a little girl was upset because her mother had no aluminium to give, so she gave her own dolls' tea set. Shortly afterwards, the area's newspapers set up a Spitfire fund, with collections made wherever possible.

In the middle of this glut of patriotism, Portland was taking a hammering from Hitler's planes, and there were rumours that the island was to see a mass evacuation. This was immediately denied, but the authorities were taking no chances. A public address was made in Easton Square, with islanders being told of the folly of running away even, as was expected, if the Germans landed. It was pointed out that refugees attempting to escape on the continent had seriously hampered troop movements.

Though there was no concerted exodus by Portlanders, a few did slip away, including a former chief ARP warden, who may not have realised that bombs might be dropped. The Prime Minister was appealing to people in areas such as Dorset to volunteer to help build the much-needed defences against German invasion. The bumbling stupidity of the Government, over the years, had caught up with it. At any moment the Germans could invade, and unpaid workers were sought to provide ditches and trenches. C.H. Stroud, Dorchester's mayor appealed for volunteers, and was disappointed when just twelve turned up. Weymouth did better, on the first night, when fifty willing men turned up for digging duty. But they did not come back, leaving five women — four from Brunswick Terrace and one from Upwey — to struggle on with the work. Aid came from the Borstal institution at Portland, where the formality of volunteering didn't apply.

What and who to believe was the biggest problem of the time, particularly regarding reports of air attacks. To the astute observer, the truth lay somewhere between the underplayed British reports of the effect of raids, and the German exaggerations. Reversing an old adage, it was a case of what you don't know does worry you, and the Government arranged a "Tell the people" programme all over the country. To all but the really gullible it was apparent that the people were to be told only what those organising the campaign wanted them to hear. Two open-air assemblies took place at Dorchester, at Fordington Green and in Victoria Park. Professor Roland Chaput and Sir Philip Colfox MP, made stirring speeches, and offered helpful advice. A prudently selected set of war photographs were on display. When the gallant words and encouraging pictures could not hold the crowd's attention any longer, patriotic songs were broadcast on the Ministry of Information's loudspeaker system.

An indoor session in Weymouth, at Alexandra Gardens, made more sense. A.W. Sinclair, whose exposures (of things wrong in the war, that is) had brought him instant radio fame, pulled a crowd in the town he described as a "front line city". Sparing no-one the grim truth, he dissected the Nazi mind and ideals, then displaying either remarkable foresight, or inside information, told the crowd that Hitler wouldn't cross the Channel to invade England — as was the popular and logical assumption — but would turn elsewhere for land battle.

This was good news, if you could believe it. Most people had become too cynical to believe anything. Air attacks were more frequent and heavier, and it was said that the police had toured houses in Wyke Regis, telling the occupants to move further inland. An instant denial once again sprang from the authorities, but a London newspaper did not help the situation when it claimed that the people of south Dorset were buying up old trailers, loading them with personal belongings, and getting ready for a mass evacuation.

All towns from Bournemouth to Weymouth quickly issued a statement saying that this was a lie. But damage had been done. Even those to whom moving out had never occurred, began to wonder if they should.

While all this was going on, an Owermoigne man was making history by being the first person in the county summoned in court for refusing to accept evacuee lodgers. Albert Louis Bulley of the Bungalow, Owermoigne, was fined £5.

Reminders of desperate air battles over the county came with the bodies of German airmen floating ashore around the coast. One at Portland was in such an inaccessible place that soldiers and police had to descend 300 foot cliffs to reach the body. Six more policemen scrambled over a quarter of a mile to reach the spot. It took three hours to get the body up the cliffs. As was the usual procedure, no inquest was held and the RAF claimed the body.

Escape from death made more pleasant news, and many shared the joy

One of Portland 9.2 inch guns of 102 Coast Defence Battery (left). The righthand picture was taken at the same gun emplacement, and this was its original caption: "Ever ready. Men on duty keep watch as a searchlight sweeps the sea."
Photographs: Imperial War Museum.

of three Dorchester families who received cards from soldiers who had been reported as dead. Mr and Mrs H. Moore, of the Half Moon Inn, North Square, heard from their son, Sergeant Major William Moore, aged 27, whom they had given up for lost. In the Dorsetshire Regiment since sixteen, he was in a Belgian hospital with a leg wound, and a prisoner of the Germans. William was a noted welterweight boxer, and his father was formerly a prison officer at Portland.

Mrs Mullins, of Bowling Alley Walks, heard that her reportedly dead husband, Staff Sergeant Douglas S. Mullins, of the Dorsetshire Regiment, was a captive of the Germans. The good tidings came in a card from him three months after being told he was dead. Another member of the Dorset Regiment, Corporal Scott, sent a similarly welcome card to his wife, Mrs W. Scott, of 6 Hardy Avenue.

Relief came to Weymouth also, when Mrs Martin, of Quebec Place at Park Street, learned that her 21-years-old son, Private Thomas Martin, of the Dorset Regiment, missing since 16 June 1940, was in a German prison camp.

Private air-raid shelters were being issued in the county, but on an unsatisfactory basis. Criticising the way schools were being issued with shelters, and having a general go at its local council, the Dorchester

A shell from the loading tray (left, centre) is positioned ready for action on Portland. The photographer spent the whole day with 102 Coast Defence Battery of the Royal Artillery. Right, for the camera, they fired into the night.

Photographs: Imperial War Museum.

Chamber of Commerce met in Mrs Major's cafe at Cornhill and described Dorchester council as being "inoculated with the drug of inactivity". The Chamber stressed that vacancies on the local authority should be filled by younger men who would bring fresh ideas and impetus to the town.

In the hope of confusing the Germans when they arrived — there being very little point in saying 'If' at that time — placenames were being removed from railway stations and streets, including signposts and milestones. War memorials were causing problems, as the names were etched deep into stone on them. Maps were cut from directories in public telephone kiosks, and, in rural areas, the list of call charges to various places removed. The policy assumed the German invaders would not look down. Most of the drain covers in the Bournemouth area had the town's name cast into them. The move to remove signs, like that to collect scrap, was psychological rather than practical.

Maximum retail prices were put on most commodities but, human nature being what it is, items that were scarce could be made to appear if a higher price was discreetly paid. Among a group appearing in court charged with buying butter at more than the stipulated price were Viscount Cranborne, Member of Parliament for South Dorset, and Lord

Shaftesbury, Lord Lieutenant of Dorset. The days of surprises were long gone, and nobody was shocked that those you were supposed to look up to turned out to be just as bad, or perhaps worse, than anyone else. What did cause amazement was the fact that their cases got as far as court. Society was changing.

Crime was soaring in the county, but it was of a type that could be described as adult delinquency rather than criminal. August bank holiday was looming up and the government, now all-powerful, cancelled it. The shopkeepers of Dorset reasoned that if Monday was not a holiday they would stay open — and they did.

A Weymouth woman with more than a squashed holiday to worry her, was Mrs C. Emsell, of 81 Kitchener Road. Her husband, Lance-Corporal Cyril Emsell, a clerk in the Royal Army Service Corps, had been missing since the evacuation of Nantes. Neither the British nor Germans offered a solution to his fate and, fraught with worry, Mrs Emsell made a plea in the local newspapers, asking a Dorchester man whom her husband had spoken of as his 'mate', to contact her. She was hoping to learn some clue from this other man. A Yorkshireman, Emsell had come to Weymouth five years previously, and had been an agent for the Royal Liverpool Insurance Company.

Not all the military danger was across the sea. In the heart of hunt country, at the Fox and Hounds Inn, Cattistock, a young soldier was larking about with his rifle. It went off, shooting his friend in the leg. The wounded soldier was taken to Dorchester Hospital, and he died there.

On the night of 7 September 1940 all Dorset's invasion fears came to a head. A seven-mile German convoy was reported in the Channel, heading in the direction of the county. Coastal defences were on full alert through the night. Few people could credit it when dawn arrived without a shot being fired, or the crunch of jackboots over the beaches.

When this biggest crisis of all was over, or at least postponed, the county became ultra patriotic. The first cheque in the Spitfire fund, for £2,000, was sent off to Lord Beaverbrook, signed by mayor Stroud, and A.E. Clayton. Dorchester and area had raised £1,214, Purbeck £612. 15s. 6d., Weymouth £593 2s. 9d., West Lulworth £75 1s. 0d. (collected by H. Thompson) and Cerne Abbas £28 15s. 0d. that was collected by F.C. Winter of the New Inn.

Conscription has never brought satisfactory services. A 20-years-old Dorchester soldier was court martialled for refusing to obey an order given by acting-Captain T.S. Beasley. Before being called up for the

German air reconnaissance photograph of military camps to the south of Wimborne at Merley (top) and Oakley (bottom) showing the tents clustered in threes, protected from bomb-blast by rings of sandbags. Photograph: German High Command.

army, the accused soldier had tried to register as a conscientious objector, not through a lack of guts, but for the same reason that he refused an army order — he wanted to be in the Royal Navy.

As the year was drawing to a close, so was the Parliamentary career of the butter-eating Viscount Cranborne, once controversial and now quiet, who became a baron. An unopposed Lord Hinchingbrooke succeeded him as South Dorset's representative in the Commons.

Local political activity centred around the selection of mayors, unexciting as most towns had the same man going round again and again. The exceptions were Blandford, with J.E. Conyers for the first time, and Bridport, where S. Gale popped into the main seat. Slipping the chain on for the first time at Dorchester was A.R. Jeffery, chief officer of the Fire Brigade since 1927. At Lyme Regis, W.J. Emmett was starting off on his fourth year as mayor, while it was third time around for Poole's J. Bright, with an equal innings at Shaftesbury for R. Pearson. It was three times at Weymouth, as well, for J.T. Goddard, while A.T. Moss, at Wareham, had a year's lead by becoming mayor for the fourth time.

The police force was having a reshuffle. Inspector Galpin left Weymouth to become a superintendent at Bridport. Inspector A. Foster was transferred from Shaftesbury to Weymouth, staying at the same rank. Sergeant Malkin moved from Dorchester into better things at Shaftesbury, where he was promoted to inspector. Sergeant Lill moved from Broadwey to Dorchester, while Pc. King was made an acting sergeant and moved from Weymouth to Broadwey. At Wareham, acting-Sergeant Oliver could get the missus to sew on his stripes permanently, when he was promoted to sergeant.

With Christmas cards at a penny a stamp, the only other thankful thing about this gloomy Yuletide was that it did not take place under the swastika. Dorset men had been killed, taken prisoner, and left in that mind-bending limbo stated officially as 'missing'. Towns and villages were battered and scarred by bombs, and a great deal of each day was spent in air raid shelters. Total war had arrived. There was much worse yet to come. Although, in international terms, 1941 was to be the quiet year of the war (with German divisions actually being stood down) it was to be active enough for Dorset.

By the close of the summer of 1940, German planes were being shot on to English soil in increasing numbers. Claims were often wildly optimistic, even so, in that on 15 September the British Air Staff claimed to have destroyed 186 enemy aircraft. The actual total turned out to be 62. It all explains the absence of too much mess: "German aircraft brought down in Britain are not allowed to litter the countryside for long. Damaged machines are transported to vast dumps, there to be broken up. In this picture, workmen are carrying part of a fuselage to a graveyard of Nazi raiders."

Dorset at War

Mighty at sundown our Air Patrols go out
To search for those marauding German planes
Who choose this time their deadly mines to sow —
Our men will give them something for their pains!
Of magnetic mines the enemy take a load
To place them cunningly right in the road
Of innocent passing merchant ships, but we
Soon put a stop to this wicked piracy.

Cumberland Clark, the white-
mustachio'd war poet of
Bournemouth, in his verse 'The
Heligoland Base'.

FOOTNOTE: As this book went to press *Ultra goes to War* by Ronald Lewin was published and is a detailed history of the Government Code and Cipher School. Stationed at Bletchley Park, employing several thousand cryptanalysts and wrens, it decoded intercepted German radio signals throughout the Second World War. It was responsible through M16 to the Foreign Office. One example of the benefits that came from reading the other side's mind, quoted by Lewin, was issued by British Intelligence at 0152 hours on 19 August 1940: "From a reliable source, information has been received of an impending attack on Warmwell aerodrome this morning. Aircraft to be ready to leave at 0700 hrs." Another warning was issued at 0740 on 25 August: "It is reliably reported that air attacks are to be expected during the course of today 25th August 1940 at WARMWELL, LITTLE RISSINGTON and ABINGDON aerodromes and reconnaissances by a single aircraft in the area SOUTHAMPTON-ALDERSHOT-BRIGHTON." Less dramatically, but still of importance, signals intelligence also told the airfields when attacks would cease — enabling them to relax again.

January 1941 —
June 1941

*I am not going to suggest what the course of
this war will be. I am only going to make one
small prophecy. It is this. When Germany
breaks she will break very rapidly and
completely.*
— Sir Charles Petrie Toller, addressing Dorchester Rotarians,

February, 1941

AFTER A short but welcome period of quiet, the drone of German
aircraft filled the Dorset skies once again, on the evening of 2 January
1941. A new style of attack began. Any pretence either side had shown
about attacking only military and industrial installations had long gone.
Civilian morale was now the target, as was pointed out to Dorchester
council by the ARP controller Douglas Jackman. He drew attention to the
fact that the raids were now occurring early in the evenings, when
workers were going to and from their places of employment, though that
was only for the practical reason that it enabled the bomber to fly across
the safety of German airspace and locate its target whilst it was still light.

Incendiary bombs were being dropped as well, and hundreds of fires
were ignited with each raid. The sirens, always hard-pushed to get going
before the bomb doors opened, now failed to give warnings because they
were iced up in the January weather.

A radio broadcast by the Prime Minister accelerated the fear of gas,
when he warned that such attacks were a distinct possibility. All citizens
were asked to carry masks at all times, and to attend centres to have their
respirators checked for efficiency. As a hint of a protection against blast
from bombs, two half-filled sandbags were delivered to every house on a
Sunday morning.

A young soldier who had fought the backstepping battles of Belgium
and France, returned to England confused as to when the killing had to
stop. At 1.30 am, on 27 January 1941, Police Sergeant Lill charged 20
years-old Private David Jennings with the murder of Dorchester tailor,
Albert Farley, of 12 The Grove.

Later that morning, Dorchester magistrates — A.R. Jeffery (the mayor), Mrs A. Comben, F.C. James, W.J. Fare and W. Clark — were elevated from the trivia of blackout offences and petty crime, when the defendant appeared before them on the murder charge. Police Superintendent Lovell asked for a remand in custody, and got it. The soldier, who pleaded not guilty, was later sentenced to death. It may have been murder in the legal sense, but not in its normal form. The defendant's crime had been to kill by accident whilst carrying out a felony. He was breaking into a licensed club, for money and drink, and war had given him a new means of access — he shot the lock off. Standing behind it, unknown to the intruder, was Farley. A member of the jury, asked in 1972 by a reporter for *Dorset County Magazine* why David had not been charged with the lesser offence of manslaughter, replied: "We didn't think of things like that, we were at war".

The Government, whatever had happened to justice, now did an about turn on a pledge given to farmers that their workers would not be called up. Young farmers between the ages of eighteen to twenty had to register. All others liable for conscription had either gone, or established a good alibi for still being at home. The pursuit of dodgers had abated and there were now unofficial family competitions to see who was doing the most for the country. Hoping to claim a record were Mr and Mrs R.J. Brennan, of The Model Bakery at Worgret, Wareham, who had five sons serving in the RAF — Edwin (33), Archibald (31), Peter (27), Eric (21), and Samuel (20). Their two other children were girls, and Mrs Brennan was also caring for the motherless children of her eldest son.

This claim stirred the pride of Mrs Copp at Acorn Yard, Maiden Newton, who had four sons in the army and one in the Home Guard. They were Private E.J. Copp (34), Gunner R. Copp (32), Private H.G. Copp (26), Private C.H. Copp (24) and A.R. Copp (18), who was in the Home Guard. Mrs Copp's husband had been killed in France during the Great War.

The 'tub thumping' was going well now, and Sir Charles Petrie Toller, of Sherborne, proved himself a super optimist by telling Dorchester Rotarians that Germany would break rapidly and completely. This was wild talk at a time when we still stood alone. Heavy air-raids were continued day and night, and, in February, the extensive damage that one bomb could achieve made it obvious that Germany had a new type of bomb. Weymouth, the most prominent target on the Dorset coast, received much of the Luftwaffe's attention. One unfortunate section of the town had a bad attack at 4.30 am on 9 May 1941 when no alert had been sounded. A single German plane penetrated radar cover and dropped a stick of five bombs. Damage was widespread and casualties high. A family had returned to their house after an earlier 'all clear' had sounded. The sneak raider scored a direct hit on the house, killing six of them — the mother, Mrs Lilian Adnam, a married daughter, Mrs Violet Hood, and her single sisters Dorothy, Vivian, Margaret and Mary. Two other daughters were injured.

War had seemed to earmark this part of Weymouth for death and destruction. On 17 November 1940 Chapelhay was smashed in a different type of air attack, with twelve people, including children, being killed. Now rebuilt with the dreary regularity of modern design, Chapelhay was then a zone of tightly-packed small houses. The Jack Buchanan radio programme, highly popular at the time, had just come to a close. It was 9 pm, and the occupants of those snug houses were stirring to get supper on that dark night. For some, it was their last movement on earth. At low altitude, a German raider swept in over the town, switching off his engine as he did so. Gliding silently, he opened his bomb doors.

All was quiet as a mine drifted down by parachute. Then there was a terrific explosion. Seventy-seven houses were smashed beyond repair. A further 181 buildings were seriously affected, while blast damaged another 879 houses. No written words, especially after so much time has passed, can effectively describe the horror of that night. But it strains the most ardent religious belief to understand why a child is killed in one part of a house while relatives are saved in other rooms, to grieve for the remainder of their lives. Or to comprehend why a war caused by some men and fought by others who had no argument, could lead to a young boy being reached by rescuers who find him still kneeling in the position for prayer, but dead.

Understandably, the German pilot was condemned as a murderer. But he did not set out on that flight with the intention of killing innocent civilians. Markings on the remains of the device showed it was a sea mine, intended for the harbour.

Hitler's planned invasion, Seeloewe ('Operation Sealion'), was still very much on the cards, though dependent on the Luftwaffe being victorious over England. At least this plan spared Dorset the military capabilities of General von Runstedt, the man who, as a field marshal, all but ended the Allies advance across Europe in 1944. The counter attack he launched in the Ardennes, became known as the Battle of the Bulge.

In 1941, von Runstedt was to command the eastern of the two landings projected for England, with Dorset being left to Field Marshal von Bock, who was to land in Weymouth Bay. Large airborne landings were planned for the Midlands, but a smaller parachute force, under General Student, was to drop between Weymouth and Dorchester linking up with troops landing by sea. How ready were we for such an attack? Despite the Home Guard and other coastal defences being constantly on the alert for parachutists, the answer must be — inadequately. A German flier shot down over Dorset wandered around trying to give himself up, without success. Completely lost, he first wandered along a dark road, and was relieved to see a British soldier coming in the opposite direction. But the soldier called out a friendly 'Good night', then passed on. Coming to a level crossing, the German found the gate closed. Patiently he stood waiting, dressed in Nazi uniform. Then the signalman came down from his box, and without looking at the German he opened the gates for him. The flier then met several more people, all of whom ignored him. Eventually, fed up and with nowhere to go, he stopped a civilian, mustered all the English he knew, and asked to be directed to the nearest police station. The startled civilian asked the German to oblige by staying where he was, while the man to whom he had surrendered ran away to find a member of the Home Guard. This mission complete, the German was taken to the police station, where he made a few faces red by relating his recent experiences.

Apart from the air attacks, the war now had nasty side effects that struck a blow where it really hurt — bank balances. Britain's wartime totalitarianism found a lot of rebels when it was decreed that all personal gold must be sold to the Treasury. An official must have swept an eye over Dorset's downs and concluded "Thar's gold in them thar hills".

He was right, and a 48-years-old retired civil engineer, Sir John Henry Sherlock, of 'West Wings' at Clarence Road, Dorchester (also of Pitt Orchard, Axminster) came up before Bow Street magistrates on a charge of not making the gold he owned available to the government. The case had been adjourned so that he could sell what he had to the Treasury. It was a considerable amount — 3,647 sovereigns, 4,590 half-sovereigns, and 66,888 ounces of gold worth another £499. He was allowed to keep 51 sovereigns and 86 half-sovereigns, but fined £4,000 with £100 costs. His sister, Mrs Olive Marjory Tufnell-Barrett, aged 42, an artist, of Axminster, was fined £200 with £30 costs for a similar offence.

A semi-carnival was held in most towns under the heading 'Warship week'. Portland held its event in the Tophill district, a platform bedecked with flags provided a saluting base at the side of Easton Square, from which General Sir Henry Jackson, connected with Dorset and well-known for his fine military record, performed the opening ceremony. With him was Lady Jackson, in Auxiliary Territorial Service uniform. The message that money was needed came with a light tank bearing a notice that it had cost the nation £5,000. Five bren-gun carriers had a £1,500 price tag on each, not much different from these days when armoured cars and tanks are put through their paces at Bovington for the appraisal of Arab buyers. The rest of the 1941 parade was made up of the island's fire fighting services, plus the Home Guard, its wardens in their dark blue uniforms. The week ended with Portland's target doubled, to £67,200.

Heathland tank training, early in 1941. The furze and heather of Purbeck and Bovington was to become increasingly churned as the war developed. This tank is an A13. It was a cruiser tank, a long-range vehicle, and the first British chassis to use Christie suspension. The idea for this was developed in the United States and smuggled to Britain as a "tractor with a number of cases labelled 'grapefruit'" in 1936.

Photograph: Imperial War Museum.

Weymouth followed up with an equally successful week, enhanced by a thrilling display put on by the RAF. Dorchester held its week from 17-24 May, with the intention of enticing residents to donate a total of £120,000, sufficient to buy six bombers. But the cream of these grand events was soured by horror and tragedy that May, particularly in Weymouth. To most residents there did not seem to be any time of day that was free from air attacks. Houses were flattened, death and injury becoming accepted if not acceptable. Among a formidably long list of people killed in air-raids were the wife and baby son of a man serving overseas in the Royal Navy. This sailor had never seen his baby.

Lives of heroes of the air were short, and reported missing was Flying Officer Archibald Weir, of Pensbury House, Shaftesbury. On 1 June 1940, the eve of his 21st birthday, Weir shot down his first two

Messerschmitts, and then fought in actions over France, at Dunkirk, and over the Channel in the Battle of Britain. On 8 August, when his squadron had set up a record by shooting down twenty-one planes, he accounted for three of them himself. For this, and his work at Dunkirk, he was awarded the Distinguished Flying Cross.

Another Dorset aviator reported missing on 27 March 1941, was Wing Commander Edward Collis de Virac Lart, who had been born at Lyme Regis in 1902. Luckier than these two fliers, but only just, was the prospective Conservative candidate for the Yeovil division, John Fox-Strangways, second son of the Earl and Countess of Ilchester. Serving in the Middle East, he was wounded in the foot and taken prisoner of war.

Gallantry was rewarded with a George Medal for Captain (acting major) G.B. Matthews MC TD of the Dorsetshire Regiment. His action was announced in the London Gazette of 24 February 1941:

> An explosion occurred in a minefield, causing a number of fatal casualties to NCOs and men. Four men, though wounded, survived the explosion and were left marooned in the minefield, surrounded by unexploded mines and mutilated bodies. The field was enclosed by barbed-wire entanglements, which made the task of extricating the survivors more difficult as it was known that more mines were buried under the wire. Major Matthews decided that the only way to reach the survivors was to place planks over the wire and so enter the minefield and assist the survivors to safety. This he did, though fully aware of the danger of exploding mines, not only in the field but under the wire. He did, in fact, only miss treading on a mine by some six inches. There is no doubt whatever that his resourcefulness and courage saved the lives of the four men, who were unable to move unaided.

In support of the men in uniform, the civilians of Dorset were sparing no effort. Bridport had earlier raised £6,000 toward the purchase of a fighting plane named 'The Brit', and the town's War Weapons week began on 14 May 1941, with a target of £45,000 to buy three medium tanks. When the week ended, the mayor addressed a large crowd outside the Town Hall, telling them the war had made us a nation of brothers and sisters. Then he walked to the huge indicator that had recorded the week's finances. There was a mighty cheer as he moved the hand to show the final figure as a fantastic £52,000.

The results in the county of War Weapons' weeks confirmed what most had suspected — there was now more money about than at any time in living memory. This new affluence began to affect rationing regulations. The food control executive committee at Lyme Regis received a complaint that some people, who could afford to, were registering with three or four grocers, and when these retailers had supplies of rare unrationed goods, the greedy customers got a share from each. It was also claimed that some retailers were showing favouritism to a small section of customers, to the disadvantage of others. Then, as now, there was little real chance of winning with a complaint against authority. The Lyme Regis food officer, Gilbert Atterbury, explained that he would need to have specific and detailed complaints before he could take action.

A similar problem at Dorchester was brought to light in a court case. A butcher, Arthur Wake of Cambridge Road, was prosecuted by solicitor Morton, on behalf of the borough food office, for selling meat in excess of the coupons tendered by a customer. Morton said that a Mrs Tickler had purchased 4s. 4d. worth of meat from the shop, while supplying only one coupon from her ration book (worth one shilling) and a leave coupon also valid for a shilling's worth of meat.

She said she had left her son's ration book at home. Though pleading guilty the butcher pointed out that Mrs Tickler had not taken her ration of meat the previous week, but Morton said that rations could not be held over for a week, and a fine of £5 was imposed on Wake.

Risking prosecution, and being warned about it by the Air Ministry, were the souvenir hunters who descended on crashed Nazi planes. The ministry warned how dangerous a practice this was, as many had been killed by unexploded bombs or high-octane fuel tanks blowing up. Taking souvenirs was not only illegal but was an action against the country, as crashed aircraft provided salvage that gave vital information to the authorities, like that which reached Dr Ronald Jones from the sea off Bridport. Rodney Legg explains its significance:

Earlier in the war, on 6 November 1940, a German bomber of Kampt Gruppe 100 (a flare-dropping pathfinder squadron directed by radio beams, code name Knickebein, on 31.5 mHz) suffered a compass failure and was misled by British signals into thinking it was over France. In fact, the plane was still over Dorset, and out of fuel it crashlanded on a beach at West Bay near Bridport.

The plane, a Heinkel 111 call sign 6N + AH, carried a complete X-Gerät direction finding system , restricted to an experienced two percent elite of the German bomber force. It was the first such device the British had captured, and it eventually reached Dr Ronald Jones, the head of Air Ministry scientific intelligence.

However, it was nearly lost to the sea, and the lost days that resulted turned out to be vital. What happened at Bridport was that a coastal defence army officer had left soldiers in charge of the ditched bomber with the order that no one was to touch it: "I don't care if even an admiral comes along. You are not to allow him near it."

What was beyond the experience of the officer was that the sea is tidal, and the plane had touched down between the high and low water marks. Later in the day the army prevented the navy from hauling it up the beach. The result, Jones remembers in his memoirs, *Most Secret War*, was "that the whole aircraft was awash".

The radio equipment filled with sand and its light alloy components had corroded by the time they were salvaged and being studied by 80 Wing of the RAF. Goering himself had been told by the Luftwaffe that night bombing was useless without radio location devices — and here the key equipment had fallen into British hands and been allowed to fill with seawater at Bridport.

Jones is scathing about what a little Dorset incompetence caused: "This failure to save the aircraft intact may have contributed to the disaster eight days later at Coventry".

For the Royal Aircraft Establishment at Farnborough found that the filter of the X-Gerät was tuned at 2000 cycles per second ("a high pitch note corresponding roughly to the top 'C' on a piano) whereas British jamming at the time of the Coventry raid was at an ineffectual 1500 cycles per second ("corresponding to the 'G'") and might as well not have existed. Jones was angry that the inadequate precautions came about because of inattention to a most trivial detail: "Of all the measurements in connection with the German beams, easily the simplest was to determine the modulation note, because this could be done at any time in comfort, and yet whoever had done it had either been tone deaf or completely careless, and no one had ever thought of checking his measurements. I was so indignant that I said that whoever made such an error ought to have been shot".

Sir Robert Cockburn, at the time the head of the beam-intercepting Telecommunications Research Establishment at Worth Matravers on the Purbeck coast, has said: "I was really quite appalled to hear that such a gross boob had been made. It must have been a failure of communication; somebody rung up and given the wrong frequency."

Too late to save Coventry, the information was to be of crucial importance throughout 1941 for it led the way to effective jamming of the German beams, and prevented what could have otherwise become a raid of Coventry style precision and proportions carried out whatever the weather every night of the week.

Radar saved Britain, by not only forewarning of imminent attack, but allowing economy in the use of fighters — patrols only had to be airborne when the enemy was known to be coming. This advantage meant that inferior forces could be conserved against a foe who had all the numerical advantages. Britain's radar system was masterminded by the Telecommunications Research Establishment at Worth Matravers on the Purbeck coast. By June 1941 the authorities were confident enough to release some of the secrets and this photograph appeared with the following caption: "Radiolocation stretches far beyond Britain's shores to send back warnings of the approach of enemy aircraft. Highly skilled men and women are required to share in this valuable duty. This picture, one of an official series, shows the mechanic at the main switchboard of a power generating station."

Dorset at War

Down in our Air-Raid Shelter
There's no cause for alarm,
It is so sure and strongly built
We cannot come to harm.
Let the bombs bounce round above us,
And the shells come whizzing by.
Down in our Air-Raid Shelter
We'll be cosy, you and I!

Cumberland Clark, Bournemouth's poet, in one of his 'War Songs of the Allies'. He can, however, provide us with no further chapter tail-pieces. Cumberland Clark was killed in January 1941 when a German bomb destroyed his flat in St Stephen's Road.

July 1941 — December 1941

I do not know when the end of the war will
come, but when it does it will be a quick finish.
— Bernard Newman, broadcaster, lecturer and
author, speaking at Weymouth. August, 1941

FUND-RAISING was still a civil responsibility, but by the latter half of 1941 the war was familiar enough to breed a measure of contempt. Scattered evidence of this was cropping up — like at a Bridport council meeting where Councillor W.S.B. Northover raised the subject of fire-watching, and revealed that a lack of volunteers made compulsory duty seem probable.

Again at Bridport, more than a few consciences were pricked when the chief billeting officer for evacuees, Councillor T.J. Dale, handed in his resignation. Council members pleaded with him to change his mind, but he was adamant. He publicly stated that he had been sickened by the refusal of many residents to even consider housing evacuees.

Things were not much better at Beaminster, and it began to look as if evacuees would be forced on residents by law. This possibility, and disgust with the circumstances that had brought it on, made the town's billeting officer, Major Horner, throw the towel in as well. He said that compulsory billeting would be best enforced by a salaried, independent outsider. After two and a half years in the job, he had had enough.

But it was not all apathy in Beaminster. An energetic executive committee there — of L. Skyrm, E.P. Bailey, W.J. Bailey, L.D. Colborne, R.W. Ryall, W.A. Stibey and with Hon. Sec. P.W. Barrett as secretary — planned a Warship Week for 12 to 19 July. The target was £25,000.

With America not yet in the war, the Weymouth in the States was feeling sorry for the hard-pressed Weymouth over here, and asked what help was needed. The mayor of Weymouth in England, suggested to the mayor of Weymouth in Massachusetts, that a contribution to his war fund might be a good idea. Without delay, 1,200 dollars were cabled by the generous Yanks.

Now that sides, flexible until then, were beginning to take shape, the unexpected inclusion of Russia on ours caught people unawares. Few knew much about this huge new ally, and Mrs J.L. Stocks, principal of Westfield College, gave a talk from personal experience of Russia, in a crowded Bridport Town Hall.

While it was all happening, ladies still took interest in a bit of vanity. Silk stockings were as rare as a Christmas tree in Kingdom Hall, and a liquid leg make-up, in natural tan, was selling well at a shilling for a two ounce bottle.

Tales of miraculous escapes were numerous enough to be boring, but a Bridport incident just had to be retold. Cause of the trouble was a single German plane, usually doing more damage than a mass raid. This particular lone wolf let go an incendiary bomb that wrecked two houses in a street, and brought Mr and Mrs Edgar Barnes very close to death. The couple were in bed when the bomb came through the ceiling, passed down through the end of their bed — fractions of an inch from their feet — then on through the bedroom floor and the ceiling below, to ignite when striking the ground floor. The couple escaped through a front bedroom window.

Once cowed by criticism, the Civil Defence was now a proud organisation. The experience of one man, E. Godden of Weymouth, will, albeit in a macabre way, vividly illustrate the gory work. Having spent a night of hard duty in a bad air attack, tending to the dead and injured, he returned to the scene the following morning. A policeman came from his house and beckoned Godden over, saying there was something unusual in the back garden that he wanted to show him. There, lifting an upturned flower pot, the policeman revealed a human heart. He explained that he had covered the gruesome object with the pot to "keep the cats away".

Though not tested in battle, the Home Guard had also found respect in the eyes of the public. This was a big step from the early days of disorganisation, when the body was known as the LDV, for Local Defence Volunteers. Cynics had corrupted this to Look, Duck and Vanish. Churchill had the name changed. Home Guard, in fact, had been used as the title for Bridport's local defence volunteers in 1915.

Mostly no longer young, Home Guard members were often experienced veterans of the previous war. This made a fatal accident at Sherborne even more surprising, as it involved a rifle handled by a knowledgeable old soldier.

Neighbours Harold Sweet, a 46-years-old partially deaf dental mechanic of 12 Winfield Road, and Sergeant Thomas Read, aged 50, of

62 Winfield Road, Sherborne, finished a spell of night duty at 5.30 am. Returning to the house used by the unit, Sergeant Read squeezed the trigger of the American type rifle he thought he had unloaded. From the other side of the darkened room, he heard a groan and found Sweet lying on a bunk, shot but conscious. The wounded man said "I don't blame you" and then died. At the Sherborne hospital inquest, Read pointed out that he and the dead man had been close friends. The coroner for North Dorset, W. Creech, recorded a verdict of death by misadventure.

Special constables were having their big day at Dorchester, being paraded and praised by Lord Shaftesbury, the Lord Lieutenant of Dorset. Having survived the court appearance for unlawfully obtaining his butter, Lord Shaftesbury told the Sunday afternoon paraders: "Carry on and go forward in the way you have begun, with no relaxation of effort or flagging of spirit, to make sure that when the call comes you will be either individually or collectively a powerful support to our Chief Constable and the Dorset Constabulary as a whole."

Relief came to Mrs Sly, of 14 Fairclose, Weymouth, when a letter arrived from the husband she had been told was "missing believed killed". Lance-Corporal Cecil Sly, who was a driver with the Post Office at Weymouth before the war, wrote to say that he had been captured by the Germans.

Also in the "Lucky brigade", and even more so, was Air Mechanic Morgan Jeffery, a survivor of the sinking of HMS *Ark Royal,* who was home on leave with his parents, Mr and Mrs H. Jeffery, of the Bridge Inn, Dorchester. Morgan, who celebrated his 21st birthday a week after the sinking of his ship, joined the navy as a boy and had transferred to the Fleet Air Arm two years previously.

Weymouth, in the front line for the bombing of Dorset, was also a target for every orator heading west. Broadcaster, lecturer and author, Bernard Newman started a speech at the Alexandra Gardens with a sound observation. He told a large audience that Hitler's biggest mistake had been to attack Russia. Then he slipped into understatement by saying that if he had invaded England, the dictator would have had a fifty percent chance of victory. He would, in fact, probably have had something like a ninety-nine percent chance. The only thing that made Churchill's "we will fight them on the beaches" speech subject to admiration rather than ridicule, is that the Germans did not arrive.

Optimistic speakers already had an armistice fund going in the north of England, and Newman looked like bringing this madness south, by saying that the bombing of our cities had not broken morale, but the German people would not be able to stand up to the bombing of their cities in the same way. "One week we shall be fighting with our backs to the wall," he told the people of Weymouth, "and the next thing we shall know will be that it is finished".

This was dangerous, stupid talk, which suggested that the people of Britain had some kind of innate superiority. The German people, later in the war, stood up to far worse air attacks than had ever been launched on Britain. It is apparent why the bombing of civilians was never listed among war crimes. Had it been so, the Germans on trial would have had to shuffle along their bench to make room for a number of distinguished Englishmen.

As for the war ending suddenly in our favour, there was no hope of that. Historians knew, and the astute British public was aware, that demoralising as it seemed, Britain had never before won a war alone against an armed opponent. This conflict was to be no exception. Always, Britain had been one of a winning team, and the only chance of victory lay in the participation of the United States in World War Two. At the time of Newman's speech, this country was practically totally dependant on American finance, and to the USA for ultimate victory.

By this time, harassment of shipping had cut imports drastically, resulting in just about everything being in short supply. Motorists were asked to drive on tyres for as long as possible, even if the canvas was showing. The armed services needed all available rubber. A new traffic law was introduced, making it an offence to leave a vehicle without immobilising it. This was to deprive enemy agents of the chance of stealing cars. The usual fine for offenders was ten shillings.

If the Germans had the exact result of an air-raid on Weymouth during the night of 1 November 1941, they might have been pleased. For the mayor of the town, J.T. Goddard, respected by all and decorated for bravery in the Great War, was trapped under rubble for almost an hour when his home, the Adelaide Hotel, in Abbotsbury Road, was hit. A rescue squad, headed by Bill Docksey, a mace-bearer for the mayor, was able to save the mayoral medallion and the mayor's war decorations. They freed Goddard by cutting through a beam, and he was taken to hospital.

Without the publicity given to the injured mayor, this would have been just another night in Weymouth — three people killed and eleven injured in the Abbotsbury Road area, with 171 houses damaged. Gas mains were affected and the road blocked to traffic. For those without gas, or possibly no stove or kitchen left for cooking, the Cookery Nook at the Rock Hotel was opened up for meals.

It had all begun at 11.20 pm when four high explosive bombs fell. It was all over quickly for the dead — never ending for the bereaved.

The NAAFI, always better material for a comedian's jokes than a mother-in-law, brought a bit of fun to the war with a national contest to find 'Miss NAAFI'. Some 28,000 girls entered. Main judges, ostensibly, were a soldier, sailor and airman, but stage and radio personalities, plus Lady Astor, did most of the thinking. Winner was a Bridport girl, 21-years-old Miss Eileen Bishop of East Street, a former assistant in the town's branch of Woolworths.

Christmas was again on the horizon by this time, and the towns of Dorset did what they could for those who could do little in the way of festivities for themselves. Cinemas organised free shows for evacuee children, most of the managers managing to find a gift for each child. Mayors were asking householders prepared to take soldiers into their homes for Christmas, to say so early, so that a list could be drawn up.

Warship weeks were now the big money-raisers, and there was a friendly intercounty championship to see who could raise the largest sum. At this early stage, Dorset was lying eleventh, far ahead of neighbouring Devon and Cornwall. Most amazing of all was how the total figures averaged out per head. The majority could not afford really large sums, so a few towns must have given a lot. At Sherborne, £178,149 had been raised (an average of £13 14s. 1d. per head). Shaftesbury had £119,654 (average £10 2s. 3d.). Wimborne pulled in £143,611 (£6 1s. 7d. per person).

Russia, taking a break from being hated, needed help, and the ladies of Charmouth, Wootton Fitzpaine and Monkton Wilde Red Cross groups organised a "Russian Flag Day". At Charmouth, Mrs Dixon, Miss Flanagan, Miss Goodfellow, Miss Niblett, Miss Maluel, Mrs Matthews, Mrs Taylor, Miss Tucker and Miss Williams collected £15 13s. 1d. Miss A. Fowler, Mrs A. Powell and Mrs F. Rapsey, worked hard to get £3 19s. 1d. at Wootton Fitzpaine, while £1 0s. 11d. was picked at Monkton Wilde by Miss Moss and Mrs Neale.

Still held under Section 18b of the *Defence Regulations*, Captain G.L.H.F. Pitt-Rivers, of Hinton St Mary, thought it would be pleasant if he were home for Christmas. But the King's Bench felt he would be safer inside where he could be kept an eye on, and dismissed his writ of habeas corpus. Christmas this year, the most depressing one of the war, had a boost when the United States first declared war on Japan, following the sneak attack on Pearl Harbour, and then on Germany. A further indication of a more affluent future came from the Ship Inn thrift club at Bridport, one of the few carrying on under pre-war rules. £700 was paid out to 112 members. The officials were T. Conway, Mrs L.M. Northover, C.W. Crabbe, T. Tuck, J. Ward, W. Legg, B. Canterbury, D. Tattersall and W. Ryan.

Dorset pubs were granted an extension from 10 to 11 pm on Christmas Eve and Boxing Day. At Beaminster sessions, J. Roper successfully applied for extensions at Askers Roadhouse, from 10 pm until midnight on 26 and 31 December and 9 January. This was for dances held by the

RAF Benevolent Fund, Askerswell and District Young Farmers, the Red Cross Fund and BBC Social Club.

A new year was coming, and Britain no longer stood alone. But it was too early for general optimism, and generally it was not a happy Christmas.

January 1942 —
June 1942

*Maybe some of you aren't doing anything to
help win the war — probably just sitting there
handing out summonses.*

— a Dorset woman war-worker addressing the
Weymouth Juvenile Bench, May 1942

NEW YEAR'S Honours gave the county a lift into 1942 with a few OBE's.
In Weymouth they went to the mayor, J.T. Goddard, the executive
officer for War Agricultural committee, T.R. Ferris, and Mr Reddell,
general manager of the Whitehead Torpedo Works. Such frivolities were
soon overtaken by other events. At an ARP meeting, Major W.J. Van de
Weyer was saying: "In Dorset there is a great deal of lack of thought
regarding an invasion by the Germans".

Adding that he would like to see the possibility of such a happening
emphasised more in the press, he went on: "In this neighbourhood people
seem to think there is not going to be an invasion. I have heard people say
'What is the use of the Home Guard, they will never be wanted?' But the
Prime Minister keeps talking about invasion."

The possibility, Rodney Legg points out, had in reality gone, as
Enigma decoding of German operational radio traffic confirmed. But
pretences had to be maintained, as no action could be taken on Enigma
knowledge unless it could be justified by other intelligence information,
to avoid revealing its real source. In fact, in February 1942, there was to
be a miniature invasion in reverse, and it was to restore a little of the
morale shaken by the fall of Singapore and the escape up the Channel of
the German warships *Scharnhorst, Gneisenau* and *Prinz Eugen* from
Brest to Kiel.

In Dorset, W.B. Lewis, the Deputy Superintendent of the
Telecommunications Research Establishment (TRE) at Worth
Matravers, had studied close-up aerial photographs of a German radar
scanner, called a Würzburg, on a 400-foot French clifftop at Bruneval.
On 27 February, in deep snow, a small party of paratroops landed,

dismantled it, and brought back key parts of the apparatus for examination at Worth Matravers.

The success of the raid led to fears of a reprisal against the research station at Worth where, less than a mile from the Purbeck cliffs, all British radar development was taking place, only a short distance up the valley from Chapman's Pool. Dr Jones, of Air Ministry scientific intelligence recalls in *Most Secret War* that with Hugh Smith he drove to Swanage to see the examination of the Bruneval equipment: "We said nothing about the possibility of a German retaliation, but merely carried our tin hats everywhere and had revolvers ostentatiously strapped to our belts.

"We also contrived to give the impression of nervousness and an anxiety to get back to London as soon as possible. The next we heard was that TRE was moving in a hurry to Malvern where, as the Royal Radar Establishment, it still is." As an indication of the calibre of the work that was carried out on the Dorset coast, in April 1942 the simple British radar-jamming countermeasure that was to involve strips of metal dropped from bombers was given the codename "Window" by A.P. Rowe, the superintendent of TRE. When finally introduced, after more than a year of argument and hesitation, it was to cut air losses over Germany from 6.1 percent to 1.5 percent, and save 75 planes in a single night.

Such superiority seemed far away in the spring of 1942. Shortages of materials had the authorities pulling down iron railings for war salvage. Owners of iron fences were first sent a postcard notification that their decorations would shortly be cut down and taken away. In Weymouth, the gates of the Grammar School, through which many an education-jammed head had proudly passed, went to the melting pot.

Much of the war-scrap was useless for a nation whose industry needed high-grade steel, and shiploads of rusting waste were dumped in the Western approaches. Its salvage had been psychological, to emphasise the severity of the crisis in a way that everyone would notice. History was often the loser, and the Royal Armoured Corps' collection of the world's first tanks was literally broken up. These vehicles had been preserved in Dorset at Bovington Camp, as a result of being seen by Rudyard Kipling in 1924. He appreciated their historic significance, and as a result of his visit a couple were rescued from a scrapheap and put in a shed.

Luckily, in 1940, a few were again spared — this time for use as stationary pillboxes. These were gathered up once more in 1942 for the making of the propaganda film *Victory*. It was filmed on the Dorsetshire heaths with "British light tanks seen advancing under heavy artillery bombardment from the enemy in the war of 1914-18". They were put back into their museum in 1948.

Elsewhere on the civilian front in 1942, to ease the mental suffering of

The Channel Dash of February 1942: German battleships Scharnhorst (right), Gneisenau and Prinz Eugen escape from Brest to Kiel.

relatives of prisoners of war, the Red Cross and St John Ambulance Association set up a Weymouth branch of the Prisoner of War Organisation. Open from 2.30 to 4.30 pm each Thursday and Friday, the branch gave advice and information. Secretary was R. Butcher, and treasurer Mrs K.P. Colson, both with sons in German prison camps.

Petty Officer Coates, the 35-year-old son of Mr and Mrs H. Coates, of 92 Corporation Road, Weymouth, found that his early-war luck was

Bovington's historic collection of the world's first tanks was scrapped in 1940. Those machines that had not been broken up, and were merely lying around as pillboxes, came back to life for an admiring audience in 1942: "A realistic scene from the British film 'Victory' which was filmed in Dorsetshire. British light tanks are seen advancing under heavy artillery bombardment from the enemy in the war of 1914-18."

OPPOSITE TOP: *"Look, I think we could get in there," Dr Ronald Jones, the director of Air Ministry scientific intelligence, said after studying a pair of stereo aerial prints of a field at Cap d'Antifer near the village of Bruneval on the French coast. He had located the parabolic aerial of a Würzberg radar station, operating on 53 cms (between 558 and 560 mHz) at the top of a low cliff on the Cherbourg peninsula. Lord Louis Mountbatten, the head of Combined Operations decided on the 'Biting' plan, a raid by C Company of the 2nd Battalion of the Parachute Regiment, to retrieve the station's aerial, receiver and cathode-ray tube, plus one or two of its operators. The Navy's job was to get the men out again. In February 1942, shortly before the operation, there was a rehearsal (above) in the waters off Portland.*

OPPOSITE, BOTTOM: *Here, about seventy miles to the north of the Cherbourg coast, a recovery operation was to be staged in which the waiting men would be on a similar-looking piece of the adjacent Dorset shore.*

OVER, TOP LEFT: *Redcliff Point was chosen — an uninhabited 150 ft. high cliff at the east end of Weymouth Bay, midway between Weymouth and Ringstead. The Bren guns were to give covering fire in the actual raid, and silence the Germans firing from the beach.*

OVER, BOTTOM LEFT: *As the boats arrived the paratroops came out of cover and moved down towards the water.*

OVER, TOP RIGHT: *Some poised on the shingle ready to give protective fire.*

OVER, BOTTOM RIGHT: *It is possible this is not quite what was planned, as the tide seems to have gone out a little faster than was expected, and the first landing craft appears to be stranded on the beach.*

holding out. At the evacuation of Dunkirk he had survived when his ship was sunk. He was serving aboard HMS *Prince of Wales* during the *Bismarck* episode.

But luck had run out for Petty Officer Bert Ayles. Eight years before, after a boy-and-girl courtship, he had married Stella, the daughter of Mr and Mrs Kirkaldie, of the Dolphin Inn, Park Street, Weymouth. It looked like the final story, too, for a well-known Dorchester journalist, J.B. Whalley, when his ship went down. His friends grieved when they heard of the sinking of HMS *Vimiera,* commanded by Lieutenant Commander A.A. Mackenzie, of Sherborne. Of 1917 design, the ship was one of the over-age destroyers allocated to convoy duty, and had the distinction of shooting down three enemy aircraft. Whalley had been serving on her for some months, but there was widespread relief among his many friends when it was later learned that he had been home on leave at the time of the sinking.

As always, Weymouth council looked in danger of sinking. The sad council, with its long history of getting nothing right, made a hash of the Minister of Education's directive that meals had to be provided for all schoolchildren. Weymouth went its own way and decided that only needy children in the borough would have meals. The ministry rejected this as objectionable on social and educational grounds, as the children concerned would be subjected to a means test. The borough treasurer, M. Lodge, said the scheme would cost £8,000 — over £2,000 of which would be borne by the council. Alderman Peaty pointed out that children with millionaire parents would be getting meals provided by the ratepayers, not that there was evidence of any parents in Weymouth having that financial distinction. But the objections were only tokens of dissent, and the minister's instructions were obeyed the second time around.

Death, by natural causes for a change, brought sorrow to Dorset, when the county lost a popular schoolmaster, Henry Eli Brickell. He died while cycling from Wareham Senior School, where he was headmaster, to his sister's funeral at Shaftesbury.

A new and particularly distressing dimension had been added to the worry about men who were prisoners. The Japanese were capturing

TOP: Waiting to leave, and hoping it is soon! The men may be well dressed but they were still cold that February day, as several rubbed their hands and stamped their feet. The cliffs towards Ringstead are in the background.

BOTTOM: The right way to beach a landing craft. The final evacuation from Redcliff Point, almost as successful as the real thing — where two were to die, and six taken prisoner. The background metalwork dates from the invasion days of 1940, and ran along the beach from Redcliff to Shortlake. The cliff to the right is Black Head. This series of photographs has been provided by the Imperial War Museum.

Britons on a scale not even approached by the Germans. Things looked bad to Mrs Whatley, 17 Lynch Road, Weymouth, when her husband, Able Seaman Louis Whatley, aged 33, was reported missing in Hong Kong, where he had served for two and a half years. Final confirmation of his death seemed to come when the Admiralty stopped her marriage allowance. Mrs Whatley then received a telegram saying that he was safe, though it gave no further details, such as his location.

The education authorities were now finding that conscription had brought a severe shortage of teachers, and Dorset remitted the rule that women teachers had to retire when they married. Bringing a fresh concept to Home Guard service was the decision to form a mounted patrol in the county. It was hoped that the scheme would appeal to farmers, who lacked the time to join in the ordinary way. Each volunteer had to provide his own horse, which would have to be one that could survive on grass alone, as no forage coupons would be granted. Saddlery also had to be personally supplied, but the mounted men would be excused all foot duty. The idea was to set up a means of communication that would cover ground a motorcycle and rider could not traverse.

With the likelihood of German invasion still treated seriously, official instructions were issued for essential workers in the Home Guard, such as farm workers, who found themselves engaged on an important task when the Nazis landed. Their orders were to finish the job and then change into uniform and report for duty. The success of this loose sort of timetable would obviously depend on the unlikely co-operation of the invading Germans.

Arriving in Weymouth, after having left Singapore on 31 December 1941, just in front of the triumphant march of the Japanese, were Mrs Edith Neale and her three daughters, Marjory, Doris and Margaret. All were shivering in the shock of a British winter, and Mrs Neale said: "I am thankful that we got through safely and I am now awaiting news of my husband."

The family had been in Singapore for five years, where the husband, Lieutenant Neale of the RASC, was stationed. With the Japanese advancing, they speedily packed their belongings, left their home behind and boarded a boat. Among the passengers on this first leg of the sea journey were Air Marshall Sir Brooke-Popham and Lady Brooke-Popham, Mrs Peggy Bailey, and Commander Denby, also of Weymouth.

The Neale family later found itself in the company of Brigadier Lyons, who had been responsible for the evacuation of Penang. Mrs Neale, taking a realistic view of the situation, said at Weymouth: "The war was short and rapid for us, being all over in five weeks. You have had two and a half years of it."

British restaurants, a boon in these times of rationing, had popped up everywhere, and Dorchester had its turn when Major Gwilym Lloyd George performed an official opening ceremony for a restaurant there. In his speech he said that he did not think anyone in this country had cause for complaint where food was concerned. He should have known whether this was true — as he was Parliamentary Secretary to the Minister of Food.

Viscount Hinchingbrooke, the new member of Parliament for South Dorset, had a bit of a problem when addressing his Party at the Burdon Hotel, Weymouth. This was a time of rousing speeches in which the orator was expected to say nice things about Britain's allies. But how does a true-blue tory face the flag-wavers of Dorset — while showering praises on communist Russia. Worse still, in acknowledging the Soviet Union and the United States he was writing Britain's obituary as a power in the post war world. But he made it, saying: "Since I spoke to you last we have gained two great allies and found another enemy. In Russia and the United States we have two allies without whom it would be safe to say we could never win the war. In Japan we have a most abominable enemy who will have to be exterminated as completely as Hitler and Mussolini."

How many right-wing orientated listeners, in that town half flattened by the Luftwaffe, asked themselves the old question again — would it have been best to unite with Hitler.

It became easier each day to hate the Japs. They sank the 10,000 ton cruiser HMS *Dorsetshire* in the Indian Ocean, with another cruiser of the

Japanese airpower ended the myth of British naval supremacy. The cruiser HMS 'Dorsetshire' went down in the Indian Ocean. These are the survivors, swimming towards the rescue boats from a destroyer which arrived on the scene shortly before nightfall.

same tonnage, HMS *Cornwall,* going down at the same time. It was known that there were 1,100 survivors, and relatives spent a terrible time waiting to learn who the fortunate ones were. Completed in 1939, the *Dorsetshire,* commanded by Captain A.W.S. Agar, VC DSC, mounted eight-inch guns.

If there is a fate worse than death, a Dorset man, together with countless others, was just about to experience it, by becoming a prisoner of the Japanese. He was leading Aircraftsman J.W. Savidge, of Brownlow Street, Weymouth.

Back home, astoundingly in circumstances of war, a different kind of prisoner was being worried about. At a Dorchester meeting of the Dorset and Bournemouth Prisoners Aid Society, chairman R. Sykes stressed the need for subscribers to keep donations coming in, even if they were reduced by war. He pointed out that prisons were full, for various reasons, and discharged convicts still needed help. No record exists as to the response to this, but it is doubtful that even a handful of people gave a damn about discharged prisoners at that time. The forces were willing to give him bed, board and a uniform, and if he did not meet requirements there was full employment available elsewhere.

News of boys overseas was always welcomed, and a letter received by Norman Windust, a pupil at Weymouth Grammar school, was of great interest. It was written by one of two 'Masterminds' of Dorset, Lieutenant A.E. Walkling. From 1928 to 1937, he and R.R. Head had attended Weymouth Grammar school. Both of extremely high intelligence, they had always been neck-and-neck where gaining scholarships was concerned, with Head eventually pipping Walkling at the post. But they had both gone on to Oxford.

In his letter of April 1942, Walkling, who was serving in the Libyan desert, wrote to Windust: "You will be amazed when I tell you who I ran into the other day. About a month after the campaign started, I was wandering the desert in a truck, looking for Jerries. I spotted a large column early one morning and crept up on it as stealthily as an army truck will allow. It was a friendly column, and out of the nearest vehicle popped a long thin figure with glasses. It was Head. I don't know which of us had the biggest surprise. It seems strange to me, but there was both of us, with more than our fair share of brains, yet we had nothing better to do than chase our fellow men around the desert."

Walkling was the son of the late Mr and Mrs Walkling, of Bovington, where his father had been headmaster of the school. Sadly, shortly after this letter arrived, Head, whose parents lived at 5 Queen's Street, Weymouth, was reported missing.

With relief, Dorset noticed that air raids were now abating. One of the reasons for this was clear in the announcement that on the Soviet front, between 22 March and 19 April, the Luftwaffe had lost 891 planes, while Russian losses were just 239. The action had moved east. On the western front, Germany was beginning to fight a defensive war.

New legislation was being churned out without thought to side effects. Appearing before Weymouth juvenile bench was a woman forestry worker. On war work, she could not leave or take time off — so had to keep an older child home from school, so that her younger children could be looked after. She was summonsed for not sending her eldest daughter to school. Irate because of the unfairness of the situation, she shouted at the magistrates: "Maybe you are doing nothing to help win the war! Just sitting there wasting time and handing out summonses."

On the bench, R.R. Conway became equally angry and defensive, possibly because there was some truth in what the woman said. "I think she ought to be put in her place," Conway said. "I have never heard such insolence in my life."

The woman replied that he should have done so, for he deserved it. Then, after further debate, acrimony, and a report from the school attendances officer, the woman was fined £1, and left with the same problem of being in two places at the same time.

More sympathy went to a Portland mother whose two-years-old daughter died indirectly from an air-raid. The child was recovering after having pulled a kettle of boiling water on to herself, and was asleep in her cot when the siren sounded. Sitting up swiftly, the child then fell back — dead from the shock.

The loss of the cruiser *Dorsetshire* was a bad blow for the county's morale and the Lord Lieutenant, Lord Shaftesbury, called a meeting to discuss proposals for raising money to replace the warship. At the same time, Dorset workers were moaning that the shops closed too early, depriving them of the chance of buying what they wanted. Shopping early, and buying in bulk, was Dorset county council, which purchased eight tons of soap for issue to all departments.

The 'missing' tag attached to so many men on active service was still blighting the lives of relatives. Included on the list was 2nd Lt. John Marcus Benzie RASC, whose wife lived at the Broadway in Broadstone. He had been serving in Malaya. Also unaccounted for was Lieutenant Adrian A. Huxtable, 88 Field Regiment Royal Artillery, elder son of Lieutenant-Colonel C.H.A. and Mrs Huxtable, of 'Vancourtland', Wyke Regis. Life had also turned an unfortunate circle for the younger Huxtable, as he had been born in Malaya. Another officer missing presumed killed, was Lieutenant John W. Harbottle RN, second son of the late Kathleen Harbottle and Captain Harbottle RN, of Lavender Farm, Broadstone. More violence, of the civilian kind, was being meted out at Dorsetshire assizes when Mr Justice Charles sentenced an escaped

Portland borstal boy to twelve strokes of the birch for robbery with violence, and a year in prison for burglary.

As if touched by midsummer madness, Anthony Eden, then Secretary of State for Foreign Affairs, was calling for a Second Front to take some of the pressure off Russia. Britain's biggest problem at the time of this speech still seemed to many, how to stop the Germans coming across the Channel, not how to cross and have a go at them. Not content with this, Eden rambled on about a partnership between Britain and Russia, both in war and peace. Coming from a man in Eden's position, this struck many as naive.

Churchill, on 23 April 1942, spoke to a secret session of Parliament, assuring MPs that: "Members should realise our affairs are not conducted entirely by simpletons and dunderheads as the comic papers try to depict, and in particular that the Admiralty which I regard as an incomparable machine for British protection in spite of all the misfortunes and accidents that have happened, deserves a very broad measure of confidence and gratitude. Any featherhead can have confidence in times of victory, but the test is to have faith when things are going wrong for the time being, and when things happen which cannot be explained in public."

Arthur Legg of Wallisdown, Bournemouth, serving with 30 Corps Signals, Middle East Forces, wrote to his brother Ted, a Winton boot repairer, on 21 January 1942 with an accurate though greatly accelerated summation of the eventual course of the war:

> What do you think of the Japs now? I think you ought to have seen they meant business the way they put down the unsinkable battleships. They are still doing well, but they ought to have come in earlier. The Yanks, although taking a long time, will see them off, I'm certain. The Russians are too much for Jerry at present, and come a few months after the spring, it will surprise me if the war don't end suddenly. But the Far East will still be fighting.

July 1942 — December 1942

*Three years ago he sailed from Weymouth
with the Home Fleet, and we haven't seen him
since.*

— A Dorset sailor's wife, after learning that her 47-years-old
husband was a prisoner of the Japanese. August, 1942

RIGHT FROM the start of hostilities, speakers with as remote an idea of war as their audience had been firing words in Dorset. But a visit from Lady Hanbury, the widow of Sir Cecil Hanbury, former Member of Parliament for North Dorset, brought a change. She had been around, and knew what she was talking about, even if some of her ideas seemed a bit way out. For, riding into Weymouth like a refined Calamity Jane, she was guest of honour at a meeting of the Women's Round Table, in the gardens of 8 Melcombe Avenue. Controversy was expected from her. At the beginning of the war, when saying exactly what you thought was not in fashion, Lady Hanbury had been a warden at Westminster until, in her vernacular, she was "given the boot" for visiting underground shelters and then shouting about the disgusting conditions down there.

"Germany could lose this war in Russia," she told her Weymouth audience, "and, hopefully, in Egypt. But she could win the war by invading here and conquering us. I do not think that there is any doubt that Germany will take a final crack at victory on the shores of our tiny island."

She accused the Government of having a total lack of imagination and initiative, with the exception of Churchill. Having visited many parts of the world, being in Barcelona during the first air-raids of the Spanish Civil War, she was able to talk with authority. Recounting the atrocities she had witnessed in other countries, she asked: "What are we going to do with the children when the Nazis get here? We must make our own arrangements for their safety. In my district we have decided to bury them, and the person in charge has instructions to deliver a knock-out blow to any child that cries and endangers the others. Such a blow will

Winston Churchill watches his tanks, in the second half of 1942, possibly at the Royal Armoured Corps headquarters at Bovington on the Dorset heath. No longer would they be outgunned in the desert, for the new British tanks were substantially modified, with heavier armour and 6-pounder guns. Its name — a Churchill!

only give them a headache."

Never had advisers and would-be advisers enjoyed such scope as in this period of the war. A lot of it was useless, most of it uncalled for, but everyone thought that everyone else needed guidance of some kind, and a Citizen's Advice Bureau opened up at 3 Johnstone Row, beside the Esplanade at Weymouth.

No one could advise about the fate of the British in the Far East. For servicemen and civilians alike out there, it was all conjecture at home. But a Red Cross report arrived via Geneva, which said that Britons in an internment camp at Yokohama were being treated well by the Japanese, and it was hoped that letters from the camp would soon be delivered in England.

The Weymouth YMCA had the nerve to organise a jumble sale at the Sidney Hall, and probably regretted it from the moment the doors opened. There was a mad, undignified rush for ration-free clothing, that ended in a stampede and several scuffles. It did not improve morale for individuals to see themselves stripped of decorum by privation.

There was some pride left, though, and Weymouth was pleased to be associated with Leading Seaman Frederick Caddy, a former member of

The newly introduced Churchill tank tops a hill in one of its early manoeuvres on the Dorset coast.

Weymouth lifeboat crew, who was awarded a certificate for devotion to duty on convoy work in the Channel. Aged 41, he had served in trawlers and minesweepers during the Great War. But all was not well for those who go down to the sea in ships, as E.C. Burden, chief fishery officer at Bournemouth pointed out, when he complained about the controlled price of mackerel. He protested that 3s. 6d. a stone was not sufficient inducement to encourage fishermen to devote their attention to catching these fish.

The urge to get rid of kids for the day, as soon as they could balance on bent legs, had a less selfish motivation than it has today. To assist mothers on war work, a day nursery opened at Elwell Manor in Rodwell Road at Weymouth. Perhaps attendance there was better than it was at the real schools. Though poor and difficult to control in wartime, the officer responsible for attendance said it had been picking up, and then an outbreak of chicken-pox, coupled with children being off because their fathers were on leave, had hit attendance badly again.

School was only one casualty of this half-expired war. At a Dorchester meeting of the Diocesan Association for morals and social welfare, the bishop of the diocese, Dr Neville Lovett, pleaded with mothers to keep their daughters under control because war conditions were dangerous and there was a "rampant evil" about. Adding a flowery euphemism, he said he was appalled by women who were not prepared to help the Mary Magdalens war had manufactured.

The stupidity of war was illustrated by Lieutenant Alan Slee, whose mother was a Portlander. He was among the minefields surrounding Tobruk, when a German soldier surrendered to him. Both Englishman and German adopted the wary, cautious stances of the situation, then the German exclaimed: "You are Alan." Slee replied: "Hello, Karl." The captor and captive were old friends, having been fellow students at

A Churchill tank speeds away from British tank landing craft number 316, in an exercise which may have taken place at Lulworth Cove or Worbarrow Bay.

Westminster College in 1937. Both had intended becoming schoolmasters, but had ended up shooting at each other in the desert of a country foreign to them both. Thomas Hardy wrote a poem about that sort of thing during the First World War, on killing people you would otherwise buy a drink in a bar.

Back in the mundane life of Dorset, the Chief Constable, Major Peel Yates, had recovered from a serious illness and resumed his duties. A. Barrett, who had put in 43 years of police service, was rewarded by promotion to assistant chief constable. Things were not so good for the boys in blue who were under 25 years old — they were called up.

Retiring after 22 years of dealing with the people in the police court, was Mrs R.S. Comben, the county's first woman magistrate. At the time of her appointment on 30 August 1920, she was the wife of R.A. Logan, a well-known Dorchester solicitor. She later married Mr Comben of Weymouth.

In view of the current circumstances, the county council was thinking about keeping the schools open during the summer holidays. Seeking the views of heads of the schools, a questionnaire was sent to each. The majority were ignored, and most of the others came back marked "Don't know," so the idea was abandoned.

Night air attacks had shown a sudden increase, but improved defences made them costly for the Germans. In just one week, 21 enemy aircraft were destroyed. But it was an act of God, not of Hitler, that brought big problems for Weymouth showman Richard Townsend. Fire broke out in a shed housing fairground equipment worth £500, on a Tuesday evening. It was noticed by Charles Little, who attacked the fire without success, then called the Townsend family and the fire brigade. It took units of the national fire service, under Company Officer Pitman, three hours to get the blaze under control. The machinery destroyed had been purchased in 1939 for a royal visit to the Townsend fair in Suffolk. War stopped this and the equipment had never been used. Mr Townsend had returned from Poole that very evening, having arranged the first outing of the amusement equipment. This could not take place.

A sadder show business story than the Townsend setback was the tale of Danish composer Jacob Gade. Fifteen years before, he had written a tango, unsuccessful at the time, that was put into a 1942 London show, under the title 'Jealousy'. It was an instant success, with £2,000 royalties piling up in a few weeks. Sadly, Jacob Gade was then an inmate of a German concentration camp.

August bank holiday came and went without Dorset really noticing it. Only 500 people arrived at Weymouth railway station that weekend, most of them servicemen coming home on leave. Returning to Dorset was a

Lines of Churchill tanks, apparently on the Purbeck coastal army ranges.

sergeant in the ATS, Violet Cross, of Broadmayne. She had been nursing with the French army when captured by the Germans, who asked her to establish a hospital among the 15,000 people in a town held by them. She worked there until she could do no more. When France capitulated, she made up her mind to escape.

With French papers made out in the name of Violette Cross, she obtained permission to go to Paris and get a pass for Spain, where she said her husband was living. Nazi officials were crowding the Chamber of Deputies in Paris when she got there, and she closed her eyes at the sight of so many Germans together. The next thing she knew was a German tapping her on the shoulder, and then another Nazi was offering her chocolate, after the first one had tendered a glass of water. At first mystified by this unusual show of concern, Violette Cross then realised that they thought she was ill. She immediately put on some authentic-looking fainting fits. Embarrassed and eager to get rid of her, the Germans gave her a pass for Spain without checking her phoney papers. She had also been a nurse in France during the Great War, and on coming home Violet was wearing six medal ribbons, including the Croix de Guerre and the Medaille de la Reconnaissance Française.

The war had ended a happy retirement for naval pensioner William Bright, aged 47, of 16 Penny Street, Weymouth. In 1939, when the Home Fleet was assembled in Weymouth Bay, he was recalled for service. On 18 January 1942, he was reported missing in the Far East, but his wife had never given up hope that he was alive. She was right to a certain extent, for he was a prisoner of the Japanese, and news of this came through in September. Mrs Bright said: "Three years ago he sailed from Weymouth with the Home Fleet, and we haven't seen him since."

Hopes of ever seeing Wing Commander John Chapman, reported missing presumed killed in a raid over Germany, again looked slim. He was aged 34, and the eldest son of Mr and Mrs H. Chapman, of the Old Bell at Cerne Abbas. His wife, Barbara, later heard that John was in fact dead, buried in Holland. A civilian "doing time," Japanese style, was H.J. Pearce, deputy director of public works in Hong Kong. His brother, Major J.E. Pearce, of 161 Dorchester Road, Weymouth, was told that he was interned in Camp Standley, Hong Kong.

German reactions were tested on 6 August 1942, and war could now and again still be a game. The amplification and relaying of echoes from eight of our own Defiant aircraft off Portland turned out to be so effective that thirty German fighters were scrambled from airfields on Cherbourg peninsula to meet them. There was also a more serious sequel.

Accustomed now to having the Germans just across the Channel, people living in the Dorset coastal districts were startled by the sound of gunfire and explosions sliding over the still sea of an August evening.

There was speculation that the Second Front had opened. Next morning the BBC radio scuttled this theory by announcing that it was a reconnaissance raid in force. What was actually a wasteful, murderous mistake by military leaders, was described as "an exceptionally tough job with severe losses". It was soon learned that Dorset men were among those who perished on this much-criticised raid.

Mrs Cox, of Myrtle Cottage, East Knighton, Winfrith, was told that her son Stoker John Cox had been killed in this attack on Dieppe. Aged 29, he had been called up in 1940. His father, who had died in 1934, had been in the Dorset Regiment during the Great War, and had been a prisoner of the Germans for two years. A 21-years-old man who had served a four-year apprenticeship with Messrs Barlow, the Weymouth bakers, also lost his life in the raid. He was cook Frederick Stone, only son of Mr and Mrs Stone of 33 Norfolk Road, Weymouth. He was soon to have married a Cardiff girl.

Our new allies, the Americans, were on their way over — a knowledge that was causing almost as much concern in Dorset as a Nazi invasion would have done. In an attempt to smooth the way for the US servicemen, Professor Newell, a well-known American current affairs commentator, was in Dorset making a plea for doors to be opened in friendship to the Americans. He threw in a touch of humble pie by saying that his country had a lot to learn from Britain, Russia and China in this war. He also promised that there would be none of the American "I'll show you how" attitude of 1917.

Just how much fruit was missed was shown by the person who paid £4 when three bananas and one lemon were auctioned as one lot at the dance held for Weymouth Hospital week.

More rare in Dorset than expensive fruit was murder. But the village of Piddletrenthide managed to throw up a mystery thriller that could have used the talents of film detective Charlie Chan. On a Wednesday evening, while it was still daylight, farm worker Louis Aubrey Stickland left his house in the village, telling his wife that he was going to buy cigarettes. He was a long time gone but his wife did not worry, at first, because he would get the cigarettes at the bakery, where he often stayed to chat with the proprietor, who was a close friend. But it was at 5 am the following day, September 17th, that Stickland was seen again — lying in a lane, shot through the head and dead. Scotland Yard was called in to work with local detectives, but apart from the knowledge that Stickland had been shot with a revolver, and he had a fresh packet of cigarettes in his pocket, the killing was a mystery.

Meanwhile, acceptable murder — the sort committed whilst wearing uniform — was still going on, and a notable Dorset man, Wing Commander G.H. Stainsforth, was killed by the Germans in the Middle

East. This aviator had been quite a character. An old Weymouth College boy and Schneider trophy pilot, he had set up a new air speed record of 407.5 mph, an event which was commemorated by a weather vane in the shape of an aeroplane being placed on top of the college. Unveiled by O.N. Sempill, it was handed over to the civic authorities for use on a suitable occasion, when the college closed.

Numerous records were gained by Stainsforth. Before flying upside down for 11 minutes 7 seconds, he had trained by being strapped into a chair that was suspended upside down from the ceiling of his room. His first air speed record was made in 1929, at 246.6 mph. In 1931 he achieved an average (highest) 379 mph. Among his other achievements was that of RAF revolver champion, and he also held a rifle championship. Starting his service career in the army, he served in France, India and the Middle East, resigning in 1922 and entering the RAF. Among several close things while flying, was the incident where his propeller broke into pieces, and he landed safely after gliding for two miles. In his fast but short life he became a crack night-fighter pilot, and held the record of being the oldest fighter-pilot serving in the Middle East campaign. During a night air battle, his last, luck slipped from him to embrace the Nazi pilot who sent him hurtling to his death.

A victory here and there promoted thoughts of post-war life, and the Bishop of Sherborne, H.N. Rodgers, was warning the Dorset ruridecanal conference that vicars after the war would need to be specialists. His God had not given him the gifts of a prophet, for the post-war world has had less use for vicars than at any time in Christian history.

Time was slipping by fast, and the big boys from London were still tramping about with the Dorset 'dicks' at Piddletrenthide. Then they swooped, arresting Frederick Charles Davis, aged 36, of the bakery, Piddletrenthide, charging him with the murder of 42-years-old Louis Aubrey Stickland, of Swan Lane, in the same village. Charged also, as an accessory after the fact, was widow Mrs Dorothy Maude Ford, Davis' housekeeper.

Up before the Dorset county bench, Davis claimed the death of Stickland had been an accident. Afterwards, he had become frightened and, with the assistance of Mrs Ford, had carried the body across a field and placed it in a lane. Both pleaded not guilty and were committed for trial at the Hampshire assizes, Winchester, in December.

It was in October 1942 that Franklin Delano Roosevelt paid homage to blitzed London, and walked through the bomb damaged St Paul's Cathedral. The supporting propaganda photograph, to emphasise that Britain was not alone in material help either, was taken somewhere in southern England — probably on the downlands of Wiltshire or Dorset — and shows a 155 mm heavy field gun, capable of firing a 95 lb projectile fifteen miles. Beside it, the unmistakable stance of Americans at war.

Back in Weymouth, having got away just before the Japanese took over Sumatra, where he had lived for thirteen years, R.G. Lock did not have an uneventful escape. He had been torpedoed twice on the way home. Giving a talk at a servicemen's club in Weymouth, he confirmed what most people already had assumed — the war in the Far East had been a bungling disaster for Britain, so far. Lock told how conditions in Sumatra favoured the Japs. How they had planted spies in native villages long before the war had begun, and had infiltrated the jungle while our troops guarded the roads and key positions such as railways. He said that our troops had found themselves miles in the rear of the Japanese, without having seen one Jap soldier. A lack of air superiority and a serious underestimation of Japanese equipment were factors, Lock claimed, that greatly contributed to the British fiasco in the Far East.

The war still was not going too well, so the Government continued to provide diversions. One of these was Lady Mountbatten, who turned up to open the Weymouth YMCA, at the Sidney Hall. In her speech, she declared that, as a sailor's wife, she had an affection for Weymouth. This unsnobbish approach may not have been totally convincing as it was impossible to imagine her queueing on a Thursday morning to draw her allowance at a post office.

Out at Piddletrenthide, the plot was thickening. On a grim, dark, Thursday afternoon, Sir Bernard Spilsbury, Home Office pathologist, arrived at Piddletrenthide, to step about in a misty churchyard as the body of 32-years-old Mrs Freda Annie Davis was exhumed. Mrs Davis had died at the Dorset County Hospital on the previous August 2nd, shortly after admission for an illness diagnosed as ulcerated colitis. The place was alive with interest, for Mrs Davis had been the wife of the man accused of murder. At the graveside were Chief Inspector Arthur Thorpe and Detective Sergeant E. Griffin of Scotland Yard with Superintendent S. Lovell MBE of Dorchester police and CID Superintendent Frank Howe. Apart from the grave-diggers, the only civilians at the scene were Kenneth H. Mooring Aldridge, the defending solicitor, and his chief clerk, Mr Shiers.

Moves were still being made towards having local government reshaped, and the chairman of Portland Urban District Council, A.N. Tattersall, got in early with the use of Americanisms, by referring to it as "something cooking". His council decided that no such reformation should take place until the men fighting in the war were at home to have their say. Noble though this gesture was, the men coming home were only given a short spell of having their say, barely long enough to be respectful, and then those who had not gone were running things again.

Lunching at Claridge's, in London, was Mrs Roosevelt, wife of the President of the USA, together with chums from her old school

Allenswood at Wimbledon Park. Among the old girls was Mrs Colmer, wife of Company Officer Colmer, NFS Weymouth Division. With their ages ranging between 52 and 58, the excitement of meeting the President's wife was equalled by a game of "Guess who I am," for most of the ladies had not seen each other for 41 years.

Setting a record, which no-one would envy, was pilot Neville Hussey Carter, who was the first former member of the Dorset Constabulary to lose his life in the war. Aged 22, he was the only son of Superintendent F.W. Carter, of Poole division of the force. An old Dorchester Grammarian, Neville had left school to become a clerk in the taxation department of the Dorset county council, and was a member of the Territorials. He later joined the police and was stationed at Wimborne and Weymouth. A rewarding career with the police looked promising when he received commendation for arresting an armed soldier house-breaker.

The loss of another Dorset hero, said to be one of the most daring men in submarine service, brought grief to the Sherborne family of Lieutenant Commander Michael Willmott. Aged 32, he was the commander of the submarine *Talisman,* which was sunk by German bombs. The *Talisman* flew a number of strange flags, to commemorate incidents in action — the sinking of a U-boat, the chasing and damaging of an enemy destroyer, and the sinking of a 50,000 ton troopship. At Benghazi, the *Talisman* had surfaced and gunned two enemy schooners, one of which broke up while the other was beached.

A half-dead Christmas was limping along on the horizon of 1942 and the prospects were so unexciting that the county's chamber of commerce associations left to the discretion of members as to what time shops be closed. Between 5 and 6 pm was recommended.

Perhaps the best Christmas gift of all was given by the jury at Winchester, after an absence of 45 minutes, to Frederick Charles Davis, the Piddletrenthide baker charged with murder. He was acquitted. Mr Justice MacNaughten spent 70 minutes summing up, and said a charge of murder could only be substantiated if Davis had fired the gun intentionally.

In 1942 there were thousands of people playing, cleaning and showing off with revolvers and rifles with which they were basically unfamiliar. Accidents were inevitable, and had a high chance of proving fatal if two people were examining a gun in the closeness of a living room.

The weather then gave Dorset a grand finale to a traumatic year. Tremendous waves crashed over Chesil beach for a distance of more than a mile and inundated more than a hundred homes in the Chiswell district of Portland. A relief fund for the victims was opened jointly by Rev C.H. Brammer, a congregational pastor, and Councillor B.S.W. Fancy. Knocked about and unhappy, the county stumbled up to the end of the year, which was roughly the halfway mark in the war.

January 1943 – June 1943

Hitler will be dead by this time next year —
it is doubtful we will ever know what happens
to him.

— David Wehl, Ministry of Information, speaking
in Dorset. January, 1943

HAVING LOOKED a loser shortly before Christmas, the fund-raising to replace the cruiser HMS *Dorsetshire* suddenly leapt to success. The target of £3,000,000 was topped by £57,703. This was quite an achievement when it is considered that a large part of the war was fought on charity, with the public constantly harrassed to donate to one scheme or another. Running at the same time, in Wareham, was a joint effort by the St John Ambulance and nursing corps volunteers to raise funds for local men serving as prisoners of war. Money came from the usual flag day, dances, whist drives and similar projects, to total £390 12s. 4d.

The Ministry of Information was still spreading well-meant falsehoods, and David Wehl, a speaker at Weymouth's Guildhall, didn't let his superiors down when he claimed it was "almost Hitler's midnight". It may have been the Fuhrer's teatime, but he was nowhere near ready for bed.

"Hitler will be dead by this time next year," Mr Wehl confidently predicted. "It is doubtful if we will ever know what happens to him. He will probably disappear. Over his tombstone might be written the epitaph: 'My last territorial claim in Europe'."

Wehl described the war as a great drama in which we knew the fates that would overtake the actors. The Nazis had started the war with the incredible idea of conquering the world. It had not been possible in 1914, but Hitler thought it was in 1939. "Last summer," Wehl went on, "the Germans had made a final attempt when they tried to join the Japanese through the near East and India, to bind the world in an axis ring. Hitler is now expanded to the fullest and is bound to contract slowly but surely.

Hitler is nearly at the end of his day. It is about 9.30 pm before his midnight. He is definitely going and is due for liquidation. We are witnessing the greatest military disaster in Russia since 1812."

There was good news for Dorset farmers living within 25 miles of a camp holding Italian prisoners of war. They could apply to the War Agricultural Committee (WAEC) for Italian labour, and have the services of good-conduct prisoners. These prisoners could live in, either at the farmer's house, or with an employee, or failing that in a warm, comfortable farm building. Most of the Italians could handle English reasonably well by then, and an extra help for the farmer was a specially prepared Italian-English phrase book. One drawback was the number of Italians who took great care of their hair and even made-up their faces with improvised cosmetics. Today, when television has made effeminate men acceptable, this would not have raised an eyebrow, but the Englishman of 1943 found it difficult to stomach.

Farmers, who could tolerate the 'pretty boys', paid the WAEC £2 a week for each prisoner hired, for the first three months, and then £2 8s. 0d. a week thereafter. The employer was responsible for the safe custody of his foreign employees and had a guinea (£1 1s. 0d.) returned to him for the bed and board of each prisoner. No financial transactions were allowed between farmer and Italian, but the War Office paid the prisoners direct. None of them got rich, for overtime rate was just a shilling an hour for the first three months, then 1s. 3d. for the remainder of his employment.

Comforts for British troops were sparse, and one of the highlights was the chance to send a message home on a radio programme called 'Cairo Calling'. Welcome as this programme was in those days, it must take the blame for launching the sickeningly-sweet, long-running 'Two way family favourites' that came later. Recipients of a message from Cairo were Mr and Mrs W.A. Trevett, of 'Myrtles' at Damers Road, Dorchester. Their son, 28 years-old Sidney Trevett had been recorded in Malta, where he had been stationed for two and a half years.

Now that there was a glimpse of hope, even if it was still on a distant horizon, the fashionable thing for politicians was to talk about the good things that were to happen after the war. Captain Quintin Hogg MP championed the adoption of Sir William Beveridge's famous report, the cornerstone of the reform of British social history. This topic had north and south Dorset involved in a political and non-violent, though verbally passionate, version of the American civil war. Representing the south, Viscount Hinchingbrooke distanced himself from the pre-war style of Toryism. He advocated a much fairer and more tolerant Conservative party, saying that men returning from the war would not stand for the vicious wielding of a Tory whip in the style of the 1920s and 30s.

Hogg and Hinchingbrooke were two of only forty Tory MPs who pressed for legislation on the Beveridge report. Their preaching of the new conservative sermon upset the member for north Dorset, Captain A.V. Hambro. The latter criticised Hinchingbrooke publicly, whenever the opportunity presented itself. Hinchingbrooke retorted in the local press: "Captain Hambro seeks to use my recent statements of post-war financial policy to cast a general slur on the political faith which I hold, and on the pledge on which I was elected to Parliament — that is a very grave matter. Captain Hambro comes from a distinguished banking family and is schooled in the old tradition of orthodox finance, and it is not reasonable to think that in his circumstances he could embrace these new ideas which war and economic nationalism is forcing on the world. I feel the right to speak for the new conservatism, or radical toryism as I prefer to call it, as he claims the right to speak for the old conservatism, which has, alas, over the last fifty years had grafted on many corrupting growths."

This nasty old war, confusing from the start, had caused a revolution inside Dorset's traditional ruling caucus. Here was a Tory not only saying that the Party needed to change, but claiming that it had formerly been corrupt. It was becoming difficult to have faith in the Conservatives, while Labour was fast gaining respectability and popularity. This eagerly anticipated new world was going to be a peaceful one. The education authorities in the county, probably with a gutful of violence, were taking a look at corporal punishment in schools. It was decided that only head teachers, and certificated assistants delegated by them, could administer corporal punishment. Each head had to keep a log with dates and details of those he had given the power to administer punishment, and also a record of any teacher he had deprived of this power, and his motive. Corporal punishment could only be administered for a grave offence, and then only after all other methods had been tried, and failed. Only an approved cane could be used, and even this was prohibited on any child under the age of seven.

Making an early return to this Dorset of promise was Driver Leslie Templeman RASC, son of Mr and Mrs A.J. Templeman of 'Halgarth', South Court Avenue, Dorchester, and husband of Mrs L.J. Templeman.

Dateline the Wessex frontline, 1 March 1943 — the appearance of 'The Advance Post' would have made its own news but for the fact it was "not to be published". Such was the growing sophistication of the Second World War that it marked the appearance of the "first daily newspaper of its kind to be printed specially for the purpose of a military exercise in this country". Exercise 'Spartan' was the invasion of southern England by the British Expeditionary Force. The message may have been a little premature, but it was to have history on its side: "We are not on the defensive; we are passing to attack, but if we carry the Spartan determination in defence into attack, then the battle will be won."
Courtesy: Imperial War Museum.

"The Advance Post"

Published by the British Army in the Field

No. 1	1 MARCH, 1943	Free Issue

ON TO EASTLAND!

OUR ADVANCE CONTINUED

Enemy Infiltration from the North?

Waiting for Zero Hour

The following official communique was issued at Headquarters of the British Expeditionary Force in SOUTHLAND to-day :

Operations by the British Expeditionary Force in SOUTHLAND are proceeding according to plan.

During the past few days there has been increased air activity on the EASTLAND border.

On the 24th February our fighters and fighter-bombers attacked enemy M.T. and troops approaching the frontier. Considerable enemy fighter opposition was encountered. Successful reconnaissance flights have been made over enemy territory.

From these operations one of our aircraft is missing.

The civilian population of SOUTHLAND continues friendly and co-operative, and our forces are received with acclamation wherever they go.

HERE is the story of the Exercise on which we are engaged.

In theory the island of GREAT BRITAIN is

(Continued overleaf)

A NAME TO LIVE UP TO

SPARTAN   1943

We are all about to take part in an exercise which will be a test of endurance. It will need the most strenuous efforts from everybody to make it a success.

The name of the Exercise has been carefully chosen. It is "SPARTAN"; a name to live up to. In ancient Greece, the battle of Thermopylae was a heroic and successful defence by 4,000 fighting Spartans against ten times as many Persians.

We are not on the defensive; we are passing to attack, but if we carry the Spartan determination to outface into attack, then the battle will be won.

We are all well trained men, hardened and fit; so let us go forward into "Exercise Spartan" so that the lessons we learn will help us to take our places at the side of our fighting comrades elsewhere.

Finally, in words which echoed through the Eighth Army before El Alamein. . . . " there will be no belly-aching. And to these we add. . . "BE A SPARTAN."

R.A.F. OVER EASTLAND AGAIN

BRING BACK VITAL INFORMATION FOR ARMY

GROUND AND AIR TARGETS SUCCESSFULLY ATTACKED

THE Royal Air Force will be playing its part in full in co-operation with the Army throughout this Exercise. There will be fighters, bombers and reconnaissance aircraft constantly in the air by day and by night.

Already many "Spartan Sorties" have been made by our own aircraft, flown by young veterans of many a battle over this country and enemy territory. The Spartans of old have taken wings, and the same Spartan endurance which will be shown on the ground will also be in evidence in the air.

The R.A.F. has taken every advantage of good weather to make reconnaissance reports and follow the movements of the enemy, and also to hamper his motor transport and troop convoys.

Surveys have been made deep into the enemy lines despite the determined opposition of his fighter aircraft, and the only deterrent to the work of the flying men has been fog on the Eastland frontier and further into enemy territory.

Reconnaissance pilots have been able to bring back valuable information, and some of them have seen repeated signs of friendliness on the part of the civilian population, workers in the fields waving to them as they flew over northern Southland on their way to Eastland.

The enemy has shown his concern about our inquisitiveness by sending up strong formations of fighters to try to intercept our aircraft. On the afternoon of 24 February our fighters and fighter-bombers, strafing enemy troops as they moved towards the frontier, encountered more than 50 fighters.

THE AIRCRAFT IN THE BATTLE.

THE value of air support and cover in present-day warfare cannot be over-estimated. This has been proved time and time again and the lessons learned in those earlier encounters, both offensive and defensive, will prove invaluable in this exercise.

Immediate recognition of our own and enemy aircraft is vital. Our own fighters, fighter-bombers and reconnaissance aircraft will carry NO special markings, and our light bombers will be Bostons.

The enemy fighters, fighter-bombers and reconnaissance craft will have the under side of the port wing treated with black wash, while his light bombers will be largely Venturas with possibly a few Mitchells in addition.

Throughout the exercise all aircraft will be acting in a realistic manner, flying at operational heights and speeds, and you will have no difficulty in knowing by their actions whether or not you are coming under fire.

Light bombers when attacking from high or medium levels will dive Vacsy lights, and when bombing from low levels will come in with their bomb doors open.

Fighters will give no visible notification of attack, but their markings will be clearly distinguishable when flying low, and the action of the aircraft themselves will indicate when an actual attack against a ground target is being carried out.

Remember, when an air attack develops, it takes place and is over, all in a matter of seconds, so keep on the alert.

SPARTAN'S NEWSPAPER

Army field newspapers are not unknown, but "THE ADVANCE POST" is the first daily newspaper of its kind to be printed specially for the purpose of a military exercise in this country.

Written and produced by a staff of soldier-journalists—some of them not undistinguished in their peace-time professions—its aims are :—

1. To put you in the picture and keep you there, day by day, as the "battle" develops.

2. To increase and widen the range of your outlook on the scheme.

3. To try to simplify your own particular job by giving you what we hope will be useful tips on what you should or should not do.

Our readers may note a certain unusual character about "THE ADVANCE POST." This arises from the unusual composition of the Southland Force itself—we have troops from the United Kingdom and from Canada, and the latter of course include French-Canadians. All three sections go to make up our reading "public": our staff, and the appeal of their work, are designed accordingly.

Where We Stand To-day—March 1st

(Shaded part is territory already occupied by British.)

WORLD WAR NEWS

TUNIS.—German retreat from Kasserine continues. Enemy landing grounds strafed by fighter-bombers. Enemy counter-attacks beaten off ; 800 prisoners taken.

RUSSIA.—German counter-attacks in Western Donets basin driven off with loss of 36 tanks.

AT HOME.—No enemy air activity over this country in daylight.

R.A.F.—Air offensive over France and Holland continues. Mines laid in enemy waters.

FAR EAST.—Japanese transport and corvette bombed by U.S. planes and left blazing.

U.S.A.—New aircraft carrier and four destroyers launched.

Flight personnel of 263 Squadron lined up for their photograph at Warmwell beside the Whirlwind 'Bellows'. Theirs was an Empire unit. From left to right are Flight Lieut. E.C. Owens (Adjutant), Squadron Leader G.B. Warnes (Commanding Officer), Flight Lieut. H.K. Blackshaw (Flight Commander), Sergeant S.D. Thyagarajan (from India), Flying Officer C.P. King DFM (British West Indies), Flight Serg. F.L. Hicks (Australia) and Flying Officer J.P. Coyne (Canada).   Photograph: Imperial War Museum.

Those taking part in the 'Spartan' invasion were forbidden to buy anything in shops and pubs, "as the exercise must be made as realistic as possible". The invading force made "rapid headway" after its capture of Salisbury, and there is an interesting warning about taking the fantasy too far: "All vehicles, especially armoured fighting vehicles, should avoid operating, or coming to rest within 400 yards of RAF wireless stations. The RAF, you know, will probably be engaged with the real enemy and we want to avoid interfering with their functional efficiency."   Courtesy: Imperial War Museum.

No.1.　　　　　　　　　The BULLDOG.　　　　　　　　　**No.1.**

THIS CONCERNS YOU!
No Vists To'The Local' During Spartan.

You'll probably think this really is a spartan war, but during the period of the exercise you are strictly forbidden to make any purchase outside home stations at shops, canteens (including mobile canteens), hotels and public houses.

There are several very good reasons for this order. One of them is that the exercise must be made as realistic as possible and there would be very little to buy in the shops of an invaded country.

Reason number 2 : One of the objects of the exercise is to test the supply arrangements in an overseas operation; and the third reason, and one which all will admit is fair and reasonable, is that local inhabitants will suffer hardship if the limited supplies in the shops are all bought up by troops taking part in the exercise.

This order applies to all ranks and will be strictly enforced.

Cigarettes and tobacco will be available but you will have to control your thirst until you have disposed of the enemy.

NO LEAVE DURING SPARTAN.

Privilege will not be granted during the period of the exercise, but all personnel due to begin leave during the exercise will be granted privilege leave on its termination.

It has also been decided that a maximum of 3% instead of the normal 1½% of unit personnel may be sent on leave after the exercise until all personnel whose leave was postponed have been despatched. The usual regulation will apply - no travelling on Saturday or Sunday.

BRITISH ARMY IN SOUTHLAND
(Continued from Page 1. Col.1.)
This they did shortly after the fall of their capital, Salisbury.

Since the fall of Salisbury, the invading force has made rapid headway. The shaded portion on the map shows the areas now occupied by the British. The interstate boundaries between Eastland and Westland and Southland are also shown.

It is learned in reliable diplomatic circles that Westland's government has declared her intention of remaining neutral and is prepared to defend her neutrality against any aggressor.

A large scale battle is undoubtedly imminent.

B.B.C. NEWS SUMMARY

There is no official news from Central and Northern Tunisia to-day (1300 hrs Sunday).

In the South the 8th Army is continuing its probing of the Mareth Defences.

The Russians are still meeting strong German counter-attacks at the Western end of the Donetz Basin.

SITUATION MAP. For security reasons it is not possible to indicate the actual locations on this map, which will be published daily, but it will show the general situation and will assist you to follow the progress of the battle.

YOU CAN'T FIGHT WITHOUT FOOD.
(Continued from Page 1. Col. 1.)
All vehicles, especially armoured fighting vehicles, should avoid operating, or coming to rest within 400 yards of R.A.F. wireless stations. The R.A.F., you know, will probably be engaged with the real enemy and we want to avoid interfering with their functional efficiency.

With regard to digging and wiring, the orders are that the digging of weapon slits, gun-pits etc. and the erection of wire obstacles will be carried out at all times as in actual battle. Where the ground and tactical siting permit, digging should take place, if possible, along the line of hedges and fences.

All units should take fulladvantage of the facilities provided, and these special arrangements will add greatly to the realism and training value of the exercise, but the army must demonstrate that it is possible to apply sound common sense to the use of land under these conditions without abusing the facilities provided.

Aircraft of Bomber Command laid mines in enemy waters and bombed objectives in Western Germany.

The Prime Minister has sent a message of good wishes to the Wings for Victory Campaign.

He had been taken prisoner at Fort Mecheli, near Derna, on 8 April 1941, a year to the month after having joined up. He had been repatriated from a camp in Italy, not for the usual reason of being wounded, but because he was attached to the Royal Army Medical Corps, a respected unit.

But all things were not bright and beautiful. The bishop's warning came true at Stinsford, where an inquest heard Detective Sergeant Fudge tell how he had gone to Slyer's Lane in the the village, when responding to a message. At a point seventy yards from the Cross, a parcel was pointed out to him. It rested in a wide but not thick hedge. Inside, he found the dead body of a newly-born male child. From the condition of the undergrowth and the wrapping he concluded that the parcel had only been there a few hours. Medical evidence at the inquest showed the baby was a full-term child and had existed as a separate entity, even if briefly. There was no trace of food in the stomach. Death was due to lack of care, cold and exposure.

On the good side in the county was the glance, more than a passing one, the War Agricultural Executive Committee was casting at Rothesay House, Dorchester, which had recently been sold for £6,750. Miss Olwell, County organiser of the Women's Land Army (WLA), was asked by the WAEC to secure the building as a hostel for WLA girls. It was proposed that Land Girls would be accommodated at the house.

The latest thing in the seemingly endless ways of raising funds, was Wings for Victory, and it proved to be a long-running campaign. Though there was still a period of eleven weeks to go, there were signs that the improving war situation, together with boredom, was taking the urgency and keenness out of war money-raising. Results for various Dorset towns at that stage were as follows, with only Bridport and Shaftesbury emerging with real credit:

Town	Target	Total raised
Shaftesbury	£130,000	£150,000
Weymouth	£250,000	£9,230
Beaminster	£44,000	£15,684
Blandford	£25,000	£29,000
Gillingham	£50,000	£17,115
Dorchester	£200,000	£59,894
Portland	£50,000	£13,836
Wimborne	£160,000	£41,808
Swanage	£65,000	£16,543
Sherborne	£160,000	£39,758
Bridport	£133,000	£209,920

Wareham	£120,000	£26,973
Lyme Regis	£42,000	£7,593
Sturminster Newton	£75,000	£12,253
Poole	£880,000	£122,832

A war bonus came to a Puddletown widower, Mr Spracklen, when his 21-years-old son, Able Seaman William Spracklen, was repatriated from a German prison camp. But war balances the good and bad and a sailor home was followed by news of a soldier who would not be coming back. Aged 21, Lieutenant Maxwell Chenevix Trench, Royal Engineers, second son of Brigadier and Mrs R. Chenevix Trench, of 'Woodend', Studland, was killed in action in North Africa.

Perhaps the most overlooked facet of war is the inconvenience it creates. This was obvious to people living at Lytchett Minster and Lytchett Matravers, especially if they were sick. Most were registered with a partnership of doctors Lord, Smith and Hatfield, which brought its problems as Lord was in the Royal Navy, Smith was dead, and Hatfield was called up for military service. Sir John Lees brought the people's plight to the notice of Wareham and Purbeck council.

Four Burmese pilots flew with 257 Squadron at Warmwell in January 1943. They had been training in India when the Japanese invaded Burma. (Pictured left to right) are Pilot Officers M.H. Yi of Pegu, H.Y. Lau and S.J. Khin of Rangoon, and T. Clift from Shan States. *Photograph: Imperial War Museum.*

Mrs Hatfield had struggled to carry on the practice, but her health had broken down, leaving her ill without a doctor. The council asked medical officer Dr E.J. O'Keefe, what could be done about the serious matter, and he replied that he had protested to the County medical authority about the call-up of doctors, to no avail. He advised that the only course left was representation to the Minister of Health. Being a wise man, O'Keefe added that this wouldn't make a bit of difference.

Putting this unfortunate predicament to one side, the council had history repeat itself by once again re-electing long-serving chairman Major F. Holland Swann, then added a bit of variety by replacing I.S. MacDonald with Sir John Lees as vice-chairman. The dust of this little reshuffle had not settled before Councillor W.G. Marsh was on his feet shouting through it to claim, and meeting no denials, that fifty to sixty percent of the houses in the district were not fit for cattle to live in.

Odd things were happening in the Wareham Home Guard at this time. Private W.E. Bugler was court martialled and sentenced to 28 days detention for refusing to carry out an order of his commanding officer. Then the general officer of southern command took a look at some medical evidence. No details were made public, but the sentence on Bugler was quashed and any record of the court martial expunged from his documents. It was assumed that the order disobeyed had been given by a man who had lost some of his marbles.

A fingertip of the permissive society was tapping away at Dorchester. In 1938, the town had considered, and thrown out, suggestions that the strict rules of how Sundays were spent should be altered. By early summer 1943, the vicars of Dorset were losing their grip, and the council again discussed a scheme for brighter Sundays. By eight votes to seven, it was decided that games could be played in the borough gardens and recreation fields on the Sabbath during summer months.

Victory had come to the allies in North Africa and one snippet of information, which may or may not have had any effect on the fighting there, was that British troops had smoked a total of 450 million cigarettes between them throughout the campaign. Our current obsession with statistics should have some 'expert' work out which was the most dangerous in the desert fighting — lung cancer or the enemy. One of the first victims of the habit turned out to be the man who helped set the trend, King George VI, who was only to live another eight years.

A bit of North Africa — or in this case Afrika — turned up at the New Inn, South Street, Dorchester, in the form of an unusual Nazi arm-flash. It was in white on a black background, bearing the word 'Afrikakorps'. It had been sent by the only son of the landlord, Lance-Corporal H.R. Ham, whose proud father fixed it to the wall, where it attracted a lot of interest but no suggestions as to its origin. The flash had been found by

Ham at a Nazi headquarters between Medjex el Bab and Tunis in the final push for victory. Aged 23, the Dorchester soldier had landed in North Africa in November 1942. Prior to the war he was in the Territorial Army at Bournemouth, where he was articled as a municipal engineer with the borough engineer and surveyor.

'Bellows,' a named Westland Whirlwind of 263 Squadron, seen here at its Warmwell base, was piloted by 22-years-old Flying Officer J.P. Coyne of The Pas, Manitoba. They were photographed together in 1943. Coyne had just won the Distinguished Flying Cross.
Photograph: Imperial War Museum.

July 1943 — December 1943

*Where will I find the Dorsetshire Regiment? I
have a hankering to have a yarn with those
Dorset boys. I come from Texas and my name
is Hardy, Thomas Hardy. They tell me that is a
well-known name around Dorsetshire.*

— An American Army sergeant, during the Sicilian campaign.
1943

BRIDPORT HAD decided that Police Sergeant Goodchild was a decent
sort. Having been in charge of the Police War Department in town since
1939, as a popular and co-operative officer, he was moving to Sherborne.
The Civil Defence and Special Constabulary each presented him with a
memento of his stay in Bridport. The presentations were at a ceremony
conducted by ARP controller W.S.B. Northover, who wished Goodchild
success and happiness in his new appointment.

The war had suddenly taken on a brighter look. The Nazis were
experiencing an innovation — retreat. The British and Australians in
North Africa had been joined by the Americans, though the latter's first
assault on the enemy was a tragedy for everyone but the Nazis. But a
revision of tactics soon had the US Army fighting as a valuable ally.

A Bridport man, Driver S.S. Loveless, showed how confident the Axis
powers had been of victory in North Africa, when he sent his wife a medal
specially struck for the Afrika Korps for a victory that never came, so the
medal was never issued. Mrs Loveless was living with her parents, Mr and
Mrs H. Symes, at 2 Hope Terrace, St Michael's Lane, Bridport.

Having joined up in January 1939, Dvr. Loveless had been through the
whole of the Libyan campaign, and was one of the guard of honour when
the King and Winston Churchill visited the Middle East forces. His
parents, Mr and Mrs H. Loveless, lived at 13 Rope Walks, Bridport.

The Home Guard was now a really efficient organisation, and had
rules to match, which brought two of its members before the magistrates
at Dorchester, accused of not attending parades. In a case prosecuted for

the War Office by Superintendent S. Lovell, the difficulties of trying to serve two masters were explained by one of the accused. Through his solicitor, Kenneth H. Mooring Aldridge, he admitted being absent, but told the bench that he felt it best to be before them on this charge, rather than a more serious one connected with his employment.

The man, Arthur Drake, aged 41, of 11 Prospect Road, Dorchester, was an engine driver with the Southern Railway. He pointed out that it was impossible to drive trains and be on parade at the same time. In reply to questions by Aldridge, Lieutenant Bernard Hoey, of 7 Cromwell Road, Dorchester, who was in charge of Drake's platoon, agreed that a petition had been passed to him that May, signed by seventeen men protesting about attending parades. He had passed this on to his commanding officer but had received no reply. He added that Drake had attended only three parades in six months. Evidence was also given by John Viney, of 19 Alfred Road, and Montagu Stanley Northam, 158 Monmouth Road, both sergeants in the platoon. The magistrates showed an understanding that was rare at the time, and dismissed the charges.

The family rivalry over who had most members doing their bit was still going on. Possibly topping the lot in Dorset was Mrs Chubb, of 20 Council Houses, Maiden Newton. Her proud record was a husband, seven sons, six nephews and two nieces all in uniform. At the age of 60, her husband was a uniformed employee of the Government. He had served in the Dorset Regiment in the South African war, and was an Old Contemptible in the First World War, being wounded on Hill 60. Son Jack, aged 37, was in the Devons but had changed to the RASC, and had sixteen years service in the army. Next came Bill, aged 36, who had joined the Somersets when he was 16, but was then attached to the RAOC; Dick, at 35, had put in eighteen years service, and was then a Lance Bombardier in the Royal Artillery. Aged 34, Bert had been in uniform for 15 years, first the army then transferring to the RAF. The family novice was Bob, aged 29, with only four years service in. But in that time he had managed to serve with the Devons and finish up in the ACC. Douglas was a corporal in the RAF, at the age of 24, while Derrick (Sam) the youngest son, was in the Air Training Corps.

Bert and Jack were serving in the Middle East. They had a reunion at Tripoli and often saw each other after that. Writing home to mother, Bert said it was a wonderful experience and he was greatly encouraged by Churchill's visit. He had been just a few yards away from the Prime Minister. Bob was also in North Africa, not near his two brothers, though, while Bill wasn't likely to bump into any of the family, or Winston Churchill, for some time. He had been taken prisoner in May 1940 and was then at a prison camp in Bavaria. The eight nephews, all in various service branches, were Arthur and Walter Beavis, Gerald,

Graham, Jack and Walter Chubb, George Hole and John Davey. The nieces, Jessie and Ilma Chubb, were in the WAAF and NAAFI, respectively.

Uncertainty was causing trouble for Mrs Day of Eype near Bridport. The Air Ministry told her that her son, Aircraftman Robert Sprake, was missing presumed killed. This was followed by a telegram saying that he was alive but a prisoner of the Japanese in Java. Mrs Day was told that she could write to her son once a month. The mastermind who imparted this bit of information forgot to give an address to which Mrs Day could write. So it was a long, painful wait to see if a letter would arrive from her son. Robert Sprake had joined the RAF in July 1941, and went overseas five months later. Before going into the service he was employed by G.P. Elliott, a grocer at East Street, Bridport.

On Sunday 15 August the double ration of daylight lost half its bonus, as double-summertime ended. This year, with things looking brighter in the war, and fewer air attacks, the approaching dark nights were not so fearfully anticipated as in previous years. The Dorsetshire Regiment was now in Sicily, and that island had been all but won.

At Lyme Regis, officers and ship's company of HMS *Lyme Regis* were given a grand welcome at the town hall. The party, consisting of Commander F.G. Tidswell, DSC, Lieutenant Goff RNR, and several ratings, were received by Mayor W.J. Emmett, members of the borough council, the committee responsible for arranging the evening, and members of the public. Possibly the sailors, whose ship had been named by the Admiralty in 1941 and adopted by the Dorset town in 1942, must have forced their smiles, for they were sacrificing part of their precious wartime leave to attend the function.

Sex equality was apparent in the fireguard team on Portland, where a special quorum of six councillors, under the chairmanship of B.S.W. Fancy, decided to apply to the regional commissioner for one male and one female fireguard. Not that the pay was equal, as the man was to be paid £5 13s. 6d. per week, and the woman £3 19s. 0d. The same meeting boosted the salary of fireguard officer, W. Stevens from £200 to £300 a year.

Though all administration looked terribly muddled at that stage of the war, the dependable 'snooper' was still around, and Alfred Boswell, an old age pensioner of Newplace Mill Cottage, Hinton Hill, Crewkerne, was summoned to the local petty sessions. In a prosecution brought by the Yeovil area officer of the Assistance Board, he was accused of making a false statement when applying for a supplementary benefit under the Old Age and Widows Pension Act, 1940. He had said that the only income of his wife was her 10s. 0d. weekly pension, and that two sons in the household were bringing in £1 8s. 6d. and £1 10s. 0d. respectively. This resulted in a supplementary pension of 8s. 6d. weekly being paid. F. Proctor, prosecuting, said it was later ascertained that, in two periods, Mrs Boswell had been in receipt of dependant's allowance from the Army of £1 2s. 6d. The total sum paid in pension by the Assistance Board was £9 3s. 0d. Major Eric Craven, chairman of the bench, decided there was no doubt that Boswell had made a false declaration. He did not, however, think that he had done it on purpose. Had he thought this, Boswell would have been heavily fined. Instead, he was ordered to pay back the £9 3s. 0d. and also pay 16s. 4d. costs.

The Admiralty announcement that the only Royal Navy losses in the Sicilian campaign had been two submarines, three motor-torpedo boats and one motor gun boat, made it seem that a double tragedy had happened for one Dorset family. One of the submarines was the *Saracen*, commanded by Lieutenant M.G.R. Lumby RN, whose father, Lieutenant Colonel Lumby, of South Eggardon Farm, Askerswell, had recently met his death in a flying accident, at the age of 52. But, the following Sunday, hope came to the wife of Lieutenant Lumby — who lived with her mother and baby son, at 'Spyway', Askerswell — in an Italian communique that stated five officers, including the captain, and 41 men serving on the *Saracen* had been taken prisoner.

Meanwhile, Viscount Hinchingbrooke was passing hope around like it was a bag of sweets. Predicting that the end of the war was near, he told the Women's Council of the South Dorset Conservative Party: "Without putting an actual date to it, I can say that we are approaching that favourable state of affairs. To those who say a Second Front has not been launched to help Russia, I would reply that it is safe to say, in view of the obligations we have in all parts of the world, this Second Front has already been opened."

All good friendly chat, but of a 'Mary Poppins' nature that showed just how unaware of the true situation most politicians were. Hinchingbrooke's speech did not encompass a fraction of the majestic but terrible Normandy landings, or the year of tough fighting that followed. When it was all happening elsewhere, the unlikely locality of East Anglia saw a gallant effort by a Dorset man. A woman's decision to end her life was to risk that of Captain John Bartholemew RE, son of Mr and Mrs R. Bartholemew, of Bothenhampton, near Bridport. An inquest on Miss Lucy Lister, aged 34, of the Bakery, Hingham, Norfolk, revealed that she had suffered a nervous breakdown, and while visiting the coast had jumped up from a seat and plunged into the sea. Captain Bartholemew saw the woman's body drifting away from the shore. Without hesitation, he negotiated his way through a minefield to reach the shore, to swim out and bring Miss Lister back to the beach. He tried artificial respiration without success, then led a constable and first aid man through the mines, telling them to tread in his footprints. He later repeated this feat by leading a stretcher party through the danger zone.

Dicing with danger caught up with Flight-Sergeant Ronald Floss, whose parents lived at 49 South Street, Bridport. His wife, an Ebbw Vale girl he married the previous April, was serving in the WAAF at the same station. She was in the information room when it came through that he was missing on an operational flight over Germany. This was a time when the RAF was ever-busy over Europe and the toll in fliers' lives always increasing. The mother of Flight-Sergeant Charles Goddard was officially notified at her home, Hooke Farm, Bridport, that he was missing.

What few knew at the time was that east Dorset was at the forefront of the wartime race to perfect radar techniques. Work from the Telecommunications Research Establishment (TRE) at Swanage had progressed into the field at Sopley, near Christchurch, where rudimentary equipment proved itself an effective interception screen against enemy bombers. Coastal defence radar installations were at Worbarrow Bay and Portland Bill. Rodney Legg has researched the county's contribution to the development of radar for *Dorset County Magazine,* including the airborne version invented by the British for detecting towns:

Codename H2S, this was manufactured by the Government's top security Research Prototype Unit which was set up on a site now occupied by Max Factor's cosmetics factory on the edge of Northbourne golf course, north-west of Bournemouth. The aircrews knew the equipment as the Black Box or Magic Eye. To the scientists it was known as H2S — a navigational bomb aiming device given the chemical name for the gas that smells of rotten eggs, because Churchill's chief scientific adviser, Frederick Lindemann had told the unit at TRE (about themselves): "It stinks! It stinks!"

Steve Inglis took control of the project in November 1942. "We went to all manner of lengths to maintain security", he has said. "Apart from a handful of people, no one working at the unit ever knew exactly what we were making until the war was over".

The equipment was installed in the planes of the British Pathfinder squadrons which spearheaded bomber raids. H2S ensured accurate flare dropping, marking the target area for the benefit of the following drones of Lancasters, by giving the Pathfinders a virtual radar street-plan of the German city below. It worked, but that is not the point.

Strategically, the existence of H2S can be said to have led to one of the worst Allied defeats of the war. Such technical accomplishments encouraged Bomber Command chief Arthur Harris to promise that the wrecking of Berlin from end to end "will cost Germany the war". Hitler had the same thoughts about bombing London in 1940-41. Neither offensive broke the civilian will to resist, and both campaigns against the populace took the pressure off factories and the systems providing the logistics of war.

From the start, massed bomber raids were torn apart by the Luftwaffe — to the extent that the United States Air Force refused to carry bombing missions beyond Allied fighter cover. Still Harris persisted. He embarked on a course of action that prolonged the war. German fighter strength was being increased at the rate of a hundred planes a month, and other munitions production kept pace. Berlin became the prime target on 18 November 1943.

The effectiveness of the German night fighter 'boxes' was at this stage minimised by the ease with which their half-metre radar waveband could be jammed. Then the position changed. First, the Germans used intense flares to illuminate the sky over targets and silhouette the waves of attacking bombers. Next, Nazi fighters joined the British bombers as they crossed the German coast.

Not only was H2S jammable, but the German fighters had their own devices to home-in on its signal. Some British crews turned on their H2S sets before they even crossed the Channel, and gave the nightfighters the time they needed to plot and intercept the bombing stream. Losses mounted monthly. The percentage of losses per night almost touched one in ten in a raid over Leipzig. Worse was to come on 30 March 1944 when 94 bombers failed to return from Nuremburg and another 71 were damaged. Harris was finally forced to abandon his policy.

Morale in Bomber Command had collapsed to a point where hundreds of tons of British bombs were jettisoned in the North Sea and Pathfinder commander Donald Bennet spoke of crews "baulking at the jump". The proportion of bomb loads carried as far as his marker-flares was insignificant. The despair is understandable — the average bomber crew could expect to be dead before they completed the fifteenth in their 'tour' of thirty sorties.

A new mood of re-assessment has spread amongst war historians. Typical is Donald Watt, reader in history at London University who writes about the mass bomber offensive: "Yet all the time Harris had a faster, more accurate weapon to his hand in the Mosquito, which could outpace the German fighters, carry a surprisingly heavy bomb load and whose losses were running at [only] 0.4 per cent."

The public throughout this time had no real information on which to question the conduct of the war, and their technical adventures seldom stretched further than housepaint. The proliferating electronics invented for war were to provide the playthings for the generation that came next. Ordinary life had not yet become that complicated.

Decorating the house might cheer things up a little, as emergency wartime paint could be bought without a permit, in any colour you liked — providing it was dark brown. Pints of this gloomy gloss came at 1s. 9d. and a quart was 3s. 6d. An oil-bound distemper was also available unrationed. There was more variety here, with shades of cream, old gold, bath stone and reseda: seven pound tins were 4s. 6d. each.

The sound of gunfire tragically came nearer home at this time, with both the victim and the gunmen on our side. In Portland dockyard, a soldier, Private Edward Dickie, was on guard when a group of apprentice lads started to take the mickey out of him. A witness at an inquest, Private Stanley Clerk, of the Buffs, said there was a mocking comparison made by the boys regarding the sentry and the Home Guard. There was a sudden burst of tommy-gun fire and one of the boys, John Groves, a boiler cleaner of Williams Avenue, Wyke Regis, fell dead. He was 17-years-old.

Invited by the coroner, P.M. Wickham, to make a statement, Dickie declined, pointing out that he had already said all he could say, and that it had been all written down two or three times. The coroner said he did not think that any man would deliberately fire on boys, even in retaliation for the taunt about the Home Guard. He did not know that sort of thing went on, and if it continued something would have to be done. A majority verdict of carelessness amounting to manslaughter was returned against Dickie.

A hero in the news was Major Roger Streatfield RA, second son of Symondsbury's rector, who was awarded the Military Cross. With the 1st Army, he had seen considerable action, being one of the last to take part in the Dunkirk evacuation. At Cambridge at the outbreak of war, he had been a member of the special reserve of officers there, and had two brothers serving in the Royal Navy — Lieutenant C.E.J. Streatfield and Lieutenant D.H.C. Streatfield, the former having been an officer aboard HMS *Cornwall* when she was sunk in the Indian Ocean.

Another army officer, wounded and repatriated, was telling a story of bravery and devotion relating to a former Portland schoolmaster. The officer was Major S.T. Pester, and the Portland man was Sergeant Mallory. Major Pester had been badly wounded in Greece when the lorry he was attempting to escape in was hit by a bomb. With the Germans advancing rapidly, Mallory insisted on staying behind to care for the seriously wounded major. Also telling the story, with an extra twist, was another repatriated prisoner, M.Q.M.S. Ballard, of Weymouth. He said he had seen Mallory stay behind, even though the advancing Germans were close on their heels. Ballard had not expected to ever see Mallory or Major Pester again. Two years later, he was aboard the repatriation ship, *Drottingholm,* when he was told his comfortable bunk was needed for a sick officer. He took a dim view of this until he learned that the officer was Major Pester, when he gave up his place gladly.

The major said he owed everything to Sergeant Mallory, who, in spite of heavy machine-gun fire, showed a complete disregard for his own safety. His knowledge of first aid stood him in good stead. Having tied a tourniquet on Major Pester's leg, Mallory then got him into another truck and took him to a Greek institution. "By that time," said Major Pester, "the water and electricity services were out of action. The only available light for a Greek surgeon to work from was a hurricane lamp."

Mallory remained cool throughout and made no attempt to get away. The major praised the Greek nuns as "simply marvellous". After fighting in the streets outside, which was marked by incessant machine-gun fire, the Germans occupied Kalamata, discovered Pester and Mallory, both of whom were taken prisoner. In the action leading up to this, a New Zealander, Sergeant Hinton, won the Victoria Cross.

The journey home for repatriated prisoners was via Sweden, with a

Preparations for an air-sea rescue exercise at Warmwell in August 1943. Ground crew load a dinghy into a Mark II Spitfire of 276 Squadron, ready for the drop — as the original caption puts it — to airmen "in the drink". Photograph: Imperial War Museum.

Silence sign on a telegraph pole beside the Dorchester road near Puddletown, photographed on 5 May 1944. The indistinct notice above is more positive: "In case of fire call N.F.S. Dorchester. Telephone: Dorchester 766. You are at: D3."

Photograph: Imperial War Museum.

welcome all the way. But a welcome, on this earth, would never be needed for another Dorset man, G.H. Stevens, a Chideock mariner. In 1918 he had won a county scholarship at Chideock council school, which gave him three years training on the *Mercury*. In the Royal Navy for 20 years, he had joined HMS *Aurora* in the early months of 1943, and was on the ship when it took the King from North Africa to Malta. Stevens and his gun crew were killed in action in October, and buried at sea. He left a wife and baby son at Gosport, while his mother lived at 'The Retreat', Chideock.

Earning the tragic distinction of being the first lad from the village of Loders to lose his life in the war, was Signalman F.D. Symes RN, second son of Mr and Mrs F. Symes. David, as he was known, had an older brother in the RAF.

By now, the Government was confident enough of victory to stop talking about it. Instead, the public was bombarded with ambitious plans for post-war Britain. Most prominent of all was an epoch measure of education reform, laid out in a White Paper.

Christmas was coming, and the general belief that this was to be the last one of war had people eager to celebrate. But circumstances would not permit it. No extra drinking hours were granted, and transport

A secret decision had been taken by Churchill's war cabinet to requisition and depopulate several square miles of western Purbeck. Lulworth's tank gunnery ranges were to be extended. Today, the hulk of a discarded Churchill tank rusts on the slope above Worbarrow and Tyneham. Photograph: Dorset County Magazine

problems restricted movement severely. Family reunions were cut down but Dorset again opened its arms to servicemen, and the festive season passed pleasantly and quietly. One man not having a good time was Richard Gallagher, of Bridport. In a graphic illustration of the lack of freedom in war, Gallagher had been sentenced to fourteen days imprisonment for leaving his job, at Pymore Mills, without permission of the National Service officer.

His counsel, Mr Willett, asked that the sentence be postponed so that he would be free over Christmas. He said Gallagher had been employed at Pymore Mills for about four months. In that time he had made two applications to leave, but these had been refused. On September 15 he had walked out and had not returned. His client was of good character and wholly patriotic, holding the General Service, Afghan and Victory medals. Of these, he could only produce the Afghan, as he had gone to

Such was the speed at which technology moved through the Second World War that by 1944 these light tanks at Bovington were regarded as obsolete. They were used to train wireless operators. Field Marshal Sir Bernard Montgomery strides by (centre right).
Photograph: Imperial War Museum.

London to find that his premises had not only been blitzed but had also been looted, with many of his personal belongings stolen. The chairman of the bench, E.R. Sykes, said that he had no authority to postpone the sentence, and Gallagher spent his Christmas in a cell.

At the western end of the Purbeck Hills it was the British army, not the Germans, who brought the Second World War into Tyneham valley six days before Christmas in 1943. There, in 1940, local magistrate Ralph Bond formed the Tyneham Home Guard and made himself its platoon commander. But in 1943 he had to leave his home along with all his servants and farm labourers. Rodney Legg describes Dorset's greatest wartime evictions, carried out to provide a vast empty training area for the army that was to invade Europe:

All 3,003 acres of the parish of Tyneham and other land beneath Dorset's Purbeck Hills were evacuated by direct order from Winston

Field Marshal Sir Bernard Montgomery (centre right) talking to officers of the Royal Armoured Corps driving school at Bovington. In the months that followed he was commander of the Allied assault force for the invasion of Europe.
Photograph: Imperial War Museum.

Churchill's war cabinet. Local councils were not allowed to question the correctness of the decision and censorship prevented any mention in the press of the requisition of a vast extension to the Purbeck tank gunnery ranges. Never for one moment were the Tyneham area inhabitants led to believe that their evacuation was other than a temporary measure necessary for winning the war. All the tenants were informed by the War Department land agent that, if they wished, their tenancies would be maintained.

The notice served on each of them contained these words: "This means that when the War Department has no further use for the property and it is handed back, you have every right to return to the property. It should not be assumed by you that, because the War Department has turned you out, you lose your right of occupying the premises again."

Even though no mention of the Tyneham takeover was permitted in the press, anyone could have sensed the truth from the auction columns of the *Dorset County Chronicle* on 2 December 1943. Western Purbeck sounded like a disaster zone. Auctioneers Henry Duke & Son offered 313 dairy cows and bulls, nine working horses, 71 sheep, 33 pigs, 167 poultry, four Fordson tractors and over 700 separate lots of farm implements from the Tyneham valley alone. The farmers were fleeing:

"Tyneham Farm, Tyneham, for Mr S.G. Churchill, quitting.

"Lutton Farm, Steeple, for Mr A.E. Cranton, quitting.

"Baltington Farm, Tyneham, for Mr A.J. Longman, quitting.

"North Egliston Farm, Tyneham, for Mr H.J. House, quitting.

On the other side of the Purbeck Hills there was a similar pattern of tragedy. Thomas Ensor & Son announced dispersal sales at West Creech Farm (for R.C. Cake); Povington Farm (T.W. Wrixon); Searleys Farm, Povington (Arthur Cooper); Jiggiting Corner, Povington (J. Cooper); Weld Arms Farm, East Lulworth (Mrs B. Bonham); Mrs S.P. Damen, The Cat, East Lulworth (Mrs S.P. Damen); Whiteway Farm, East Lulworth (H.J. Sampson); Broadmoor Farm, West Creech (H.C. George); White Hall Farm, West Creech (W. Cake); Rookery Farm, West Creech (Frank Cranton); Hurst Hill Farm, West Creech (A.E. Swain).

There was a sad note at the end of the lists: "The Auctioneers wish to draw special attention to the before mentioned sales and sincerely trust that all farmers from over a wide area will endeavour to attend as many as possible, to assist in the dispersal of the stock on offer, all of which is thoroughly recommended by the Auctioneers".

Frank Cranton was the lucky evacuee as he was able to secure another farm, keep most of his stock, and cancel the "away-going" sale at Lutton.

Miss Helen Taylor was evicted from Tyneham and moved to a council home at Corfe Castle. She preserved the eviction note which was signed by Major-General C.H. Miller of Southern Command on 16 November 1943:

"The Government appreciate that this is no small sacrifice which you are asked to make, but they are sure you will give this further help towards winning the war with a good heart."

John Gould, who was born at Tyneham in 1911, was serving with the Devonshire Regiment in India when he heard of the occupation of his village: "It's always in my thoughts. My home will always be there. If I could, I would go back tomorrow. It is a wicked shame that the pledge hasn't been kept".

Many of the elderly villagers, like fisherman Jack Miller of Sea Cottage, Worbarrow, failed to survive their uprooting and died before the war was over. The young were able to adapt and make new lives for themselves. Sarah Braisley lived at Egliston in a secluded valley above Kimmeridge

Bay. She was the last girl to marry in Tyneham's thirteenth century parish church: "It was quite a wrench when we moved out. But it was for the good of the country. It was rather exciting in a way for me, but it affected my parents a lot. It meant selling everything".

Poppy Budden, her sister, was then 18. She said later: "We were given an understanding that we would move back there some day. Most people expected to go back. But I don't feel any bitterness about it and I look back on the years at Tyneham as a very happy time".

The reaction of Mrs S.B. White was different: "I find it too painful even to go back and look at Tyneham again. Members of my family are buried in the tiny churchyard and my mother's old homestead on Povington Heath can just boast a pile of stones, part of the chimney stack and a lonely and gruesome-looking yew tree".

As the last residents evacuated the valley they pinned a farewell notice to the church door: "Please treat the church and house with care. We have given up our homes, where many of us have lived for generations to help win the war to keep men free. We shall return one day and thank you for treating the village kindly".

This was never to happen, but that is another story.

January 1944 —
June 1944

We've got to face it, the good times are over.
After this war has ended we are going to have
to pay £135 a year for a maid.

— Miss Blanche Randell, president of the
National Council of Women's Household Committee,
addressing a Dorset Meeting. 1944

AS 1944 eased into being, an ally was altering Dorset more profoundly than enemy bombing had. The American, wild and woolly, had taken over the county. Huge trucks thundered around narrow roads, the negro drivers visible inside only as white flashing teeth and eyes. Fields became mammoth stores and arsenals. The leaders of local dance bands struggled to learn jive and boogie woogie, both of which were replacing the waltz and foxtrot. These Americans knew that for the war to end they would most likely need to die, so they lived their Dorset months to the full.

Local newspapers, aware of the tastes of new readers, began to print results of baseball games played in the United States. This game was played in Dorset, and one intrepid local reporter set out to write about a match. Aware of his inadequate knowledge, he added a rider to his newspaper report that suggested any critical, smart-ass of a GI Joe should try reporting an English cricket match.

Initially, girls who went on dates with the Yanks qualified for the phrase that held a wealth of contempt in those days: "She's no better than she ought to be". But this sort of criticism faded as time passed, and many a 'nice' girl dated, and eventually married, an American, to add yet another lasting description to a long list of wartime euphemisms — GI Bride.

Those for whom the soon-to-die Americans were a licence to go on living, went on about their usual tasks, with the odd few altering their lives just enough to twist money out of the rich servicemen from across the Atlantic. Most local authorities in the area were upset by the county rate made on 25 February and the borough councils of Poole and Weymouth appealed against the rate, and had their appeals adjourned for the quarter sessions. Even the Abbotsbury parish council, snuggled peacefully in the thatched-cottage village, wrote a letter to the Dorchester rural district council, asking that a strong protest be registered against the county rate.

Other worries were on people's minds, particularly a Sherborne schoolteacher and those around her, for it was confirmed that she had smallpox. It was thought she had been infected during a visit to South Wales. Vaccinations for the public were quickly arranged.

With most of those preparing to go across the Channel to hit the Germans possibly prepared to give anything not to have to go, a young sailor was protesting in a Weymouth court that he had not yet seen a German, and was anxious to get at them. At least that is what he said in a kind of excuse for breaking into a store in Franchise Street and stealing sweets and cigarettes to the value of £8 1s. 0d. the property of Ernest Phillips. Aged 19, James Patrick O'Halleran, from Walton-on-Thames, admitted the offence at the quarter sessions, but asked for another chance so that he could fight for his country. He said it would break his mother's heart if she knew he was in gaol. Either because of his good character, thought for his mother's heart, or the fear that he would take

One of the more bizarre 'Scam' projects of earlier 1944 was for a floating airfield, codenamed 'Lily'. It was tried out in Weymouth Bay, on a reassuringly flat sea, with a Swordfish biplane. The aircraft, loaded to 9,000 lb, is about to use rocket assisted take-off gear to become airborne.　　　　*Photograph: Imperial War Museum.*

Failure (left), as the Churchill tank fails to climb one of the steeper parts of the Studland sand dunes. So enter one of Hobart's Funnies (above). Major General Percy Hobart of the 79th Armoured Division designed a series of ingenious machines that could ease the way for tanks, and however strange they looked, his vehicles were to save hundreds of lives in the Normandy campaign. Here, an AVRE lays a carpet from a bobbin, across the soft sand. Photographs: Imperial War Museum.

Using the carpet that the AVRE has laid, the Churchill tank repeats its attempt at climbing the dune (centre, right). This time it disappears over the top (far right). On the lefthand side of this picture you can see the deep rut left by its first, unaided, failure. Photographs: Imperial War Museum.

BOTTOM RIGHT: A heavily laden Bedford lorry drives across Weymouth Harbour. This is one of the most astonishing photographs to emerge from the secret war. A floating pier, known as a 'Swiss Roll' had been laid over the water, and a rough day was chosen for the test. The whole of Dorset was practising for D-Day. Photograph: Imperial War Museum.

more of Dorset apart if they did not let him have a go at the enemy, the court bound him over for 12 months.

A sailor doing much better than this was Bill Tilley, RNVR, son of Alderman E.W. Tilley, of Dorchester, who was promoted to lieutenant commander on a Far East station. Tilley, whose wife was the only daughter of Dorchester's A. Clark, had been serving for four years, two of which had been abroad. He was at the time the only Dorset officer to hold the Distinguished Service Cross.

Nutty old King George III, or rather his statue, was under fire, not from the Germans but from local people — particularly the Weymouth

and Melcombe Regis Ratepayers Association — who wrote to the council saying that the statue had outlived its purpose, was a traffic hazard, and that now was an opportune time for its removal. The King, who put Weymouth on the map as a resort, and is directly responsible for fine old architecture now being ruined as gift shops, with brightly-coloured plastic monstrosities dangled outside for sale, did find a defender in Alderman Moggeridge. He doubted if one in one thousand Weymouth people had read the inscription about prisoners of war on the statue, the reason for its erection, and urged them all to read it. Mrs A. Comben recalled a conversation she had with the late Thomas Hardy, who had described the writing on the monument as "very wonderful".

More important things worried the Portland food committee — oranges. At a meeting chaired by A.R.G. Comben, it was learned that a Portland trader had sold his quota of oranges before the date authorised for their sale. The questions were turned over to M.N. Fowler, of the food executive, who said that he visited the trader and had been told that the oranges were going bad, that was why they were sold at an early date. Asked what could be done to stop early selling, Fowler replied that all island traders could be warned that they would get no more oranges if they did the same thing as this offender.

Though the Dorset standing joint committee, in control of police finance, disapproved a recommendation that the number of policewomen in the county should be increased from two to three, they heard from the county's policy and general purposes committee of a circular from the Home Office urging all local authorities to see if the number of policewomen could be increased in their districts. The Weymouth YMCA had written asking for an additional policewoman at Weymouth and, after hearing from the Chief Constable, the committee recommended that subject to the approval of the Home Secretary, they would appoint another female police officer.

Proving that this was not a young man's war was 57-years-old Chief Petty Officer E. Pitcher, of Swanage, who had already shown he was brave in a young man's war by winning the VC, DCM, Medaille Militaire and Croix de Guerre, in the 1914-18 conflict. The British awards had come from his work as a gun-layer in the famous 'Q' ship commanded by Captain Gordon Camborne, VC, against German U-boats in the Atlantic, and the French decorated him for action against U-boats in the Bay of Biscay. In 1944, after 34 years in the navy, leaving in 1933 to become musketry instructor at a Dorset preparatory school, then rejoining soon after the outbreak of war, Pitcher was training gunnery ratings.

While some carried on with fighting the war, others were engrossed in talking about what was to happen afterwards. At a special meeting of the

Practising for D-Day. A Humber Scout car (above left) drives into four feet of water off Weymouth promenade on 5 February 1944. It successfully drives through the sea (above right). Next a Humber armoured car drives down the ramp of a LCT (below left). And likewise a Daimler scout car (below right). Photographs: Imperial War Museum.

The wading exercise continues (above left). Weymouth's anti-invasion defences dating from 1940, can be seen in the background of these shots. Perhaps the most amazing sight (above right) was a Stuart tank travelling through six feet of water. Note the depth marker on its exhaust outlet. The other funnel carried air to the engine. Two other Stuarts pass in five feet of water (below left). The timekeeper raises a flag to signal that the time limit of six minutes has expired (below right). Photographs: Imperial War Musum.

Weymouth and Portland Chamber of Commerce, Dr J.A. Pridham gave a talk on a Government White Paper on Health Services, and predicted that by 1960 private doctors and private practice would be non-existent. The British Institute of Public Opinion found that 69 per cent of doctors supported the basic proposals for a National Health Service.

Road accidents were on the increase. In Dorset during April 1944, seven people were killed, 43 seriously injured and 33 slightly injured. Figures for the previous April were two, 56 and 37 respectively. Road dangers were not only concerning the civil authorities, but the Americans as well. A drive to cut down on accidents involving US vehicles was instigated at Dorchester, by Colonel Frederick R. Lafferty, 7-Base section provost marshall of the US Army. He set up five military police patrol groups, each consisting of a military policeman and two vehicle mechanics, who were positioned on all important traffic arteries in the area. They were ordered to put an end to operational abuses by US drivers.

Every passing vehicle was stopped. The policeman checked the driver's permit, trip chit and manual of operation, while the mechanics looked the vehicle over for possible faults in general condition, brakes, tyres, steering, horn, lights and windshield wipers. These new regulations did not help an RAF corporal who was cycling along Rodwell Road towards its junction with Boot Hill, Weymouth, as US Army road convoys were threading the roads to Portland. On traffic control duty at this junction was Corporal E.J. Hogan, a US Army technician. Private Stickler, a US Army driver, was coming up the hill in a massive truck. Hogan saw the RAF cyclist coming at speed, and held up his hand to halt the US Army vehicle. But the sun was in Stickler's eyes, so Hogan tried, without success, to stop the cyclist. Realising his danger too late, the RAF man attempted to turn up the hill in Wyke Road, but he struck the nearside of the vehicle and died shortly afterwards, in Portwey Hospital.

Sad though these individual incidents were, all the horror of death in numbers came during the night of 27 April. Young American soldiers, many of whom would have been at school but for the war, filed from the bone-chilling damp of camps near Dorchester. Serious-faced, they boarded landing craft at Weymouth and Portland. Each one believed that the big day had come — this was to be D-Day. After the preparation and waiting, there was a fear-spattered relief in at last being on the move.

But their commanders knew different. This was the start of exercises 'Fabius' and 'Tiger', where a close-simulation of the projected landings in Normandy was to be staged at Slapton Sands, a beach in Devon. The night was cold as the landing craft rounded Portland Bill and headed into the watery graveyard of Lyme Bay. There was no escort. The big guns of Royal Navy and US Navy ships were off the Devon coast, waiting to shell the beach before the landing parties went ashore.

Suddenly, German surface torpedo craft of the 5th and 9th E-boat Flotillas were darting in among the US vessels. It was a massacre, with the shore batteries ordered not to fire because of the danger of causing more American casualties. Though the British vessels HMS *Saladin*, *Azalra* and *Onslow* steamed to the rescue, driving the German raiders away, 191 seamen and 441 US troops had died, and twelve tanks had gone to the bottom of the sea. The dead and injured were brought ashore at the Portland end of Chesil Beach. Warnings had been given about the dangers of unescorted landing craft moving out into the Channel. These warnings were ignored. Human life, when wrapped in a uniform, was not highly prized in those days.

As the inanimate King George III turned a stony eye down on the strange vehicles of war that passed regularly beneath him in Weymouth, his carved ears heard of a reprieve. It had been decided that the statue could stay where it was, at least for the duration of hostilities, but was to undergo a process of renovation.

While the waiting for D-Day went on, English brides-to-be and their American fiancés were only prepared to wait for the priest. They were relieved when the European Theatre of Operations announced that members of the US forces could marry English girls, providing the soldier or officer concerned obtained permission. A total of 80,000 eventually did so.

Each would-be bridegroom had to give two months notice to his commanding officer, to make sure that he would enter into the marriage without violating the laws of the United States of America. In some cases (for reasons usually obvious), this rule could be waived, but this was discouraged. It was pointed out that marriage to a US citizen didn't confer citizenship on an alien, but it did facilitate the alien's later entry into America, and naturalisation after taking up residence there. The wife of a US serviceman was entitled to allowances, insurances, and other benefits, as authorised by military regulations, but was not entitled to Government quarters and medical or dental treatment. To ensure there was no slip-up, the groom's commanding officer had to send a letter of approval to the civil or ecclesiastical authority who was to conduct the marriage. Any member of the US forces who married in violation of this policy was subject to court martial.

Among the Anglo-American weddings was an Easter one at Holy Trinity church, Dorchester, where the church was colourfully decorated with spring flowers and had the additional display of the Stars and Stripes and Union Jack flags. The bride was Miss Rosemary White, of 15a Cornwall Road, Dorchester, and the groom, who came from New York, was Major Stephen M. Batori. If such a distinctive wedding needed further embellishment, it came with the best man, a brother officer of the groom, Captain Quentin Roosevelt, son of Brigadier General Theodore Roosevelt, cousin of the President of the USA.

On the home front also, while cross-Atlantic unions were taking place in church, school dinners were lurching into being, and a new problem came up, which no one had thought about. The kids had an hour and a half off each lunchtime, and it did not take this long for them to eat their meals. So up popped the question — who is going to look after the little dears when they are not eating? In Weymouth, where it was agreed that teachers were also entitled to a break, the council clerk, Percy Smallman, wrote off to the Board of Education for guidance.

Then, on a grey, wet miserable Sunday, when an ashamed daylight prayed for an early dusk, the tempo of military life changed. Long files of olive-green clad American soldiers stretched from the northern end of

Cliff climbing about to start near Bridport. One of the rope ladders being fired by rockets from landing craft to the top of a 150 ft cliff near Bridport. This exercise was part of the 'Scam' project, testing experimental invasion techniques. Grapnels were attached to the rockets. Photograph: Imperial War Museum.

161

Weymouth's Esplanade to the harbour. The locals stood across the road, watching, unable to equate the soft-soled march of the US troops with the clash of hobnails and whistling their experience of British soldiers had them expect. As the landing craft in the harbour filled up, delays made the Yanks pause along the seafront.

American humour, never far below the surface, would bubble out then. The watchers became the watched, as good-humoured jokes were fired across the road at the locals. Military policemen buzzed up and down the Esplanade in jeeps. Where children once excitedly jumped as they enjoyed Punch and Judy, the young warriors leaned against the railings smiling, but many of them were already cancelled out by the mark of death.

That night, the people of Dorset were wakened by a roar of aircraft

Men of an American assault unit walk along the Promenade at Weymouth, at the beginning of June 1944, to join the invasion armada. Barbed wire separates them from the almost empty civilian street. The men seem cheerful. US Army photograph.

that shook every building. Those who had watched the passing soldiers that day, thought about them now. Wondering if those young faces still grinned, tossed about on the rough, unfriendly sea of the Channel. Next morning came confirmation of what everyone had guessed — this was D-Day.

With this realisation came a new, sobering knowledge that marred the anticipated joy of the invasion taking place at last. It was hell over there for the first American soldiers, and this was reflected in the faces of the US troops still marching the Esplanade to the docks. Gone were the smiles and jokes of yesterday. Unlike those who had gone before them on the previous day, these men knew what awaited them in Normandy.

As people rushed to buy maps of the continent to follow the progress of the Allies (maps which were soon sold out), news of the Dorset casualties

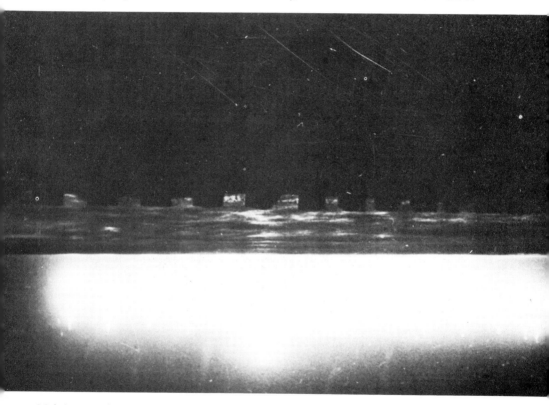

Lighting up the night. Star shells fired from two-pounder Pom-poms illuminate the Channel in a 'Scam' project exercise. In that mass of light there are forty or more shells bursting. Silhouetted against the sea are the concrete anti-tank defences of the Chesil Beach, a reminder of the days when the invasion threat was in reverse.

Photograph: Imperial War Museum.

was coming through. Invasion reinforcements were constantly rolling along the roads of Dorset to the docks, and cyclists and drivers of slow vehicles were asked to keep well to the left so that military vehicles could pass. On the subject of the left, Dorset was still a little scarred mentally from the early war anti-Party outburst of Conservative Viscount Cranborne, and it had a new shock from current Member of Parliament for South Dorset, Viscount Hinchingbrooke. Sticking up for the communists, he was one of seven MPs having a go at War Minister Sir James Grigg, accusing him of unfairly refusing to allow the *Daily Worker* to have a correspondent accredited to the invasion force, SHAEF.

Further up county, Member of Parliament Captain Hambro was telling the North Dorset Conservative Association that he would not stand at the next general election. His parliamentary career had begun in 1910,

Three LCIs drop the infantry on Slapton Sands, Devon, in the 'Fabius' exercise at the end of April 1944. The whole affair had been a little too realistic. More than six hundred men drowned in Lyme Bay a week before, when their landing craft were intercepted by E-boats. That was more than the total casualties would be in the real crossing of the Channel a month later. Photograph: Imperial War Museum.

when he was returned as Member for South Dorset, and he was there until 1922. Since 1937 he had been representing North Dorset in Parliament.

Northern Europe did not have the monopoly in the action. Inside the softer underbelly of Europe, dispatch rider Arthur Legg wrote home to his brother Ted in Bournemouth on 14 June 1944, from a room somewhere in Italy where the "typewriter and radio are tapping away". One of the world's practical jokers, Arthur enjoyed his war to the full, spending his thirties in a state of perpetual childhood thanks to the provision of an army motorbike:

> The welding went on my silencer at Taranto the other day and now she sounds just like the good old grass track days, and by the way I can't get my licence taken away out here or in Cairo yet. You want to see the

Exercise 'Fabius' was a full scale rehearsal for D-Day, using tank landing craft from Weymouth and Portland to attack Slapton Sands in Devon. Balloons protect the beach from fighter attack. Three LCTs are unloading in this sector of the beach.
Photograph: Imperial War Museum.

American soldiers being briefed during an exercise before D-Day. They wear camouflaged helmets and have blackened faces. US Army photograph.

OPPOSITE: The Union Jack would be taken back across the Channel, but first it was raised on Slapton Sands. Photograph: Imperial War Museum.

speed and noise we make especially when on an 'Immediate message'.

I have done 16,000 miles since coming to Italy in January, and if old Deacon, Roe or Bryon (Bournemouth neighbours) was anywhere around in the busy streets of Bori, or when I was in Cairo, their hair would stand on end, and I guess I can't get the sack from the job till the Ruddy War is over.

One way streets mean nothing to us DRs and the 'Red Caps' just know we are on SDR.

Mid-1944 was showing definite signs that, at last, the war was going to be won in the not too distant future. The sun was shining, some Yanks were still disturbing the Dorset peace by enjoying themselves, but most had left for Normandy. It was still a little difficult to achieve, but thoughts were now able to touch on the pleasantries of a coming victory. Half a million American soldiers passed through Weymouth and Portland on their way to France. With them went more than a hundred thousand vehicles.

General Eisenhower commanded an army of two million men. Their momentum might at times be slowed but it would not be stopped. The odds in their favour were immense. By the end of the battle of Normandy, in tanks alone, the Allies had numerical superiority of around twenty to one.

July 1944 — December 1944

After the war, the banks will be particularly
willing to help ex-servicemen. Each will be
judged on his ability and integrity to make a go
of a venture, rather than anything else.

— Mr C.H.W. Stallard, manager of a Dorset branch of
Lloyds Bank. August, 1944

A MAN who had joined the local unit of the Territorials two years before the outbreak of war, and was commissioned on mobilisation and posted to the Dorsetshire Regiment, lost his life in Normandy. He was Lieutenant Colin Frank Windebank, youngest son of Mr and Mrs R.F. Windebank of 17 Bryanstone Road, Bournemouth, who was aged 24 at the time of his death. Educated at Weymouth College, he was a well-known pre-war athlete and a popular member of Bournemouth Sports Club. Windebank was not killed in his first battle, for he had served in the Middle East and Italian campaign, returning to England the previous November to prepare for D-Day.

The country's leaders came to a decision about August bank holiday 1944 — and announced that it was to be a holiday. It was an austere affair, with no ice-cream or rock, but sunshine brought the crowds out on to the beaches. Old tins made fair substitutes for buckets, and sand was shovelled with improvised spades. There was fun on the beaches but it was tempered by occasional sobering thoughts of what had happened, such a short time ago, on shores just across the Channel.

Dorset still had a number of its guests — the Yanks played their baseball games and strolled around in the now familiar, smart uniforms — swelling every social event with their numbers. From 'Sixpenny Hops' to some of the county's distinguished annual functions, the Americans were arriving.

A lot of restrictions were being relaxed, but not all, as retired doctor Harold Chadwick, of Grosvenor Road, Swanage, was to discover. He was summoned at Christchurch police court for hiring a taxi for a journey outside the area permitted by law. Dr Chadwick had been staying at Northampton when he was taken ill due to injuries received in the 1914-18 war. A doctor decided that Dr Chadwick should return home. He was too ill to travel other than by car, and was under sedation for the whole journey.

A police constable saw the taxi in Christchurch High Street, and on checking found that it had done a 163-mile trip from Northampton to Swanage, which was well outside of the radius a taxi was allowed under war regulations. In court, it was pointed out that had Dr Chadwick applied for a permit to make the journey it would probably have been granted without question. But the law, ass or not, has to be enforced and Dr Chadwick was fined £1.

On the other hand there were signs that peace was on the way, in that the Home Guard became a voluntary service, with parades no longer compulsory, and civil defence members were released for other war work. The lifting of the black-out and lighting restrictions was promised.

Dorset waited eagerly for this big day, or, rather, night, which was predicted as 17 September, when double summertime ended. Fire watching duties had been suspended. Perhaps most welcome news of all for the county was the ending of the evacuation from London in consequence of attacks by flying bombs. Though those who had already left the city were advised not to return at present, most welcomed the fact that the old sore of evacuation was not going to be picked at and irritated further.

After nearly six years of utter darkness, street lighting was switched on again on the evening of Sunday 18 September. It was an unambitious lighting plan, with each lamp restricted to a power of fifteen watts, but it had been eagerly looked forward to since the test had been made, from 9 to 11 pm, the previous Tuesday. Windows, other than attics, were only required to be curtained so that the objects inside were not distinguishable from outside. No direct light was allowed, which, in effect, meant that curtains fitted in pre-war days were adequate. However, in the event of an air-raid, all lights had to be completely obscured either by switching lights off or fitting black-out screens.

As the towns, cities and villages were illuminated, the lights of the Church of England were going out, according to Viscount Hinchingbrooke. Having just made a few of his constituents wonder, by waving the banner for the communist newspaper the *Daily Worker,* he launched an attack on all the vicars who gave their sing-song sermons each Sunday. Speaking at Hanley, Staffordshire, Hinchingbrooke said that the Church of England had been failing in the performance of its duties for fifty years. Bishops came and went, he said, and archbishops were created and passed on, while the people's support of the Church of England declined. It was a situation that could not be tolerated any longer, the MP declared. Incompetent men who would not fight for their faith and ideals had to be dismissed.

In the Bournemouth district it was not those busy on Sunday who were the cause of concern, but the workers of the week. Raising restrictions on visitors had caused an influx of holidaymakers to the area. Apart from the austerity of wartime, the finance houses had as yet not deluded the average man into thinking he could afford a car, and public transport was still heavily used. Yet, at the time of day when local workers were going to and from work, they could not find room on buses crowded with holidaymakers.

This gave the local authority a dilemma. They toyed with the idea of issuing travel permits to local workers, giving precedence over the holidaymaker where boarding buses was concerned. But they could see the dangers of altercations, perhaps leading to violence, at bus-stops. There was the added difficulty that came with the knowledge that these holidaymakers were not the idle rich trying to avert boredom — but war workers themselves, enjoying their first well-earned rest. The problem remained.

None of this could damage the elation of knowing that the war was being won. After an agonisingly hard-won gain of territory in Normandy, the Allies were pushing on toward the goal of Germany at a better speed. The topic of the moment was now entirely what was to happen when peace came. Conditioned by years of war, the planners of the county were trying to think constructively. Weymouth council had a meeting that covered a subject worrying everyone. Housing would soon present difficulties, but they had faith in the prefabricated houses that the Government was pushing their way. The big fear, however, was that there would not be full employment for the returning servicemen. In this brave new world, paid for in suffering, there was no room for thoughts of returning to the inequalities and poverty of the 1930s. So the councillors met and talked about the problem, and felt better for having done so.

In war or peace, with victory near or afar, there are always internal grievances that flare into trouble. Though the upset was not too serious, the county starved of entertainments was depressed when the cinemas decided to close on every Sunday evening from the end of September. The cause of the trouble was the county decision to double the 7½ per cent share of takings that had to go to charity from each Sunday opening, and a new law banning children under sixteen from Sunday cinemas, irrespective of whether they were accompanied by an adult. The Dorset branch of the Hants and Dorset Cinematograph Exhibitors' Association made the decision to close the cinemas in protest, with both large and small picture-houses accepting the recommendation.

The chairman of the cinema proprietors, Geoffrey Bravery of Poole, said he regretted closing the cinemas but had been compelled to take this drastic step. The view of his association was that the existing share for charity should remain until after the war, when the figure could be reviewed in the light of prevailing circumstances. The association was also strongly opposed to the barring of children from Sunday cinema. This was seen as an infringement of human rights.

Probably not caring whether the cinemas were open on Sunday or any other evening, was Driver Jack Woodhouse, RASC, of 63 Wakeham, Portland, who was home on thirty days hard-earned leave. A captive of the Germans since 1941, having gone overseas in 1940 to the 8th Army, he was taken prisoner the following April when Derna fell into enemy hands. He had escaped from a camp in Italy when that country capitulated.

This escape took place in June, and his first friendly contact was a Polish patrol, which led to him eventually coming home on a troopship. He was spending his leave with his wife, whom he had married in the first months of the war. Free also of the Germans and home at Portland again was commando Sergeant Donald Harrington, of the Clifton Hotel, Grove Road. People at home were eager for news of prisoners and prison life, and Harrington, having spent three and a half years in captivity, supplied considerable information.

His last camp had been in Poland, where he said there had been plenty of recreation — football, cricket, and regular band concerts — but the food had been grim. Each man had received a half pound of bread and a small pot of margarine each day. All they had in addition were three potatoes every two days. He said that the Red Cross food parcels had been a great help, but had been getting smaller as the war lengthened. At this camp he had met another Portland man, Private Ernest Packer. He also told of how the boys he had left behind in the camp had already packed to come home, even though the war in Europe was still being fought.

Another Portland man home on leave was Private George Luker, of the Parachute Regiment, a hero of the epic battle of Arnhem. George, a quiet man, was reticent about the actual battle, in which he had carried a wounded comrade through heavy enemy fire to safety. He did tell of German infiltration of allied lines, and of the disappointment of seeing food parcels dropped by the RAF collected by the enemy. Snipers were an ever-present hazard, and George, just a young man himself at the time, expressed surprise at the age of some of the enemy snipers: "They looked no more than about sixteen years of age."

In a high wind and tossed by mountainous waves, a tank landing craft was in difficulties on the Chesil Beach just off Wyke Regis. The heroic rescue that followed has been documented by Rodney Legg for the Royal Naval Association's "Portland Souvenir Magazine". The boat in difficulties was an American tank landing craft, number A 2454, manned by a British crew.

Ten of them died and two coastguards who attempted a rescue — Captain Pennington Legh and Coastguard Treadwell — were also drowned. Before he was taken by the sea, Treadwell had rescued two men from the water. The brave attempt at saving the crew had to be carried out from the beach.

Because of the heavy seas, Weymouth lifeboat could only wait helplessly and watch, and an Admiralty tug failed to fight its way round Portland Bill. The heroes were Fortuneswell Lifesaving Company who ran along the beach and succeeded in firing a rocket line, by pistol, into the vessel.

When the tank craft was almost beached it was hit by a giant wave and everything movable "including most of the crew" was swept into the sea. It was at this moment that Mr. Treadwell managed to recover two of the men alive.

Two more, aboard, were also seen. They could not move nearer to the line, and more were fired into the craft, but still the men could not come closer. Pounded by the sea, the vessel shifted her position and the lines fouled. Three of the beach party, Legh, Treadwell and Rowsell, cleared a fouled line — and then another heavy wave crashed across the boat and swept them away: "Captain Legh and Mr. Treadwell were never seen again." Two others, W.C. Rowsell and V.F. Stephens, were hauled ashore, exhausted, but insisted on staying on the beach until the rescue was over.

Cyril Brown, wearing a lifebelt, finally managed to struggle aboard — with the sea still breaking across the craft — and after many attempts was at last able to haul a line to both crewmen: "Mr. Brown then let go, jumped, and was hauled ashore in an exhausted condition and taken to hospital."

One crewman then leaped into the water, and he too was hauled ashore alive. The lifeline then broke, however, and the other man was left on the boat. His rescue was carried out by Albert Oldfield, who dashed into the water — without any safety line attached to himself — and threw a line into the hands of the last man aboard. He too then jumped from the boat and was pulled ashore.

In terms of numbers the sea had won, with twelve drowned and only four rescued, but considering the swell and under-tow on the beach that day it is remarkable any were saved. The "three very brave men" who survived were later given a reception at Weymouth Guildhall and presented with the Lloyds' silver medal for lifesaving. The fourth man,

V.F. Stephens of Wyke Regis, did not live to receive his medal as he died after a car crash. For Portlander Cyril Brown there was a special honour. He was awarded the Stanhope medal for the bravest deed of 1944.

The sadness following this tragedy provided the right atmosphere for "cost counting" the loss of life, injury and property damage during the war at Weymouth. In all, 5,000 houses in the town had been affected — 346 demolished or pulled down later, 819 seriously damaged, and 3,842 needing repairs. Forty-six people lost their lives, 86 were seriously injured, and 140 were slightly wounded. A total of 429 high explosive bombs were dropped, plus some mines, and numerous incendiaries. It was calculated that 787 sirens were sounded and the people of Weymouth were under alert for 721 hours 43 minutes — or more than 30 days — the raids being largely grouped between July 1940 and April 1942.

Small traders whose businesses had been hit by war were to get Government help of up to £150 each, C.H.W. Stallard, a manager of Lloyds Bank, was telling the Weymouth and Portland Chamber of trade. He added that this proposed scheme would be for boarding house proprietors and people in similar concerns. He went on to point out how willing the banks would be to help after the war. He did not specify how institutions like the banks, who have perfected the vile habits of the parasite and live entirely on the money of other people, could 'help'

The last Christmas card of the war. This one was from the Italian theatre, sent by dispatch rider Arthur Legg to his sister-in-law, Gladys Legg, and her family at Easter Road in Bournemouth.

anyone, in the true sense of the word. Though it was reassuring that ex-servicemen would find sympathetic help, and a man's ability and integrity would be judged more than anything else when individual ventures were considered.

No statistics exist to show how many men exchanged a fight against the Germans and Japanese for a heart-breaking struggle to pay back the money, plus interest, that the banks had loaned them. The immediate post-war period saw countless ex-soldiers, sailors and airmen start out in business. Only a few survived — most came to grief.

Tarrant Rushton airfield, between Blandford and Wimborne, on the evening of D-Day. Formations of gliders, and their Halifax towing-craft, are seen assembling for take-off. A similar scene preceded the Arnhem landings, though then the airborne troops came down between two of General Walter Model's crack SS panzer divisions. Their presence at Oosterbeck had already been established from decoded German radio messages, but the intelligence reports were ignored. Photograph: Imperial War Museum.

January 1945 — August 1945

Please, Mum, don't ever cook rice for me again when I come home.

— A Dorset man, held captive by the Japanese in Hakodate Camp, Japan, writing to his mother. January 1945

NEW YEAR 1945 was a wild occasion, with Dorset's most lively spot probably being the United States Red Cross Club, in St Thomas Street at Weymouth. Five hundred US servicemen, together with Wrens, ATS, nurses and civilian girls were issued with whistles to blow at midnight. But these instruments could hardly be heard over the shouts and yells that greeted the New Year. Soldiers and sailors stripped coloured streamers from the giant Christmas tree, and draped them around the necks of girls. There was no doubt that this would be the year to bring peace.

But the war dragged on a little longer, and a battalion of the Dorset Regiment was receiving deserved recognition for its gallant action in evacuating 2,800 airborne troops from Arnhem. The whole operation was one of the most daring ever attempted, though jeopardised from the start because Montgomery ignored the information provided by the enemy's decoded Enigma signals and proceeded to have his men dropped in the midst of two German panzer regiments, front line troops who were using the area as a rest centre. "Look, you are going to jump in a hornet's nest," he was warned, and threw the message away.

Back home, it became clear that the Weymouth council's mordant desire for grandiose schemes had only lain dormant during the war, and was far from cured. A new outbreak of this illness came with proposals to clean up the Esplanade and bus shelters, clearing away all old shelters and kiosks, moving the taxi rank to some other location, allowing only local buses to pick up and set down passengers, on the seafront, constructing a shelter with seats on the roof, and a plan to lay out ornamental gardens northward from the statue. In the middle of it all was the gloomy effigy of King George III. If the spirit of the old King dwelt in the sand-swept stone image, it could at least feel secure, for the council decided to leave the statue where it was.

County towns and villages were ordering the new-fangled prefabricated houses from the Ministry of Health, while farmworkers were rubbing their hands over a raise of 5s. 0d. a week, which brought their wages for a 48-hour week up to £3 10s. 0d. Any class-climbers near the Portland naval base had a field day on 30 January, a Tuesday, when they could hang around with R.J.R. Scott, the Flag-Officer-in-Charge, at Dockyard House at noon, awaiting the Duchess of Kent who arrived to inspect WRNS officers and ratings attached to the Portland Base.

The following Sunday afternoon, in the Red Cross Centre at the Victoria Hotel, Weymouth, twelve interesting letters were being read to relatives of prisoners of war. They had been written by Flight Sergeant G. Hatton, to his family at 2 Russell Avenue. He was a prisoner at Hakodate Camp in Japan, and wrote to say that he was well but longing for news from home. Hatton said he had become the camp's shoe repairer and was getting along with the job very well. His letters ended with a plea to his mother never to cook him rice again. Other letters came from another Weymouth man in the camp, a friend of Sergeant Hatton's, and he said that there were other men from the town in the camp, including Peter Carter and Jimmy Wilde. The man's rice remark had its echoes in the Vietnam conflict when Americans released after communist internment were found to be in better general health as a result of the rice diet than their uncaptured colleagues who had continued to deteriorate under the delights of alcohol, pot and rich fatty foods.

A sweetener came for the people when sugar stocks that had been stored for emergency were released. Hitler would have then needed a miracle to cause an emergency. His last fling, in the Ardennes, was over and done with, leaving only victory for the Allies. The sugar was lumpy from having been kept in store, but was sweet, fit to eat, and very welcome. Mr. Cube was to have political aspirations in the fight for the minds of post-war Britons.

With an immediate bright look to the sky, the Wareham and Purbeck rural district council was thinking about putting things back in order for peace. The Regional Commissioner was asked when the battle training areas of Tyneham and Studland would be returned to their civilian use. The reply said that it did not think it likely that a decision would be reached by the War Office until the war was over. The Commissioner added that it would be impossible to give a definite answer about the future of the land in peacetime, as it depended on the permanent training layout of the army.

Flying into action — in a cliff exercise at Bournemouth. The war now was moving deep into Germany.   *Photograph: Imperial War Museum.*

Borstal boys, not soldier boys, were worrying the Portland urban district council. Escapes from the island Borstal institution were escalating, and the escapees had some nasty habits while on the run. It was not unknown for a boy to break into a house and use the centre of the dining room table as a toilet. Councillor W.J. Miller, moving a resolution that a complaint be sent to the Home Secretary, which was supported without dissent, said that most of the inmates were fully grown men steeped in the traditions of crime, and had an entire lack of respect for the belongings of others. Another serious aspect was that there was no compensation for loss or damage caused by the escapees.

Constant reminders that the war continued came with notices of casualties. Bernard Beale, Weymouth Corporation's entertainments manager, and Mrs Beale, were notified that their son, Lieutenant Colin Beale of the Dorsetshire Regiment, had been wounded in Burma. The communication, which arrived on 19 January, said that Colin had been injured in the right thigh and forearm and had been placed on the list of those seriously ill.

While at Weymouth Grammar School, Colin Beale had been granted a cadetship in the Indian Army, and was posted to an Indian officers' training school at Bangalore. He did so well there that he was selected with two other cadets for vacancies in the British Army. He was just under 19 when commissioned.

War in the Far East faded from significance a bit when it seemed likely there could be a minor war in the 'deep south' of Dorset. A national newspaper published a story that a small arsenal had been discovered at the Portland Borstal, and hinted that a mass outbreak had been planned. The Governor of the Borstal, B. Rashley, was asked about the newspaper article. "Outbreak?" he gasped, incredulously, it is said. "This is the first I've heard about it."

In our modern, cynical days, when public figures have perfected a wide-eyed stare of innocence into a television camera, while they spit out the biggest possible lies, such a statement would have inspired the sort of confidence that had everyone expecting armed borstal boys to come tearing over the hill like red indians. But the simplicity of life in '45, despite a world war, had nurtured a naivety, and the Governor's word was accepted.

An urge to reshape things after war, even though the fighting was still going on at the time, had Weymouth Civic Society discussing the possibility of banning cars from the Esplanade, and providing an inquiry bureau, a municipal inquiry service, municipal car parks, and library facilities. Giving a talk on the latter, Miss Holman, the Weymouth librarian, said the town was missing a lot by not having a lending library. The backwater mentality had lasted for years.

On 16 March, when everyone in the coastal areas of Dorset expected a 'full house' Easter, and looked to the railways to bring visitors in, there was a mishap at Bincombe Tunnel. The Weymouth to Waterloo train had two carriages derailed. The worn and slippery state of the rails was officially blamed for the incident. Anticipating a busy weekend, Weymouth otherwise had its attractions ready. The Command Theatrical Society was presenting a Comedy Theatre play entitled *Hawk Island,* at Bincleaves Hall, and there was a military band at the Pier bandstand. The Saturday night dance at Bincleaves had music by the Dorset Constabulary band. Most cafes and restaurants closed on Good Friday, while the Saturday afternoon had some novelty outdoor entertainment — a ladies football match on the recreation ground at Weymouth.

Like the best-made plans of mice and men are said to, the high hopes for Easter went sadly astray. Traffic on the railways was only comparable to the previous year, when the area had been tied up in strict security for the coming invasion of Normandy. The bands played to half-filled halls, and the theatre players were in danger of outnumbering their audiences. An item that came apart at the seams, metaphorically speaking if not in other ways, was the ladies football match held on the Saturday afternoon. One of the players, Miss Joan Denning, of 98 Clearmont Road, was injured in the game, and her mother created hell, publicly.

"It is a disgraceful exhibition and should be stopped," said Mrs Denning. "Women are more delicately made than men and could suffer permanent harm. I am sure the men serving abroad would not like to think of their daughters exhibiting themselves on a football pitch. I know, of course, why men went there to watch." This condemnation of women's football was unanimous, and among the men who were not going to watch was local sports outfitter Archie Bown, a former player with famous teams such as Swindon and Bristol. He emphatically asserted: "I am against women's football. It is not a women's game and those who play will inevitably suffer in later years."

Joining in a call for the game to be banned were Miss Maybee, Dorset County Youth Organiser, J. Longland, director of education for Dorset, and Major C.F. Linnitt, head of Weymouth grammar school. Agreeing with them was the Rev E.L. Langston, of St Mary's church, Weymouth, who said: "I am glad someone has taken this up. Football for girls is not seemly; there are plenty of games such as tennis and hockey which girls can play."

Not all the rats in Weymouth were sneaking round the recreation ground in dirty raincoats, waiting for a pair of female football shorts to split. There were four legged ones with long tails abounding in the port that had let the Plague into England, and since April the previous year, the council had killed 1,300. The £713 spent in rodent control was claimed back from the Ministry of Food.

Everyone wanted to do something to celebrate the victory that was surely to come, but no-one knew quite what was wanted. Weymouth council's finance and law committee was considering a recommendation from the town's Civic Society, that a scheme be inaugurated to provide a welcome-home fund for the men and women of Weymouth who had been serving in the forces. The committee was unclear about as to how such a fund would be utilised and told the society so.

Making the welcome-home brought no problems at 226 Chickerell Road, Weymouth, where Mr and Mrs J.H. Miller had their three sons home on leave at the same time, quite unexpectedly. Air crewman James Miller, the eldest son, volunteered in 1941, and was home on 21 days leave after service in North Africa, Egypt, Iraq, Cyprus and Italy. War, harsh and cruel as it is, had provided Jim with exciting adventures, and shown him strange sights that would have eluded him under normal life. Two of his most vivid recollections were of escaping from Cos just before the Nazis captured the island, and witnessing the eruption of Vesuvius, the previous year. Jim had been attached to the 8th Army when it landed in Sicily, and he said the morale of the boys had then been, and still was, one hundred percent.

His brother, George, was also in the RAF. He too had joined up in 1941, and had been stationed in South and West Africa, as well as Newfoundland. He had met brother Jim in an unplanned, pleasurable encounter, while he was in Durban.

The third brother, Robert, was in the RASC and serving with the 2nd Army. His war had included a landing in Normandy on D-Day plus three, and he was in the battle of Caen. A distinction for Bob was being the fifth soldier to take food into Paris for the hungry Parisians. Having survived a stay in Antwerp when the Germans were firing many rocket shells a day into the area, Bob was home on seven days' leave, his first for fifteen months. He added his moan to the soldier of the day's lament; that his leave was not long enough. Asked about the Normandy invasion, Bob said: "It was tough going but the chaps stuck it splendidly. We had no fresh food for the first six months. Plenty of tinned stuff, of course, but that's not the same thing."

Despite a fair degree of local animosity when the Yanks had been stationed in Dorset, the war had linked England with America in a way that was unprecedented. Evidence of this was provided on a sunny Tuesday, more fitted for fun than grief, when crowds assembled in St Mary Street, Weymouth, long before the memorial service for the late President Roosevelt was due. People stood singly and in groups, while a rustle of strangely hushed conversation whispered through the street.

Faces were depressed by sorrow, tears were in the eyes of many, and an almost tangible grief hung over the area.

In this aura of mixed sadness and expectancy for the war's end, the members of Weymouth council were displaying admirable qualities that few have given them credit for, before or since. Amost unanimously, they turned down a proposal to be paid for the time lost when attending meetings. While doing this, they also arranged details of the Victory in Europe celebrations when the Prime Minister announced that the war with Germany was over. At 3 pm, it was decided, the mayor, Goddard, would attend a thanksgiving service on the Esplanade, opposite the Gloucester Hotel. He issued a public invitation for townspeople to attend.

He did, and they did, when the big day came. The Esplanade at Weymouth was crowded for the service, and stayed crowded until the early hours of next morning, as wildly excited people revelled in the new peace. Towns and villages throughout Dorset followed suit on that big day. Then smaller celebrations continued in the days that followed, with practically every street in the county providing its children with a party. Tables were laid out of doors, while mothers combined their rations to give what was a comparative feast in those days.

Now the men began to return home. Among them was Paratrooper Jesse Roberts, of 10 Hope Street, Weymouth. A veteran of the 1st Airborne Division, he had been in the North Africa and Sicily campaigns and had been one of the first to drop on D-Day. Having recently celebrated his 21st birthday in a prison camp, he had been captured at Arnhem. When he had jumped into that now famous battle he had, he said, struck his head on the helmet of the man in front of him, and was unconscious when he landed.

Another fighting man in the news was 33-years-old carpenter's assistant John Connolly, of 4 Coastguard Cottages, Langton Herring. He was awarded the British Empire Medal for his work in clearing booby traps from the buildings and airfields in Belgium. A member of an RAF bomb disposal unit the previous October, Corporal Connolly had been one of a party of men detailed to clear mines and booby traps from six Belgium hotels that were required for military purposes. When three of his colleagues were badly injured by explosions, he carried on with the work, ignoring the danger. He also assisted in clearing over 8,000 mines from an airfield the Germans had converted to become part of their defences in the Western Wall.

Signs that peace was here, even though men were still dying and suffering in the Far East, came with a meeting of the Women's Institute at Dorchester where important topics of peacetime were discussed, including a resolution that British Double Summertime be abolished. Another omen, particularly for the young, was the sight of brightly painted wagons and steam engines moving on to the Marsh at Weymouth, as the local amusement caterers, Richard Townsend and Sons, moved out into peacetime.

In Portland Harbour the surrendering of German U-boats was the star attraction which attracted 10,000 over the Whitsun weekend. On view from 2 to 7 pm, at a charge of 6d. for adults, and half-price for children, the submarines were only for looking at — and not for boarding by the general public. The takings of £218 went to King George's Fund for sailors. One recently captured vessel, the U776, had been at sea for 42 days and only had two days fuel left. She tried to surrender at the tiny bay of Freshwater on the Isle of Wight and was redirected to Portland, arriving on 16 May. The boat carried a crew of 40 officers and men, but had only three British officers on board to bring her alongside and unload personal effects. Men of the Devonshire Regiment were guarding the German prisoners as they were brought ashore. All of the U-boats were of identical design with hull welded throughout and the same type of armaments, and all of about 500 tons. The markings on the torpedo tubes of one vessel showed that the crew were responsible for sinking thousands of tons of shipping, including a British destroyer.

The way German prisoners were handled was a sore point with a local man who had himself just returned from a Nazi prison camp in Silesia. Detailing the inadmirable treatment he had received there, he protested that German officer captives in this country were being feasted and feted, and this was sickening. Pointing out that British officers in German hands were treated in exactly the same way as prisoners of lower rank, including the issue of rations, he pleaded for a change in the soft way German prisoners were handled in Britain.

A shock election was causing more turmoil than prisoners of war, for it caught South Dorset, at least, with its political trousers down. But by the big day, Thursday, 5 July, a three-cornered fight had shaped up. Viscount Hinchingbrooke, the sitting MP who had walked in unopposed, faced his first election for the seat, and represented the Conservatives. P.S. Eastman stood for Labour, and Lieutenant W.E. Ward, RNVR was the Liberal. Hinchingbrooke's predecessor, Cranborne, who had entered the House of Lords during the war, had a 9,057 majority in the previous election, which had also been a three-sided contest.

In West Dorset, the sitting Conservative member, Major Simon Wingfield-Digby, had also been returned unopposed when Major Sir Philip Colfox had retired. Colfox had a majority of 2,090 over his Liberal opponent. Facing Wingfield-Digby in 1945 was G.E. Chappell, for the Liberals.

East Dorset was thrown wide open by the sitting Conservative member G.R. Hall Caine, who decided not to seek re-election in that constituency. He must have been a bit of a gambler for he had gained a majority of 14,171 over the Liberals in the previous election. Battling for his seat were a trio of fighting men that made it look more like a contest to join Montgomery's staff than a civil election. The Conservative candidate was Lieutenant-Colonel M.J. Wheatley, the Liberal, Lieutenant-Colonel J.A.H. Mander, and for Labour, Lieutenant-Commander C. Fletcher-Cooke RNVR. North Dorset did not produce a Labour candidate and it was left as a straight fight between Conservative Lieutenant-Colonel Richard Glyn, of Gaunt House, Wimborne, and Liberal, Lieutenant-Colonel Frank Byers.

As the sun of a not very good summer did its best to shine, Weymouth sands came back into prominence as the United States Navy relinquished a large area. There was swimming, castle building and even donkey rides, but the violence of war does not disappear easily, and it claimed another tragedy that August. The landing craft and their vessels had gouged ruts and holes below the water line. A young Midlands lad lost his life when he stepped into one of these holes and was drowned.

Even this could not slow the gallop back into peacetime. Council workers were repainting the shelters on the Esplanade and the static water pumps were removed. Punch and Judy were back in the afternoons to delight the kids. The band of the Green Howards played to large audiences on the Pier Bandstand. The biggest problem for visitors to Weymouth was obtaining something to eat. Restaurants and cafes were doing so well that an hour and a half wait to get a table was commonplace.

The distant conflict was remote enough to allow those with no relatives serving in the Far East to believe it no longer existed. One nearer reminder of the dangers of war, and a terrifying one for bathers on the beach at Sandsfoot Castle, happened at Wyke Regis one afternoon. An RAF plane dived in low, just scraped over the trees and rooftops, and crashed into the sea — bursting into flames — some 200 yards from the shore. When the sun-seekers recovered from the shock of the low-flying aircraft and its accompanying roar, they lined the shore to watch rescue workers from Bincleaves and the Air Sea Rescue station in the harbour search for the body of the pilot.

Away from the novelty of the beaches, Dorset councils were thinking about the most urgent need of all. Housing was the great priority and they discussed the possibility of employing German prisoners of war on building work. Most, if not all, of the councils decided emphatically against this. But Dorset county council wasn't in any doubt about what to do to improve the roads of the county, and announced that £50,000 was to be spent on highways.

To make up for a bad Easter, August bank holiday saw the town of

Weymouth packed to capacity. People who had never thought about taking in paying guests were helping out by accepting visitors. In Japan, thousands died from a new destructive invention of man, while others were tainted with a horror that would bring a slow, tortuous death. This ended the only remaining part of World War Two, and Dorset rejoiced. Just as on VE night, the streets were packed until the early hours with excited, laughing, dancing, shouting revellers. It was the biggest celebration the county had ever seen. Dorset's War ended as the last line of song faded into a new dawn.

The Americans
in Dorset

How it was then

IN THE way the odd memory imprints itself on the mind, I can still clearly see that American Army Sergeant. Of chunky build and rugged features, the soldier looked as tough as John Wayne has probably often wished he was. I was in the pub only because of my friendship with the landlord's son. As always in those touchy days of 1943, my eyes and hearing searched for the excitement of yet another argument or fight.

Wide back against the bar, the Yank spat words from an arrogantly-held head. The words injured his British listeners more than his bunched fists ever would if he started using them: "You don't like us because you need us. You Limeys have never won a war on your own, you've always been part of a winning team — and this one is no goddam different."

"What about Waterloo," piped up a schoolteacher type with more regard for history than his own safety. The sergeant spun on him, and I saw regret for having spoken turn to fear in the objector's eyes.

"There," growled the American, "you had the Germans to help you out."

There was no answer to that. With a challenge in his jutting jaw the American swung his head to accept any more challenges. The bar was silent, and he swilled down his beer, getting a few almost inaudible snorts of disgust as he followed it with a whisky — a drinking habit the locals despised in the Yanks. The bar was silent, but, even though I was a mere boy, I could feel the animosity riding heavily on the swirling smoke that moved restlessly under the lights.

The face appearing in nearly every newspaper might not have been handsome, but was attractive for its all-American-boy look. It was the face of a friendly young warrior arriving to fight a war of which he knew nothing. The caption said he was the first GI to land on British soil. It was a lie, as some five hundred troops had already stepped on to a Belfast quay before someone realised this occasion was one to be caught by the camera. This lad was next ashore... and a blunder lifted him from anonymity into history. In war the first casualty is always the truth.

To most Britons the photograph was as irritating as an out-of-reach skin rash. That soldier on the Belfast quay, made stupid-looking by the fuss and bewilderment, was an affront to British history as was taught in the schools. In contrast to the much-boasted pride in the British Empire, he was the epitome of the clumsy American farmboy who, unarmed apart from a bloody pitchfork, drove the well-armed and resplendently uniformed British army into the Atlantic Ocean. He was resented — but, as yet, he was also unproven.

Soon he was fighting with unexpected bravery and determination on the bloody beaches of Normandy. Later, in the bitterly cold, brutal and horrifying Battle of the Ardennes, he won himself and his army a permanent place on the rôle of military greatness. He would be viewed differently then.

"The Yanks?" laughs a retired Dorset businessman derisively. "We had them billeted next to my place. There was an air raid first night they were there. A few of us went out into the street to see what Jerry was up to, but as soon as the siren had been sounded the Yanks came running down the stairs in a panic and ran for the air raid shelters like deer chased by the hounds. We stood there and laughed at them."

It is sad. The old fellow, who had never fired a shot, and spent his war making money, had forgotten the stories of glory that followed the sixth of June '44. His memory could only evoke the time the 'Yanks' had run, and the British had stood and laughed. Were the laughers so brave when they experienced their first attack by German aircraft?

What you have to remember is all the locals had gone through by the time the American had arrived from his bomb-free country. Buildings sagged as if vandalised by a gang of giants, the quiet Sunday evening walks of the county had been somehow defiled by the brash cheeky chatter of London evacuees, and the siren wailed a constant lament for the dead of Dorset.

Along came the Americans, extrovert and wild. They laughed often, but there was a poignant sorrow, almost imperceptible, riding on that laughter. Now, when the years have tumbled away with frightening

Conquerors of their local US Army camp were these village children from Burton Bradstock. This pair, Betty ("Freckles") Mackay and Chris Kerley, called after school at the cookhouse and Corporal David W. Roberts of Iowa handed out the cocoa. Betty was a London evacuee from the Blitz days, and Chris a local boy.

Photograph: Imperial War Museum.

speed, that laughter still clings eerily to the places where they walked. "They were all bloody bullshit," growls a gnarled old countryman. "There weren't one of them acted normal."

In fact a few were reserved and did act normally, but they were often the ones who had come to accept the likelihood of an early death. That must be a pseudo-normality, even in the crazy days of global war.

They came to a country that was its most prosperous for decades. British industry was a bucket of boom without a bottom. Never had England been so affluent, though the new personal wealth was countered by an evil frustration. Even those with really healthy bank balances could find no luxuries to spend money on. The rich walked self-consciously around in drab, austere 'utility' clothing.

"It wasn't a bad time," reflects an old chap who worked through the war on the making of torpedoes. "There was some said all we did was make cigarette lighters for ourselves and our friends. Perhaps we made a few, but we worked as well, mind. And it wasn't all fun.... not with you never knowing if Jerry was going to drop a bomb on the place. But it made me, I can tell you. The money I earned put me right on my feet." Then his eyes go inward for a special bit of reminiscence. "It was best when the war in Europe ended. There weren't no more bombers then. We used to have prayer meetings in the factory — just for fun, you know — and pray that the Japanese war would go on for some time. It was too far away to do us any harm, and we didn't want to lose the big money."

Into this unreal world, which made Alice Through the Looking Glass look like a sensible arrangement, stepped the Yank. He was so immaculately dressed that even the initiated had difficulty in distinguishing the private soldier from the officer. With him came all the things of which the locals had been deprived for years. Food was plentiful, and he brought his own newspapers, cinemas and even radio programmes. Those locals who could tune in were glad of the American Forces Network (AFN) which, with its popular tunes and easy-going presentation, was a pleasant change from the alternative — the stuffiness of the BBC.

There was no denying the impact the Americans had. Apart from his money, the average GI was smooth and suave, making the Englishman gauche by comparison. The Yank got the girls — and the British male lost out. To the teenagers of the day (though the record manufacturers and other pop moguls had not yet invented the breed) the Americans

Directions from across an old stone wall at Burton Bradstock for Roy St. Jean of Springfield, Massachusetts. A GI is told the way to the village canteen. Petty Officer Podger (left) was born in Burton Bradstock and had returned recently after being invalided out of the Royal Navy. He served in both world wars.

Photograph: Imperial War Museum.

were all the Hollywood stars personified. Awkward boys tried to ape the sinuous style of Alan Ladd, while the girls risked permanent eye troubles by letting a lank of hair cover one side of their faces — in the way of Veronica Lake.

Even the very young were not immune. Children once expected to exclaim "I say, Mother," were laying the foundations for future heart attacks by piping up with "Gee, Mom."

In comparison to the native austerity the Americans were always well supplied. "Course they sold food," says the bloke who owned a lorry that was attached to an American camp at Dorchester. "Listen. I was attached to them with my lorry for months on end. Bloody good money I picked up, too... I'll say it was, and the only time I ever turned a wheel of my lorry was when they wanted me to run some black market petrol or food into Dorchester for them. They'd sell the stuff and give me a cut. I'll say that for them, they were generous. I made a nice little pile with them. But do you know what. The Yanks I was with, when they got over the other side, were all killed. The whole bloody lot of them wiped out."

An old lady, sitting in a vicarage study, also recalls the food: "I did the proper thing, or at least what was considered the proper thing at the time, by inviting a group of them to tea. They were very polite." There is a touch of reservation in her tone that suggests there was something that made the Americans not quite acceptable. "I repeated this asking of the Americans to tea several times, but it got better as it went along. You see, the first few occasions were embarrassing for me, as it indeed was for other people in Dorset who had the Americans as guests. They had so much of everything in the food line, and we were without just about everything. I was ashamed at the tea I put before guests used to much better things. But then General Eisenhower told them all that they must take their own food when visiting English homes. This made the ensuing occasions much easier, and the Americans were most tactful when they passed the food to us."

Through the fear of appearing inhospitable to the American allies, it was the grained and varnished doors of Dorset that were first opened to them. Even so, the anti-American feeling went deep enough for the Italian prisoners of war in Dorset to be regarded more favourably than the GI. This was in spite of the fact that the US soldier, though loud and colourful, was very much a man's man. In contrast, the average Italian was something of a fairy. Today, when television has made effeminate men acceptable, the Italian of wartime would cause little comment. But in the 1940s, his constant grooming of his hair, and often the use of

Tea for two Americans, on the rectory lawn in the shadow of Burton Bradstock church. Rev. Arthur Dittmer, his wife (and tabby cat) were the hosts. Their US Army visitors were Lieut. S.M. Weitzner of Ridgewood, New York, and Major E.M. Beebe of Burlington, Vermont.   *Photograph: Imperial War Museum.*

improvised make-up, sickened most Britons.

The dislike of Americans exceeded the bounds of reasonability, for the true Blue Tories of Dorset, unable to wait for hostilities to end and the return of cheese and wine parties, ignored the fact that these men came from a country that was the world's finest example of capitalism, and let their sympathies wander to the Russians. Ludicrous as it may sound, the tweed-suited, off-to-the-hunt ladies of the county found the music of the *Stars and Stripes* jangled their nerves, and they pottered about the garden humming a tribute to the Soviet Reds:

> Can't you hear me calling
> while the snow is falling
> Oh, my lovely Russian Rose.

But the Yankee personality is not built for social retreat. Outgoing enough to be thick-skinned, the GI would not let a cool reception be the foundation for relationships in the months to follow.

The 'Occupation'

IF HOLLYWOOD was to be believed, the Americans arrived in England riding chariots with Glenn Miller records for wheels. In truth, though all of us remember the warning that the *Yanks are coming,* and the crazy days when they were all here, there is a memory gap where the actual arrival is concerned. This chapter traces the GI's journey from a transit camp in the USA, across the Atlantic, and down through England for a brief sojourn in Wales. Next they moved into Dorset for a perilous rehearsal that was as dangerous as the real thing, and finally they embarked for Normandy. For this information I am grateful to one of those GIs of yesteryear, Albert Ottolino, and the efficiency of the US mail service.

One of the US Army photographs in this book, taken in 1944, featured Albert, and his home address (circa 1944) was on the reverse side. The chances of reaching him through that address looked meagre. He was a boy then, but a middle-aged man now — if he had survived the landings in France and the battles of Europe. But I wrote.

Some five months passed, then came a letter from Albert. Since the address I had, he had married and moved a total of five times. My letter eventually reached a cousin of his, and was passed on. I learned from him that he had returned to school after the war, then took a job with the Montana-Dakota Utilities Company, a natural-gas utility, of which Albert is now a district supervisor.

A tired battalion took its first step to Europe by alighting from a train at Camp Myles Standish, a transit camp in Massachusetts. There was little time to relax after moving into the tar paper barracks. An equipment shortage meant the men were tossed into a vigorous programme of body-conditioning, drill, obstacle courses and hikes — the first of which was 23 miles.

D-Day briefing at Dorchester for members of an American engineer unit. Prominent in the foreground (left to right) are Pte Albert V. Ottolino of Billings, Montana; Pfc Howard D. Kraut of Brush, Colorado, and Pte J.H. James of Woodville, Texas.
US Army Photograph.

Special clothing was issued, together with items said to be necessary overseas — gas-proof clothing, mackinaws, shoe dubbin and rifle oil. Lectures, ranging from censorship (already in force at the camp) to life in combat, filled a lot of hours. Time off was allowed, with passes authorised to the not-too-distant cities and towns — Taunton, Brockton, Providence and Boston — .which meant that a large number of lucky personnel who came from Massachusetts or some of the surrounding states were able to visit home one or more times during the stay at Camp Standish.

Even those who could not get home were never at a loose end, for basketball games were held in the gymnasium, as well as there being service clubs and theatres on the post. Toward the end of October 1943, Albert Ottolino and his buddies felt concern as it seemed the 348th was being left behind in the arrangements to move to England. Most units of the group and attached troops had left for Boston and embarkation, but things looked up for the 348th on 30 October. Swing records were played over the public address system, and the static troops waved them farewell as they loaded onto a train.

Relaxing, the new warriors of World War Two — eager but untried — travelled through the New England countryside that was brought into full colour by autumn. Gazing out at villages with prim white cottages, they went north and crossed the border into Canada, their destination unknown. The train halted at Halifax on 31 October. Forming up on the platform, the companies could see the funnels and bridge of their ship above the roofs of the warehouses. This sight was their first visual contact with the country that was to become their home for many months — for a British flag flew from the ship's signal mast.

Moving out in single file the battalion climbed a seemingly endless ramp. Each man carried his rifle and barracks bag, and there was a chalked inscription on the front of each helmet. It was a miserable scene, but a true picture of men going to war. Under miserable skies, with no bands playing and no cheering crowds, glum-faced boys stepped one by one on to a troopship.

Equipment clanked noisily as the GIs moved down a corridor to meet an official at a desk. This chair-bound war-wager sat calling out the surname of each man who approached, and the soldier replied with his first name and middle initial, in a check to ensure loading was according to roster. Passing the official, the Americans encountered luxury. No austere decks and ship's ladders here, but linoleumed floors and stairways. The mystery was solved when they learned that this was a former luxury liner, the *Mauretania.*

Another discovery was that the luxury, like beauty is said to be, was only skin deep. The GIs rushed into B-deck and staked claim to the few bunks available. The majority were left to sling hammocks, while the really unfortunate had to be content with the mess tables or deck space. It was soon obvious that overcrowding would preclude any chance of comfort.

With the *Mauretania* lying in dock until 2 November, the American soldiers heard the disquieting news that they were to cross the Atlantic without escort. But they were reassured when later told that she was one of the fastest afloat, and would be changing course every seven minutes in the hope that no U-boat would get a bead on her. She could cruise at 22 knots and reach 34 knots if necessary.

When she did put to sea it was with an assortment of passengers that her civilian years had never seen. In addition to American soldiers and nurses there were Canadian, Australian, New Zealand, Newfoundland, Norwegian, Polish and Scottish troops. The rails of the *Mauretania* were crowded. Lost in personal thought, many pairs of eyes looked wistfully at the receding coastline. One man, Master Sergeant Horn, probably summed up the feelings of all as he said quietly to himself: "You don't know how good North America looks till you see 'er a-slippin' over the horizon."

With the first trauma over, the GIs settled down for the voyage. Aside from the issue of life jackets and emergency flashlights, each person was given a Red Cross 'ditty bag' containing cigarettes, playing cards and writing material. Not many of the playing cards survived the trip, but disintegrated from over use. Letter writing held little joy, for the snatch away from his homeland had the writer feeling as if he were in limbo, penning a letter without any firm idea of when, and if, it would be delivered home. Guard and police duties filled in some of the time, while other hours were spent strolling the decks, reading, or discussing the past and the future.

Light relief came to the fun-loving Yanks through the "terribly British" accent of the ship's captain coming over the public address system. His voice giving frequent abandon-ship drills and suggestions on how to live fairly comfortably on a crowded ship, was soon being accurately mimicked by the Americans. His cautions on black-out restrictions each evening sent hordes up on to the decks for a last pre-darkness smoke. On Sunday, the speaker system was used to relay religious services throughout the ship.

Any meagre pleasure that may have been gleaned from this sea trip was vomitted out on the second day when the ship hit rolling seas. Things did not improve the following day, and by the fourth day the bows were, at times, dipping beneath the surface.

On Monday, 8 November 1943 the *Mauretania* turned into the choppy waters of the Firth of Clyde. The GIs looked out at the cliffs of Ireland from the starboard rail, and to the hills of Scotland from the opposite side. At about 11 pm the ship passed the Isle of Man. Then came a wait for the high tide in the early hours of November 9, so that the *Mauretania* could move into Liverpool docks.

In darkness, the men filed down onto a foreign quay. They marched through the blacked-out streets of the city, shivering at their first glimpse of the scars of war. The stark walls of gutted buildings towered above them like omens for their own futures. After a long march through crowded but silent streets, the GIs boarded a train at Liverpool station. Red Cross girls came aboard to distribute coffee and doughnuts as the Americans settled down in the comfortable seats. Though tired, many of the men were too fascinated by the passing countryside to sleep. They gazed out of the windows in awe at more signs of the destruction wreaked by the Luftwaffe.

Swansea, South Wales, was reached at 3 am and a transfer made from the train to a fleet of double-deck buses. The unit was carried six miles to a small resort with a quaint name that managed to tickle the journey-jaded GI humour — Mumbles. The companies were scattered at different locations around this village. Headquarters and a portion of B company were at Summerland, A company at Newton, other elements of

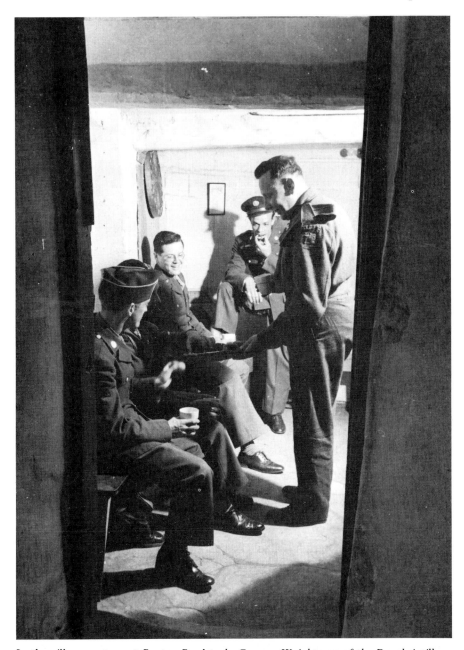

In the village canteen at Burton Bradstock, Gunner Weightman of the Royal Artillery hands homemade cakes to Corporal James Flower of Walpole, Massachusetts, Private Roy St. Jean of Springfield in the same state, and Corporal Allan Decker of Chicago.
Photograph: Imperial War Museum.

B at Singleton Park, and C company at Caswell Bay Hotel. The majority of the battalion was housed in Nissen huts. Another unit had prepared the camp for the newcomers and, in some cases, hot meals were ready for them on arrival, despite the late hour.

The battalion was among the first American troops to arrive in this section of Great Britain. There was no time for the GIs to discover how the local people would take to them, and for most the climate was unkind. Serious colds leapt to epidemic proportions.

They survived, however, to encounter less distressing problems. A shortage of American cigarettes rapidly deteriorated to the non-existence of such luxuries. Money was converted and English brands were purchased at local shops. But this presented problems to the Yanks, unfamiliar with financial terms expressed as bobs, tanners, thrupenny bits, hapenny, and half-a-crown. But they were quick learners, picking up the titles 'nut-brown ale', 'spirits', and 'half-and-half', which became substitutes for the beverages dispensed over the bars of the United States. Soon the GIs were automatically calling the drinking places 'pubs' instead of their customary 'taverns'.

Training commenced a few days after arrival, with calisthenics, infantry problems and bayonet work taking up most of the programme. Athletics were again to the fore, with softball and football being the main sports. On Thanksgiving Day, the watching local crowd possibly derived as much pleasure as the players when A and C companies played a classic game of football on the beach of Caswell Bay, with C company winning.

On the same day, the cooks of all four companies did their utmost to produce the kind of dinner expected on this holiday. By sheer coincidence, a guest of Major Powell, commanding officer of the battalion, was Major Powell of the British Home Guard. Perhaps the most significant item of that day for the men was the fact they received the first mail from home.

Fears that the winter evenings would be boring were proved unfounded. British cinemas showed American films, dances in the town were frequent, plus several rugby and football games between American service teams of the larger units. Where religion was concerned, men of all denominations were free to attend the churches in the area.

The personnel of B company, stationed at Singleton Park, worked with the 37th Engineer Battalion, improving the camp area. On 12 November, the 119th Group was reorganised into the 5th Engineer Special Brigade. The brigade included some units that were originally in the group; and, eventually, new units were added to enable it to function as a brigade. In command was Brigadier General William G. Hoge, with the former group commander as executive officer. The three engineer battalions became known as "far shore engineers".

During the first week in December the entire battalion moved to a new camp on the outskirts of Swansea — Camp Manselton. It was not a move into instant comfort, for the camp was still under construction and the main task of the battalion was its completion. Major Powell was designated as camp commander; and battalion headquarters became camp headquarters for all units in the area. Training was, of course, included in the activities in the new location.

Aside from the usual conditioning there was endurance marching, combat exercises and inter-battalion technical schools. Bailey bridges featured prominently in all training, and were built and removed several times across a lake near Manselton Camp. Complete familiarity was gained with Bailey bridges because a number of these exercises took place at night. Recreation was not neglected either. Nightly convoys of Americans with pass privileges went into Swansea. Possibly the favourite night-spot was the Pier. Each company held parties in the town's clubs and halls, and the social life was good. There was a well-stocked Battalion Post Exchange, and the needs of most American soldiers could be supplied from its shelves, even though most of the goods were made in Britain.

Christmas at Camp Manselton saw an attempt, doomed from the start, to get the hearts and thoughts of GIs from straying back home. A Swansea dramatics group presented a nativity play at the camp recreation hall during the morning. Dinner was a splendid affair with the cooks going all out to present an American Christmas on the table, at least. Many men went out on passes, either to attend a show or visit families with whom they had become acquainted. New year was a day similar to Christmas, with good food, thoughts of home, and a liberal number of passes.

By the middle of January, Major Powell had been placed on detached service, and the executive officer, Major Meharg, assumed command. On 12 January Lieut.Colonel Earl Houston joined the battalion from the 5th Brigade and accepted command. This confirmed the rumour that the battalion was to take part in amphibious operations on the continent at an undisclosed date, as the new commanding officer had participated in amphibious operations in Africa and Italy.

The special equipment needed for such operations was issued, and instructions in its use began. On 2 March the battalion moved again, this time to a camp known locally as Scurlage Castle, on the Gower Peninsula, west of Swansea. The line companies marched the eighteen miles to this camp.

Here the massing together began of the huge organisation that would train together, and eventually assault the continent as one section. Joining the battalion there was the 453rd Amphibious Truck Company; 559th Quartermaster Railhead Company; B Company of the 6th Naval

Beach Battalion; C Company 61st Medical Battalion; 4143rd Quartermaster Service Company; 2nd Platoon, A Company; 203rd Quartermaster Gas Supply Battalion; 2nd Platoon 3460th Ordnance MAM Company; 2nd Section Mag. Platoon (teams 7, 8 & 9) 210th MP Company; 294th JA Signal Company, and the 3rd Platoon 30th Chemical Decontamination Company.

The first days at Scurlage Castle were spent in making improvements to the camp. Then, on 8 March, a three-day exercise (codenamed 'Snipe') started on the beach at Eynon Bay. This was the first outing for the combined beach-team. Plans for the coming invasion of the continent were being made while these manoeuvres took place, with considerable attention given to both the favourable and unfavourable outcomes of the exercises. The second exercise commenced on the morning of 15 March and lasted two days. By mid-afternoon of the first day, 387 tons of supplies had been unloaded. There followed a longish spell, then the next and last exercise was held in April. During the interval between operations all personnel were kept busy caring for the special equipment, and at other duties around the camp.

Off-duty hours were spent in Swansea and the surrounding villages. The elaborate recreation hall in the battalion area was well patronised. It was at this time that the battalion personnel caused quite a stir and raised many comments when appearing on the streets. Both local citizens and other troops were startled by the paratrooper boots and amphibian shoulder patches that had been issued.

The final manoeuvre started at Oxwich Bay on 4 April and ended at 1300 hours on the 6th. During the following days at the camp a great amount of work was undertaken. Signs were painted by the hundred — beach and road markers were constructed. The amphibious insignia and white arcs were painted on helmets, and duffel bags. Packing boxes were marked in shipping colours, equipment was repaired, and plans were drawn up for the coming operation. A 25 percent overstrength was transferred in to all units in the brigade.

Early on the morning of 24 March, the battalion boarded a train at Swansea and travelled for seven hours to Dorchester, the county town of Dorset. The majority of the unit was dispatched to Camp D-11 but there were elements at D-8, D-6 and at other small stations in the vicinity. The overstrength and components of Force B were left behind in Wales. They moved first to Myndd Llew, and from there to marshalling camps as they were vacated by units of Force O.

Field Order 6, for exercise 'Fabius', designated the battalion with its attached units as the 348th Battalion Beach Group. It was to support the 18th Infantry Regiment of the 1st Division in the exercise that simulated as closely as possible the projected landings on the French coast. The objective was Slapton Sands, on the Devon coast, and embarkation was made on to APAs and LSTs, as well as LCTs on 1 May. The landing was executed by the use of Rhino ferries and the smaller landing craft. At the time of embarkation it was not known by most personnel whether the operation was practice or the real thing.

The beaches were shelled ahead of the mock landings by both American and British naval vessels, and a considerable amount of live demolitions and ammunition were expended on the shore. Though the manoeuvre lasted for only two days, it was 6 May before all personnel of the battalion who were in Force O were returned to Camp D-11, at Dorchester, by train and truck.

This particular camp will be remembered for its chilly atmosphere, the crowded living conditions, and the frequent raids by German aircraft. Though the training schedule filled in some time, there was little for most

In 1940 the western end of the Chesil beach was watched from a pillbox. By this stage of the war it was obsolete, and with the invasion tables turned the US troops could use it at their leisure. With the violin is Corporal Bert Markowitz from the borough of Queens in New York City. The listener on that day was G.R. Miller of Louisville, Kentucky.
Photograph: Imperial War Museum.

of the troops to do. Drivers checked the waterproofing of their vehicles, individual clothing and kit was checked, road construction material was drawn, and countless other duties attended to in order to prepare the unit for combat. Movies were shown in a large tent placed centrally in the camp. Passes into Dorchester provided the men with the meagre entertainment offered by two cinemas and the quiet pubs of a country town. Continuous liaison was maintained between battalion, brigade, and the 18th Infantry headquarters.

By the middle of the month, plans for Operation *Neptune* had been published and distributed. Immediately after this all troops taking part in the operation were given a comprehensive briefing. Photographs were studied and there were sand, table models of the Normandy coast. Much intelligence data was known — meaning that there was not a man who did not possess at least a few items of 'Top Secret' information, to use the American expression, or 'Most Secret' in its British counterpart. With the briefing completed it naturally followed that personnel were restricted to their areas.

Force O was moved to its final marshalling camps on 28 May and on 30 May the battalion began loading its men and equipment aboard the craft and vessels at Weymouth. Loading was completed in the following four days. Use was made of each available inch of deck space and there was insufficient sleeping accommodation on the vessels for all the soldiers to have bunks. The open decks served as beds for many.

The craft carrying members of Force O departed from Weymouth at different times, but the last had gone by the evening of 5 June. Departure had been executed on 4 June but bad weather had delayed the operation. The enemy did little to disturb the invasion fleet as it moved from the ports to its rendezvous zone. The absence of harassment was due to spoof attacks having taken place to the east of the Seine, coupled with the destruction of most of the German coastal radar stations and the elimination of a system that could have jammed British operational radar. Along with this, the headquarters of Luftwaffe signals intelligence in north-west France was also bombed to inaction, preventing any co-ordinated enemy response. Not a single fighter was to hinder the airborne columns.

While the invasion force was en-route to the rendezvous area in the Channel, a message from General Eisenhower was distributed to all members of the Allied invasion forces. It read:

You are about to embark on the great crusade toward which we have striven these many months. The eyes of the world are upon you. The hopes and prayers of liberty-loving people everywhere march with you.

In company with our brave allies and brothers-in-arms on other fronts, you will bring about the destruction of the German war machine, the elimination of Nazi tyranny over the oppressed people of Europe, and security for ourselves in a free world.

Your task will not be an easy one. Your enemy is well trained, well-equipped and battle-hardened. He will fight savagely.

But this is the year 1944! Much has happened since the Nazi triumphs of 1940-41. The United Nations have inflicted upon the Germans great defeats, in open battle man-to-man. Our air offensive has seriously reduced their strength in the air and their capacity to wage war on the ground. Our Home Fronts have given us overwhelming superiority in weapons and munitions of war, and placed at our disposal great reserves of trained fighting men. The tide has turned! The free men are marching together to victory!

I have full confidence in your courage, devotion to duty and skill in battle. We will accept nothing less but full victory!

Good luck! And let us all beseech the blessing of Almighty God upon this great and noble undertaking.

Dwight D. Eisenhower

Three ships brought the US 3rd Armored Division to England, the *John Errickson, Capetown Castle* and *Shawnee*. On the afternoon of 14 September 1943, the destroyers and battlewagons that had made up the escort and fussed around the valuable cargoes of fighting men like neurotic guard dogs, slipped away and left their charges waiting for the tide to enter harbour. The following day the *John Errickson* and *Capetown Castle* docked in Liverpool while the *Shawnee* moved smoothly against a quay at Bristol. Crowding the rails, the GIs looked down to be shocked by the tired, harassed, war-worn faces of the dockers. They wondered at the profusion of barrage balloons, and paled at the sight of tall buildings that pointed at the sky like accusing fingers as they begged for demolition.

Their tired eyes opened in surprise as they disembarked, and watched dockers scramble wildly for the oranges they had brought with them. A crate fell during unloading, dropping between the ship and the quay into murky waters, to be followed by diving dockers hunting the errant fruit. The Americans could not believe that anyone would go to such lengths to get what they took for granted.

There was no cold war at this early stage. Every GI, who had the chance exchanged his dollars and cents for English money. The British wanted the coins for souvenirs, the Americans wanted the English money to spend on whatever would be available, as soon as it was. Then they jostled slowly across the country in a British train, while served tea by NAAFI girls for the first time. At each small station there were English children clamouring for gum and candy. The grimy windows of the train constantly illustrated yet another sign of bomb damage. England looked threadbare — and Yankee spirits sagged.

The final lap of the journey was completed in trucks. They clambered down in Wiltshire, where the 102nd Cavalry Regiment had provided

ABOVE: An incredible mass of armoured vehicles 'somewhere in Dorset' during the build-up to D-Day in 1944. These ordnance depots filled most vacant areas in the country and were veritable 'Invasion Cities'.   US Army Photograph.

OVER: An American jeep has pulled up at A.E. Cheney's pumps at the Red House, Burton Bradstock. Cattle walk up Cliff Road. One boy cleans the vehicle's windscreen, and another operates the centre pump, while two younger ones play with their tricycle to the left.   Photograph: Imperial War Museum.

quartering details. A dense black-out added to the feeling of disorientation as men of the 3rd Armored Division were guided to billets that were either barracks or Nissen huts. Beds were straw pallets. Breakfast brought what was to be the monotonous staple diet from then until when the Germans surrendered — powdered egg. Units of the Division were split up among age-old villages with wandering streets and names that fell amusingly on American ears. Division headquarters were at Bruton, in Somerset. Combat Command B, the 33rd Armored Regiment, 391st and 67th Armored Field Artillery Battalions were at Warminster, in Wiltshire; the 36th Armored Infantry Regiment found a home in Sutton Verney; the 83rd Armored Reconnaissance Battalion at Longbridge Deverill; Combat Command A, 45th Armored Medical Battalion, at Stockton House, near Codford; the 32nd Armored Regiment at Codford; Maintenance Battalion and Supply Battalion at Codford St Mary; the 23rd Armored Engineer Battalion at Fonthill Bishop; the 703rd Tank Destroyer Battalion at Mere. Division Rear was at Wincanton in Somerset; the 54th Armored Field Artillery Battalion at Frome; and the 143rd Armored Signal Company at Cucklington.

The luckiest of these units were those at Warminster. This was a permanent camp built for the Royal Armoured Corps, complete with workshops and other facilities. A settling-in period followed, when ETO and V Corps directives were issued, examined and assimilated. In just three short weeks, equipment, including tanks was issued. Petrol was in short supply and what journeys were made proved to be hazardous. The trucks, described by the locals as "blooming big lorries", were difficult things to negotiate through narrow, meandering streets. Each turn of the steering wheel seemed to send another portion of English heritage toppling into the road.

Passing time edged out the initial homesickness, and the invaders set out to explore the area. They found tradition offered at every turn. New World hearts quickened at the dreamlike beauty of thatched cottages, and the haughty abbeys and castles. Pubs, accustomed to a couple of farmers and the occasional sheepdog in corner seats, had fresh life injected into them by the boisterous Americans. The customary Sabbath peace of a stroll in leafy lanes was murdered by wild laughter, argument, and the strange mating calls of the GI.

Girls were in large demand and fair supply. There were WAAFS, ATS, Land Army and NAAFI girls. The latter were never neglected by the Yanks, though they accused them of making the worst coffee in the world. Local hospitality was cordial. Learning the arts of war during the day, the Americans took other lessons in the evenings. Men of the 3rd Armored Division were willing pupils for the Palais Glide, the Canadian Crawl, and the Okie Cokie. They learned the words of *Roll me over,*

The first GI offensive in Europe was the take-over of Dorset's public house life. Here, at Burton Bradstock near Bridport, their pint was beer — darker but less potent than the rough cider of the locals. A poster on the wall shows the Reading premises of H. and G. Simonds. At the time the firm also had a brewery at Blandford. Another poster carries an appeal on behalf of prisoners of war.   *Photograph: Imperial War Museum.*

though shocked that such a ballad was regularly sung in the church-like country bars.

Like an exaggeration of the massive gathering of tribes for Custer's Last Stand, the magnificent armies of the Western Allies were grouping across the downs of England in late 1943. The coming assault on Europe was continually under discussion. 3rd Division Officers joined the 5th Canadian Armored Division on manoeuvres in the area east of Andover and north to Hungerford. Throughout their nine-month stay in England, hundreds of 'Spearhead' troops visited British and colonial units to exchange ideas and techniques.

The 3rd Division had initially been attached to V Corps in England, but in early November, when Lieut.General Omar Bradley's First Army was activated, the division was assigned to Major General Hugh Woodruff's VII Corps. This was later commanded by Major General 'Lightning Joe' Collins on the Western Front.

The GIs soon discovered England was no holiday. Tough and thorough training included marches, obstacle courses, maintenance and all the army drill routines in the book. Technical instruction included camouflage, waterproofing, chemical warfare and the all-important art of aircraft recognition. The ranges barked to the testing of new weapons.

Cinemas screened training films, with the inevitable inclusion of the old one so familiar to the GIs — about the boy behind the eight ball.

In the early fall the command post exercises on the downs were not uncomfortable. But as winter approached exposure in these open spaces was raw and vicious. The men of the division shouldered it all, and reached the six-weeks-in-Britain stage, when forty-eight-hour passes were issued. The tricolour patch of the 3rd Division then spread out over England — turning up in the big cities, London and Bristol, and towns like Bournemouth. A new world was revealed to the Americans by train rides that pitched them prematurely into war. They sweated through the initiation of air raids while in the English metropolis. They thrilled as a German plane was caught in the beams of searchlights. The amount of ack-ack fire through which they saw an enemy plane fly unscathed, gave them worry for the future when they would be under fire. As men of the 3rd Division watched a Ju-88 panicked and dropped its bombs as a British Mosquito night-fighter darted in for the kill. Their eyes widened as the aircraft burst into flames, and those close to the crashed aircraft looked, reluctantly, on their first enemy dead.

Piccadilly, by legend bright and gay, was made solemn by the black-out as they walked through. After treading the rubble-strewn mess that was Leicester Square, they finished their short leave with the knowledge that they were shortly to face a kill-or-be-killed situation, and training was resumed with an urgent thoroughness.

Range firing was regular. Units practised at Bowls Barrow, near Warminster, and at the Kimmeridge anti-tank range in Dorset, where the targets were alternately hidden and revealed by swirling mist. Gun crews also visited the anti-aircraft areas at St Agnes and Penhale on the west coast, as well as going to Minehead on the Bristol Channel.

In November, the 36th Armored Infantry, 'Park's Own', went on a six-day workout. Division headquarters made its first overnight bivouac on the coldest of early fall days. With all of the other units participating, Salisbury Plain, a war preparation area since the days of the bow and arrow, was awakened as never before in history. The rumble of motors rose to a crescendo that stretched its fingers of noise far out over the downs.

No amount of cold or rain brought postponements to the frequent Command Post exercises. Men slithered about in bitterly cold, driving rain, but the show went on, just as it would have to after the landings in France. Early in December, the 486th Armored Anti-Aircraft Battalion arrived at East Knoyle, Wiltshire, and was attached to the division. The ack-ack soldiers arrived just in time to join another 'Shooting Month', with firing on the Imber battle range at West Down and Bowls Barrow. Again tank-destroyers travelled to Minehead and AA units went to St

Agnes and Penhale.

With sea mist at Minehead almost as bad as at Kimmeridge, firing was difficult. Gunners not only had to wait until targets could be seen, but had also to pause while ships passed on the Bristol Channel. The training highlight of December was planned and supervised by General Hickey and the Combat Command A staff. This was on the Imber range west of Chitterne, and employed a tank battalion, an infantry company, plus an artillery battery and an engineer platoon, all demonstrating "the deployment of a covering force in lieu of an advance guard when contact is imminent, the occupation of attack positions, and the detailed fire plan necessary for a co-ordinated attack, and the employment of battalion supporting weapons in the initial stages of the attack and as a security against counter attacks during reorganisation".

Though Christmas in Britain was properly celebrated by the troops it had an underlying sadness of men away from home. There were parties for the children of the area, with the old tradition of roast turkey and cranberry sauce. Some men visited friends in the surrounding towns and villages, while others spent the evening dancing with WAAF and Land Army girls. There was a strange pathos in it for the Americans. They listened to the reedy voices of British children singing carols of hope and peace under windows that were blacked-out as a defence against the very opposite of both things. It cured any GI self pity to realise these children had never known a world without war.

There was a feeling of cheer in the old dark-varnished pubs. US soldiers who had pooled their rations and distributed gum, chocolate and Christmas candy among local children, reached for the foaming mugs of ale dispensed by busy, busty British barmaids. Usually unavailable, a small amount of Scotch whisky also miraculously appeared. Fighting men from both sides of the Atlantic stood side by side, shoulder to shoulder, singing carols that meant the same to all. There had never been such a gathering of warriors. The yellow-gold of subdued lighting brought out the significant shoulder patches of the 8th Army Desert Rats, Montgomery's finest, and the elite of America's fighting men could be seen; the lifted wings of the air forces, already harrying the Nazis in preparation for the greatest unborn invasion; the tricolour of the 3rd Armored Division, and the various shoulder insignia of proud infantry units.

When the carols ended the united nations still sang in unison, though it was now *Roll me over* and *Roll out the barrel*. Even at this time of good cheer there was no relaxation of vigilance. Outside, the blue-black of the night sky was constantly fingered by searchlight beams in search of enemy aircraft.

Just one week later, the most significant year in the modern history of the world arrived. The Continent was under constant and heavy air attack. Slow but steady advances were being made in Italy. A physically fit, finely-tuned condition had been attained by the division, and it looked as if General Eisenhower's prediction would come true and the war would end during that year. The pace of training was stepped up during those final pre-invasion months. Not a week passed without Salisbury Plain seeing manoeuvres. Teams from the division were sent down to Weymouth to learn the intricacies of vehicle waterproofing. Hindsight tells us that this was in many cases time and effort tragically wasted. The rough seas off the Normandy beaches were very different from the placid waters of Weymouth Bay, and many vehicles were swamped before even making an initial advance in the direction of the enemy.

No member of the 3rd Division could predict this as they looked around in Weymouth. Neither could they know that the tough, wild ranger units they saw practising cliff climbing would climb the cliffs at Point du Hoc, on the beach at Normandy, through deadly fire and clambering over a growing mountain of their own dead, to reach the top and discover that their target, the big guns of the enemy were not there.

An awful lot was to go wrong on Omaha Beach, but the men of the division couldn't predict this. They hoped for the best, and dutifully absorbed the waterproofing tuition. Neither was the stay at Weymouth a cheerful one. A seaside resort is a sorrowful place during the winters of peacetime. In the early stages of 1944 the town still cringed under the not-yet-forgotten threat of a German invasion. The tide had turned, so the people were told, and the allies were here to take the fight to the enemy. But the nightmare of waiting for a jackboot on the beach was slow to fade. Bustling US vehicles and throngs of busy GIs could not inject enough hope to lift the misery of the place.

So the men of the 3rd Division were not too upset when the time came to leave the seaside. Driving through roads of Dorset that looked like marshalling areas, they arrived back among the lanes and tracks of Wiltshire, now familiar enough to impart a feeling of security. All the ranges were then kept constantly busy and the crashing weapons of the division played a regular symphony in the Somerset and Wiltshire air. January 27 brought a visit from the legendary General Montgomery. The Yanks, who measured their heroes by the standards of Errol Flynn, jostled for a glimpse of the famous British fighter. They expected an image similar to the rugged General Patton, but were disappointed to see an almost fraily-built man, with a thin, high cultured voice. But his reputation, not his looks, won their support when he told them he would be leading the allied forces on the first stage of the invasion.

More 'Top Brass' later arrived at division, including Generals Eisenhower and Bradley, and Air Chief Marshall Tedder. On a day when a cloying mist swung around men and vehicles, the Duke of Gloucester

Under the tree on the green at Burton Bradstock, village children show off a machine gun belt they picked up on the beach. Examining it are US soldiers John L. Lawson of Port Jervis, New York, Robert S. Hastings of Azusa, California, and Corporal Roland Henry of Holland, Pennsylvania.   Photograph: Imperial War Musum.

inspected the armoured forces weapons on Salisbury Plain.

Spring came, and the world was poised like a diver on the high board. May was all sunshine and dry weather. The throb of motors was always on the clear air as great flights of Fortresses and Liberators passed overhead daily to smash at the continent. At night the RAF took over on constant journeys to punish the enemy.

Rumour was rife. When you are waiting for destiny, aided by generals and other ranks down to the one immediately above you, to decide when and where to throw you to the lions, as the GIs were, you listen to everything, including German propaganda. At that time, the Nazi 'mouthpieces' were alternately screaming that there would soon be an invasion — then that there would be no invasion. Perhaps most effective of all the propagandists was the female, 'Midge'. In a soft, feminine, sinuous way, she would intersperse popular crooning records of the day with predictions about the terrible cost in lives of an amphibious landing. She was putting into words what many of the young American apprentice warriors feared — and it was unnerving.

Definite action came at last to force out feelings of dread. Most units moved out to live in pup-tents on the Downs, while orders to move to embarkation points were awaited. All vehicles were waterproofed, loaded and ready. Maps of the continent were issued to officers and non-coms. The talk was all of H-Hour and D-Day. But the big day came and went. Men of the 3rd Division lay awake listening to wave after wave of warplanes pass overhead. Fit and raring to go, they chafed at the delay that left them on the sidelines.

Not that division tracks were left to cool for long on the downlands of Somerset and Wiltshire. The bivouacs were left behind and the journeys to Southampton and Weymouth began. At the ports they found themselves part of a continuous scene that had been running like an endless film for days. Each man received D and K rations plus PX supplies, motion sickness capsules and vomit bags. Well prepared vehicles rolled aboard LSTs. One face of the war had ended for the 3rd — France and many battles lay ahead. With the green fields of England behind and the tall poplars of Normandy to come, it was a time for deep thought. As the craft moved out to sea each man looked around at his comrades, wondering how many would come back.

Although separate units of the 3rd Armored Division had, for the most part, arrived at ports of embarkation on 18 and 19 June, heavy Channel storms delayed the crossing. It was not until the 23rd that the first elements touched French sand on Omaha White Beach, below Isigny. The 32nd and 33rd Armored Regiments, the 23rd Armored Engineer Battalion, and the 486th Armored Anti-Aircraft Battalion went ashore on this date. On the 24th, division headquarters, forward and rear echelon, landed plus division artillery, with the 54th and 67th and 391st Armored Field Artillery Battalions, Combat Commands A and B, and Division Trains. The main body of the 36th Armored Infantry Regiment reached France on 25 June, but the regimental headquarters had been there since the 18th, thus becoming the first sizeable 3rd Armored Division unit in Normandy.

Still delayed by stormy weather, the 703rd Tank Destroyer Battalion arrived on 28 June; the main body of the 45th Armored Medical Battalion on 2 July; Supply Battalion on 3 July; the 83rd Armored Reconnaissance Battalion, and the Maintenance Battalion on 4 July.

On Omaha Beach, the backwash of battle, a vast graveyard of broken equipment, smashed tanks and twisted ships lay rusting in the brine. The invasion armadas were there off shore, an unbelievable panorama of power. Barrage balloons swayed in the moist air, and the Thunderbolt fighter-bombers zoomed from a newly-constructed air strip close to the beach. Thousands of engineers worked on the floating piers and a steady procession of nondescript German troops, captured in the early fighting, straggled down to board outgoing transports. Past them, in the other direction, battalion after battalion of American soldiers, replacements for the infantry divisions up forward, trudged wearily ashore and up the muddy road that led inland.

Most of the 3rd Armored Division's vehicles were able to roll off their LSTs to dry land. A few, coming in on the high tide, touched in yard-deep water, but there is no record of any swamping or like mishap. Assigned to areas a short distance from the beach, troops spent their first days in France de-waterproofing and preparing for combat operations. The orders were drawn up and all were ready.

Settling in

LIKE A rolling snowball growing in size, American effervescence trundled through the county gathering friends. Within weeks the 'them' and 'us' situation had developed in a triangle — 'them', 'us', and the 'blacks'. The members of the third section of the triangle were worst off. They were fighting English reserve and the active dislike of those of their own countrymen who were of fairer complexion.

"The Yanks!" snorts a schoolteacher whom I knew to be an intelligent and fair man when he taught me during the war, "They were all trouble. They'd come to the top of the school playing field, and we'd have to go out and round the girl pupils up to keep them safe." His pace of conversation slows. "There was an anti-aircraft gun outside of my house. The gun crew were all black. We always knew when a raid was on, even if the siren hadn't been sounded, because we'd look out to see the niggers hiding under the gun."

Back in 1944 I had seen this teacher, stopping his motorcycle as he rode home to talk to the young GIs who lounged against vehicles queuing in Victoria Square, Portland, for embarkation from the docks. Despite the cheery words he had tossed to the soldiers, I knew that he was aware of what they faced. There were tears in his eyes when he left those lads, but now he had forgotten and joined the majority view. One propaganda film, made exclusively for showing to the American troops, had an old lady making tea for a coloured soldier. It explained that whatever their customs at home, white Americans had to recognise that the English did not practise a colour bar, and that over here the army was not going to have one either.

Several stations below third class in the opinion of all, it was the coloured soldier who edged the American masses into local social life. In 1944, Dorset was like the rest of England — some twenty years from becoming pagan. The church was used for Christian worship, not christenings, weddings, funerals and bingo only. Into these Dorset churches, staid and musty from years of *Rock of Ages,* waltzed the negro with his rhythmic, imaginative spiritual. In the months that followed, the negro spiritual never lost its magic for the local people.

One Sunday evening at the Portland Congregational Church, US Chaplain Captain L. Fitzgerald gave an address which was followed by a concert of negro spirituals. The conductor, Private Benedict Smith, introduced his choir as the theme song *Were you there when they crucified our Lord* was sung. The concert included a solo of the *Rugged Cross* by Private Carter, and the event had the by-product of raising £4 for the British Red Cross. Following up on this, the British Legion women's branch held a social at High Street, Portland. Two hundred

Steward's mates Asa Jones and Furrell Browning, both from Dallas in Texas, watch for enemy planes with a 5-inch gun on the USS Henrico *in Weymouth Harbour, 5 June 1944. The enemy never came, and D-Day preparations were unmolested.* US Army photograph

people enjoyed negro spirituals sung by a coloured soldier who had his comrades as a choir.

Then there were more than one thousand people packing into Holy Trinity church, Dorchester, for a concert of negro spirituals. At the end of the evening the Rev. Plaxton expressed his appreciation to the soldiers and announced that the event had raised £40 toward the Holy Trinity school rebuilding fund. Encouraged by their earlier success, the management of Portland Congregational church arranged a second Sunday evening helping, with the singers this time being Sergeant H.P. Younger and Private Skinner, with an organ solo by Thomas Lowry.

A guide to the county of Dorset was issued to the Americans. A 32-page booklet, it gave details of the towns and villages, as well as listing entertainments and places of interest. The guide had a foreword by Lord Shaftesbury, Lord Lieutenant of Dorset, in which he said that the hand of friendship was extended in every part of the county to the Americans, and that he hoped their stay would cement further the strong link between the two countries. "It's a good job they came over, old chap," a Dorset workman was to call to his pal on a cold morning in the early 1950s, referring to the fur-lined, fur-trimmed US Army combat jacket the other was wearing.

Though it all looked to be chaos, and most of it was, there was some thinking and planning going on behind the dicey socialising. As early as 1942, D-Day preparations had begun in Dorset with the establishment of a large hutted camp, capable of accommodating two thousand ratings of Combined Operations, at Hamworthy, near Poole. By the late months of 1943 this base was at maximum capacity. Another Combined Operations base, HMS Grasshopper, took the place of the Weymouth establishment, HMS Bee, which was moved to Holyhead. Grasshopper, together with HMS Turtle and HMS Attack (the latter since having once more reverted to its former name of HMS Osprey), formed Force G, consisting of three assault groups training for D-Day.

The first three months of 1944 saw Weymouth as a top secret area, with the Bombardons (artificial breakwaters) being tested. These were later towed to France and used as part of the great Mulberry Harbour scheme. Poole had become highly commercialised by this time, and was building landing craft to the Thorneycroft design. The demand was high, the need urgent, so prefabricated panels were brought into use. Bolson's, of Poole Harbour, were the largest producers of LCAs, and the work force was initially comprised of squads responsible for a particular stage or unit of the whole craft.

This system worked well to begin with but familiarity had workers bored with their repetitive task, which had no visible or rewarding end product. Production figures began to drop like many a Dorset husband's heart when he saw the Yanks arrive. Some of the American quick-thinking, quick-acting had rubbed off, and Bolsons re-organised the workshops and each squad was made responsible for a complete LCA from start to finish. Production leapt ahead when this incentive was given. There was rivalry between squads and great pride taken in craft 'we built'. Whenever landing craft were shown on newsreels in the cinemas, workers would look for their 'number'. As D-Day neared, an amazing production rate of one craft a day was being achieved at Bolsons' and Lebus, the furniture manufacturers, were also producing landing craft.

Airfields were also a major requirement for the invasion, and two in particular were made good use of in Dorset. In August 1943, the United States Army Air Force took over Hurn Airport, Bournemouth. Tarrant Rushton, near Blandford, later to play a part in the over-extended Arnhem raid, saw the formation of 298 Squadron in October 1943. It flew Halifaxes, towing troop gliders and Horsas. This squadron was joined by 196 Squadron, equipped with Stirlings for the same glider-towing purpose. At that time, the strength of the station had increased to three thousand officers, airmen and airwomen. In March 1944, 196 Squadron was replaced by number 644, and the entire complement of the station was then Halifaxes.

"Any girl could get a date in those days," recalls the woman with an overdose of 1940s lipstick. "The Americans were so loud and crude. They'd call across the road to us, it was most embarrassing. I certainly never went out with one." You listen, then do your best to reconstruct the rubble of flesh caused by the passing of three decades, to find a reason why someone would want to call across the street to her. You give up.

It is true that, at first, no 'decent' girl would be seen with an American. The area was alive with all races — American, Canadian, French, Polish — with the poor old British soldier pushed far into the background by the degradingly low wage his government paid him to die. Christine Jones, who lived with her widowed mother at Tillycoombe Road, Portland, was one of the many girls determined never to go out with a Yank. In the unlikely setting of Portland Cemetery, in Castle Road, she was tending the grave of her grandfather when she saw a GI, walking the cemetery wall, whistling *Paper Doll,* a hit tune of the time.

The general American presence could be felt by Christine and her mother as they knelt beside the grave. Out in front of them, jutting into the waters of the harbour, was the specially constructed loading jetty for men, tanks, and vehicles. Below them, sagging tiredly in the spring grass, were the tents of a US Army unit, while the windows of the Victoria Lodge Hotel, then an American Army hospital were open in the warm evening air, and the strains of Glenn Miller's music eased across to them.

The whistling Yank hung around, following the mother and daughter through Portland's main street, Fortuneswell, sadly battered by the Luftwaffe, with wrecked buildings steadily crumbling away. Later, when Christine took her dog for a walk, the GI was still there. He spoke, eventually asking for a date. Christine, her determination about not fraternising ·with the Yanks rapidly eroding under the charm of this soldier, agreed. She broke this date, and many more the persistent GI made, before eventually going to the Regal Cinema with him.

All over England there were other girls discovering what Christine had — that the Americans were not the ogres they had been classed as. It was already known that the foundations of wartime weddings were weak, and the added handicap of the Atlantic Ocean between a couple made it popular to predict that the countless growing romances between local girls and Americans were doomed from the start.

If a wedding was arranged the commanding officer of an applicant had to send a letter of approval to the civil or ecclesiastical authority who was to conduct the marriage. Any member of the US Armed Forces who married in violation of this policy was subject to court martial. Statistics later proved that a staggering total of 80,000 GI brides were married under this set of conditions. The forecasts of doom for these marriages later changed to well-enjoyed stories of how the English brides were arriving in the USA, to be met by their new husbands and their American wives. Perhaps this happened in a few isolated cases, but what were the chances of happiness for the wartime bride of a Yank? Compared with the girls marrying today, the GI bride was an outright winner where the chances of a successful marriage were concerned.

Anglo-American relationships could not be faulted in some cases, like when a US plane ditched in the sea off Chesil Beach. Local fishermen quickly put to sea to reach the crew, and one of the rowing boats had 73-years-old Abe White at the oars. The old-timer rowed for some time as the little boats fought to reach the crew of the aircraft, but was then relieved and made coxswain. When the fishermen got to the swimming fliers they found one in a bad way, but he was hauled aboard and revived with artificial respiration given by George Brown, a Portland man who was later decorated for bravery in another rescue operation in this treacherous stretch of water.

Lord Shaftesbury said the hands of Dorset people were extended in friendship, but it was greed that stretched a number of hands in the direction of the Americans. "We did alright out of 'em," wheezes an old shopkeeper sitting on a seat outside of his small but thriving business. "That's how the missus got this place." He nods to the building behind him. "Them bloody Yanks were crazy for whisky. The missus used to nearly fill a bottle with cold tea, then add a tot of whisky. Then she'd shake it all up and sell it to the Yanks for a couple of quid."

So the social and war conscious of Dorset did their best to make the stay of the Americans as pleasant and comfortable as possible, while others saw them as about ten seaside seasons rolled into one. The Yank, affable and without guile, was cheated and twisted. In view of the high casualties to come, those who fleeced the young Americans were robbing the already dead. Their activities were as loathsome as those of the scavengers who robbed bodies on the battlefields of Europe.

Dorset honesty had not quite died. A US sailor, George R. Ricci, was attempting to make a long-distance phone call from the kiosk beside the Park in Easton Square, Portland. Other people were waiting outside, and because he was having difficulty getting through, George stepped outside and allowed the other people to make local calls. When he stepped back inside the booth his wallet, which he had left with his hat, had gone.

Anxious to recover photographs and letters of sentimental value contained in the wallet, the American advertised his loss in the local press. A few evenings later, in the security of the black-out, the wallet was pushed through the letter box of Easton Post Office. The money was no longer in it, but George was delighted to get back his personal documents. Shortly after this, a WAAF was making a call from the same kiosk when a coloured US Army driver, heading for his depot in Reforne, lost control of his truck whilst taking the bend at Easton. He smashed into the telephone box, killing the girl inside. Most people, having noted the general standard of driving, were amazed that the accident collision rate was not even higher.

In the noise, bustle, and generally crazy way of living that soon became very much a part of that period, it doesn't seem possible that a large number of the American troops were actually lonely. It was a deep loneliness that sheer weight of numbers could not cure. As he balanced on a cemetery wall like a tightrope walker, and whistled his favourite tune, Chuck Ward, of the US Military Police Battalion, felt lonely. His evening had started out with two English soldier comrades, but they had found their girls and made new plans for the remaining hours, leaving Chuck alone.

He had eaten his Christmas dinner aboard the *Duchess of Richmond*, somewhere in mid-Atlantic. German U-boats were playing havoc in the region at the time, and though there was no alarm during the meal, it was made tasteless by the ever-present feeling of danger. Reaching Southampton safely, the ship discharged her cargo of GIs and put out to sea again, to be sunk by torpedoes in the Mediterranean. Chuck and his buddies were billeted in a 'tent city' at Romsey, where they were quickly issued with little booklets explaining the English currency and the difference in language that existed between the 'English speaking' peoples each side of the Atlantic. Sweets were candy, a lorry was truck, petrol was gas, and your windscreen a windshield. "Don't forget," the teacher had told us at school, tucking in her chin and hoping none of the cheekier lads would ask what the Americans meant by 'rubbers', "though homely as used by us describes someone who is friendly, the same word to the Americans means ugly."

The list was long and confusing, and after absorbing enough to get by, Chuck put the booklet to one side. He could not even put his learning to use, for every hour spent at Romsey had them confined to quarters. Suddenly, the unit was shifted to Portland. Again, they were not allowed time off, and, trapped in Quonset huts overlooking the harbour, the Americans assumed that what they could see was all of Portland.

Then, as if they were being used by some lunatic playing soldiers, they were just as swiftly taken back to Romsey. It was more fun this time, as they were allowed to explore the town, with its quaint cottages and ancient abbey. The Yanks found the Romsey people easy to get to know, and they quickly made friends. To the GIs the blackout was a formidable enemy. It would have been strange to them at home, but in a foreign land it had them completely disorientated. There were quite a few hair-raising experiences of being lost after dark.

Just when they were settling in nicely, whoever it was wanting to keep the 735th Military Police Battalion on the move, did it again. This time the destination was Radipole, a suburb of Weymouth. They found the surroundings pleasant and had begun to appreciate the move when something happened to spoil it all — their first experience of an air raid. When training back in the States they had learned about battle, but no words of an instructor could effectively describe what an attack by the Luftwaffe was like. The intensity of the raid shook them, but not so much as the calm indifference shown by the locals did. They could not adjust to seeing a child walking about saying 'Jerry's up,' when all they could think of doing was getting under cover.

With little else to occupy their time, they did something constructive about the air attacks by building a deep shelter in the garden of their billet, and stocking it with tinned food and beer. If there was a prolonged German air assault, Chuck and his buddies would survive. They soon found the Weymouth pubs rewarding places to visit, the drink, responsible for many bad things, having the good effect on the locals so that an instant welcome awaited the Yanks. They liked the impromptu 'sing-songs', which never happened in the bars at home.

Soon their day-time was filled with strenuous manoeuvres. In the evenings, Chuck explored Weymouth with two friends he had made, both of them British and in the Royal Engineers. When this trio had discovered all they wanted to know about Weymouth, they moved on to

Wyke Regis, which was well populated by Americans. Even the great world heavyweight boxing champion, Joe Louis, was stationed there.

One night, Chuck found himself in Portland and alone. From his precarious perch on the cemetery wall he saw the lovely girl with the long hair, gently placing flowers on a grave. Chuck tried to look away, for he had promised himself that he would never have anything to do with an English girl. But his eyes would not obey, and when she left the cemetery and walked up the street, Chuck was following.

"Didn't you hear about it?" asks the fellow leaning over a beer-spattered table in a Weymouth pub. It is 1944, and the practice of Yank-ridiculing is at its height. "There was these three British sailors walking along the prom, when about ten Yanks came along and said something to a girl who was passing. Anyways, our blokes take offence at what the Yanks said, and got stuck into 'em. There was only three of our boys, mark you, but they wiped the bloody floor with them. Then d'you know what they did?" A pause and dart of his eyes round the audience, delaying the climax. "They picked them ten bloody Yanks up and threw them over the railings onto the sands."

"Bloody hell," says another, young enough to have been in the war, but with a good reason for not having gone. "It's that tinned food they're brought up on. It don't give them no strength."

"The bloody Yanks can't fight," growls the storyteller, feeling better about not fighting in the war himself.

Always capable of resisting change, Dorset was now being pushed and twisted into a new shape from which it has never recovered. Still semi-Victorian, it groaned under pressure from the modern-minded Yanks. The Regent Dance Hall, in St Thomas Street, Weymouth, known for its sedate tea dances and perhaps only guilty of an occasional discreet seduction during a waltz, was shoved right into the swinging Forties. A talented musician, Freddy Goldberg, then serving with the US Forces, was pulling in delighted crowds every night. Freddy had his own band while still at school, and had later played with top American bands, including Artie Shaw's. Since being in England he had also played with the best of the British bands, among them, Harry Parry and Geraldo.

Just when the locals imagined they had seen all the fast-moving American action in the area, another shock came when the cousins from over the Atlantic took over Hawkes and Freemans store in St Thomas Street, Weymouth, and turned it into a modern club. There was room for dancing, a cafeteria of the type never seen before, but common today, and dormitories capable of sleeping two hundred. The charge for a bunk bed was two shillings per night. The cafeteria could take 150 at one sitting, with the three main meals — breakfast, dinner and tea, costing 1s. 3d. each.

No one could accuse the Americans of doing things by halves. The club included a tailor to keep uniforms smart and neatly pressed, as well as that great American institution — a shoe-shine boy. Retrospect gives the period more touches of absurdity than were apparent at the time. It was a mixture of wild living, laughter, and petty jealousies between the peoples of two nations. What made it so pathetically ludicrous was the end product — violence and death across the Channel.

Filing behind barbed wire in a wood near Dorchester, like prisoners of the war. Inside the tent, these Americans heard their final briefing for D-Day.   *US Army photograph.*

Accepted — almost

IN REVERSE to the usual reactions to novelties, when the novelty of seeing American uniforms, trucks and equipment everywhere wore off, the locals found themselves almost ready to accept the strangers. Many courtships were well advanced by then, although few Dorset mothers were prepared to dash out into the street proudly shouting: "Our Betty's going to marry a Yank." But marry the Yanks they did, bringing a mixture of joy and sorrow to the parents of every bride. They knew they weren't gaining a son, but, eventually, when the fighting had stopped and the Americans went back home, they would be losing a daughter, in many cases, forever.

At St Joseph's, the Roman Catholic church in Weymouth, a New Yorker, Staff Sergeant Russell R. Wigley married Caroline Leach, of 9 Newberry Terrace, Weymouth. Back in Dorchester, at St Peter's church, one of the first Dorset girls to join the Women's Land Army, Miss Birdie Courtenay, of Damers Road, married Sergeant Charles Wesley Miller. Bridport, a little town that had not seen much life since the final tourist of 1939 had posted the last card home, was jolted into life by a Yankee-style wedding. The local girl taking her first step across the Atlantic was Miss Vera Crook, of 88a South Street. On leaving the church with her husband, Sergeant Glenwood Morrow of Pennsylvania, she toured the town in a suitably decorated horse-drawn lorry. The streets were crowded as they rode through with a jeep escort.

A village girl, Kathryn Limm, of Grimstone, near Dorchester showed her willingness to exchange rural life in Dorset for a home in Connecticut when she married Private Gabriel Barrales. Portland was proud of its insularity, though by 1943 the cost of this remoteness could be measured in the effect intermarriage was having. Perhaps more than any place in Dorset, the island suffered worst from shock at the American invasion. Easton, in particular, was knocked completely off-balance by the arrival of coloured troops at the YMCA field in Reforne.

An innate dislike of strangers took on a new dimension for the islanders when they discovered that the dislike between the black and white Americans beat anything they could offer in the way of acrimony. Fist fights were common, but fear came to Portland when a black-white confrontation in Reforne took on a Wild West look when rifles were grabbed, and fired, in anger. Figures holding these rifles were backed in doorways, leaning out and releasing a shot each time the 'enemy' was spotted.

Such behaviour would have the British policeman of 1944 whacked, but not the 'Snowballs', the US Military Police — nicknamed after their white helmets. They moved in with their usual swift tactics, the violence and brutality of which often surpassed that of the troops they were controlling. Peace was restored to Easton.

Security was tightening in the Dorset area. This involved the British civil police in roles more in keeping with a dictatorship, as retired policeman Bill Chapple remembers: "We had to call on every house in Portland and do an inventory on the occupants. That was a job. People were often rude, and who could blame them, with us poking our noses into their affairs. Still, I was only carrying out orders, unusual though they may have been. Each person in every household was checked, and if they had no excuse for being in Portland, they were given 24 hours to leave. Then we had to call back when the stipulated time was up, to make sure they'd gone."

This "Get out of town by sunset", routine did not please anyone. But an elaborate hoax was being carried out at the time, and a spy in the Dorset area could have wrecked the invasion plans. As the RAF had almost total control of the English sky, they shunted the ever-present German reconnaissance planes towards the secluded creeks of Essex and Kent. There the German pilots were allowed to see waiting landing craft that were really dummies. Disused airfields in the east of England had a profusion of plywood gliders, which looked authentic from the air. Inflatable tanks were blown up like giant beach balls, and placed strategically.

So security in Dorset — where the real things existed everywhere — was all-important. Weymouth station was guarded by US military and British civil police. Any passenger arriving without a good reason was put on the next train out. "We did spot checks on Weymouth Road (the causeway between Weymouth and Portland)," Bill Chapple recalls. "Vehicles were stopped and the occupants questioned. Buses were halted and the passengers quizzed. Anyone without a legitimate excuse for going to Portland was taken off the bus and put on the next one travelling in the opposite direction."

"You know the railway bridge on the road into Castletown?" asks Reg Gill, who was then in business at Castletown, the docks area of Portland. "Well, when they were getting ready for D-Day, there was an American military policeman, a Royal Navy policeman, and a British civil policeman on duty there all the time. All of us living in Castletown had passes — and these three policemen would check those people in their categories who were passing — the American for US personnel, the policeman for civilians, and so on. It's amusing really, because security was so tight that when I stepped out of my back door for a breath of fresh air, I was invariably picked up. Yet an old friend came to see me one afternoon. He had retired from the Metropolitan Police, who at that time policed Portland dockyard, and he knew his way around. He came to my place via the old Merchant's railway, on which horses once pulled stone to the quays. He had tea with me and the family, then left by walking up the main road. At the bridge, he was stopped for a check. The three different policemen found themselves checking out someone they hadn't checked in. There was a lot of fuss, and at first they didn't want to let my friend go. Then, grateful for having the loophole pointed out to them, they put a guard on the Merchant's railway from then on."

In Castletown is an ancient monument, Portland Castle. This was one of a string built by Henry VIII after he had signed a peace pact with Roman Catholic France, who then feared they might attack him because he had dreamed up his own religion, the Church of England, to fit in with his liberal idea of marriage. Occupied as American officers' quarters before D-Day, this old castle underwent a post-war facelift that must be unique. It was reconverted from a modern set of quarters to an ancient monument.

"See that post there," the custodian said. It was a thick post, oddly marked with deep scars in the wood. "Well, that was a whipping post when political prisoners were held here. Those lacerations show what brutality took place, for they were made by the tips of the lash. There was a woman in here the other day. I've seen her around before, but I don't know her name. She was telling me that she remembered when the Americans were stationed here, she had them to tea very often, and then she mentioned that post. It seems the Americans like to record where they'd been, for posterity, I suppose, and they were advancing on this post to carve their names, when an officer in charge stopped them. A bit of English heritage was saved, and was protected from then on by a casing that was wrapped around the post."

"I sometimes long for a return of those days," a woman who often played host to the Americans told me, "but I know that nostalgia is deceptive, and to relive the good times would mean suffering again the anguish of knowing that our cheerful young friends were suffering and dying across the water. Names escape me now, but I do recall a Lieutenant Jack Orlando, and Johnny Dumphy, both of the US Navy. Then there was 'Doc', a really close friend who was in the US Army. He was godfather for my third daughter, and her third name was that of Doc's daughter. It's strange, but after all these years her first name has been forgotten, and she is called by the name her American godfather chose. It's fitting, because 'Doc' — a really happy, friendly man who we were all proud to know — was killed during the first few hours of the fighting on Omaha Beach. They were all generous men, especially where kids were concerned. I don't think there was a thin child in our area of Chiswell, Portland, and they regularly took the children to parties in the Royal Victoria Lodge Hotel, in Victoria Square, which was then a US hospital."

As the American was assimilated, as much as possible, into the life of Dorset, the edge went off the bad feeling. Thinking people began to realise that the boys they had envied for not having shared the bad things of war, were soon to walk into a kind of hell that surpassed anything yet experienced in the county. If the hand of friendship had not quite reached its target, there was a fragile truce between the two 'sides' — English and American.

The great convoys moving across Dorset were heading for the coast. Lines of DUKWs parked in a specially prepared marshalling area beside the Chesil Beach at Portland. The ground has since been used as a car-park for summer tourists.　　*US Army photograph.*

The last waltz

THE DO-GOODERS had done what they thought was good, and the guidelines for getting along with the Yanks had been impressed on all, but it was the good old English pub that must be praised. It was in the sweaty, noisy, smokey, 1944 bars of Dorset that Anglo-American relationships received the blessing of friendship. The pubs called the tune, from the opening number a couple of months after the Americans arrived, to the last waltz before they sailed away to war.

Standing on top of the famous Chesil Beach, in Portland, the Cove Inn has seen a few hundred years of history do some twists and turns, but possibly nothing to equal the dramatic, traumatic time preceding D-Day. Like so much of Portland's tradition, the Cove Inn was a family affair through the years — the Comben family. The wartime landlady, Mrs Elizabeth Comben, was succeeded by her daughter, Mrs Doris Saunders, who helped in the bar during the days of the Americans. Mrs Comben died some years ago, but Mrs Saunders remembers her mother's liking for the Yanks, both black and white: "A special friend of hers was an American sailor called Johnny Dumphy. He corresponded regularly with mum after returning home. Right up to the time of his death from cancer, at the age of 44. He would always put the same greeting on his letters to her: 'To my English mother'. Even after his death, his widow always wrote to mum. Now that mum has gone, and even though Mrs Dumphy has married again, she still exchanges Christmas cards with my daughter, Mrs Wendy Buckingham."

Laughter and sadness were well mixed in those days, and the Cove Inn saw both. The former came after a rather worrying time, which involved the locals as well as the GIs. With the skills and courage imparted by a knowledge that tomorrow might not come, and even if it did it could be unwelcome, the Americans and locals in the Chiswell area of Portland had a large-scale fiddle going in food and other supplies. There was a feeling of safety in these double-dealings, for, as always, the authorities needed to have anything like this pointed out to them. Unfortunately, it was pointed out, though in innocence.

What was formerly the bus garage in Victoria Square, was a store for the US Army. Two local boys broke in there one night, and stole some supplies. They were unlucky in being caught, but luckier that the sentries had not shot them on sight — which was the order of the day. The lads eventually came before the magistrates, and their break-in became the subject of a US Army inquiry. On checking the stores, the military police realised that the boys concerned would have needed to be supermen, and have had long convoys of lorries, if they had taken away all that was missing. So a house-to-house search of Chiswell commenced.

It was a silent day, fraught with worry, as the police moved diligently through the street. Precautions had been taken. The huge water tank in Chiswell had received stolen goods, wrapped in waterproofing, and crafty people had slipped packages into the sea. Tied with rope, these packages were secured to the beach. Would these makeshift hiding places be undiscovered? That was the question worrying everyone.

"I emptied out our coal bunker," Mrs Saunders smiles today, not the smile of a successful criminal, but of a winner of the spoils of war. "Then I put tins of fruit in the bottom before shovelling all the coal back. Then we just hoped for the best." Despite a stringent search, the day ended without the authorities being any the wiser about the missing supplies. As dusk came, arms braved the cold of the water storage tank, as they searched for and found sunken prizes. Furtive footsteps crept over the beach to retrieve tins of fruit and other items from where they were moored to the shore. Behind the bar stood the Combens, pouring ale into the makeshift utensils of war like vases and jam jars. On the other side of the counter, Britisher and American laughed together, a new bond brought by conspiracy against authority.

"Where's the Boot Inn? I heard about it in China."

That is the legendary statement of a British sailor, quoted many times before the war, in respect of a Weymouth public house. An exaggerated or untrue quotation, maybe, but the inference was right. "The Boot Inn?" an oldster quakes now, his wild nights out now only enjoyed in retrospect. "That was a place even before the war — but when the Yanks

Mrs Elizabeth Comben, wartime landlady of the Cove Inn at Portland, with a group of US Navy friends. Standing on the extreme left is Johnny Dumphy, who kept in touch with Mrs Comben right up to the time of his death. Photograph: Spencer, Portland.

were here... Chrrrrist... they could get anything they wanted there, and often something they certainly didn't want." Whichever way you look at it, the Americans had to rely on the pubs of the area — in some cases for the comfort and hospitality of a home-from-home, and in others for a different reason.

In the case of the Railway Arch Hotel, in Chickerell Road, Weymouth, it was the comforts of home. Taking into account that the landlady of 1944, Mrs Isobel Ainge, had been badly hurt by the war, it is a tribute to her goodness of nature that she made the Americans so welcome. At the start of the war her father had died. He was landlord of the Fisherman's Arms, at North Quay and Mrs Ainge took over that pub. The Fisherman's Arms, first licensed in 1860, had stood on a site now occupied by Weymouth's municipal offices.

Trade was initially poor, but Mrs Ainge invested money and hard work, and soon the pub was thriving. By 1940, she was just recouping some of her investment. Then the pub was closed by the most effective order of all — a Luftwaffe bomb. This was bad news, but it wasn't long before Mrs Ainge learned a harsher truth. There was no compensation. All she had lost was irrecoverable. But it did not floor her. Soon she was running the Railway Arch Hotel, and was as popular as ever.

As the town began playing its important role in the war, Mrs Ainge was asked to board men of a British commando unit. These tough young men had already been through dangerous and arduous action, and the kind hearted Isobel Ainge accepted without hesitation. She made them comfortable and treated them well. When they left they took a considerable amount of her stock with them. Badly hurt, and though it was against her nature, she vowed never to have military boarders again.

"A British army officer later called on me," she says, "and he asked if I would billet some more commandos. I explained my earlier experience, and he apologised but said that many of the commandos weren't law-abiding types. If they had been, he said, they wouldn't do the dangerous work they carried out in the war. Of course, I saw the logic of this, but still refused to board them. It was a case of once bitten twice shy. I know now that I would have done better to take the boarders when the officer asked. He came back again later, really desperate for billets, and I relented. By that time, the 'cream' of the unit had been fixed up with lodgings, leaving me with the dregs."

Just as she had those before them, Mrs Ainge made these commandos really welcome. Surely, she reasoned, it would be different when this lot left. It was — they took more than their predecessors. Cider, ale, anything they could lay their hands on, was taken. One of these soldiers had an attack of conscience while abroad and in combat. He wrote apologising for what he and his comrades had done, saying that it was inexcusable after her kindness. He hoped that she would forgive them.

Small and quaint, the Chapelhay Tavern still stands high on a hill in Weymouth. Miraculously, it survived two separate incidents in the war, when a landmine devastated all around the pub, killing many people, and a later bombing that caused more destruction and death. The soldiers, sailors and airmen of many nations came to the pub before D-Day. The ceiling of the bar was low, and the men, celebrities in their own right at the time, penned their signatures on the plaster above them.

No post-war artificial monument to the invasion could equal that ceiling. It was something to cherish. Something to save for future generations to gaze on, and wonder about the men of yesteryear who passed here on their way to rescue world freedom. Sadly, when clear varnish for posterity might be expected, philistines from the brewery sent the decorators in with tins of thick paint. The memento to heroes was obliterated — forever.

There was no blatant "the Yanks are here", about the American arrival in Weymouth. It was more of an insidious appearance of one or two expensive uniforms. These became a dozen without anyone really noticing. A dozen rapidly multiplied into hundreds, the hundreds became thousands — the Yanks were here. For Mrs Ainge it at last brought luck in military lodgers. Four arrived for lodgings at the Railway Arch and were accommodated, at £1 a week for the four.

Among the quartet was a big, quiet military policeman named Dan Ewton. A man of few words, Dan was happily married and sought no night-life in the town. When not on duty he assisted Mrs Ainge in the bar, and carried crates and barrels up from the cellar. In the year he was there he became her favourite lodger. Though it was US policy that no American should disclose his full name and address, Dan gave Mrs Ainge his. There is still speculation about this ruling, and the study of it suggests it was not for war security reasons, but to protect any GI who became seriously involved in England whilst having a wife back home.

The affluence of the Americans was a surprise to all — including themselves in many cases. Well-paid, they could buy their cigarettes (the favourite being Lucky Strike) for just 3d. for twenty. White southern Americans, from a land of inequality, resented the fact that coloured soldiers were also well paid, their £15 a month putting the black GI a long way financially above the British Tommy.

This dislike of the black man being well-paid was added to the list of hates the white American already had for him. Mrs Saunders remembers just one of many racial incidents in the bar of the Cove Inn: "Their colour made no difference to mother, and one evening I remember her giving a nice, friendly smile to a negro soldier. He was a nice boy, and was so pleased that he patted her hand. A white American took exception to this familiarity, and a really nasty situation developed. I was always frightened when they squared up to each other like this, for they often used knives. But my mother wasn't scared. I don't suppose she reached up to the shoulder of either of them, but she stepped in between them, and I heard her shout. 'Black or white, you are all the same to me.' Whether it was shock at her action, I don't know, but the two men stepped back. The heat was gone out of the moment, and peace came to the Cove Inn again."

In Weymouth, Mrs Ainge realised that if her house was to keep its reputation for orderliness she would have to be referee, prosecuting counsel and judge rolled into one; "I felt very sorry for the British soldiers. Through no fault of their own, the war had made them into third-class citizens, even when compared to soldiers from other lands. The Americans always tried to be friendly with them, but our boys would only give a rebuff in return, then sit there seething with resentment. I couldn't stand this any longer, and after one particularly rude rejection of an American offer of friendship, I called my English customers together. Thinking back, I can't believe that I did it, but I gave them a right lecture. 'Why won't you be friendly with the Americans?' I asked them. 'They have gone out of their way to be pals with you.' There were various choruses of 'They think they own the place because they've got more money than us,' and 'Because they get better pay than us they look down on us,' with the worst one of all included 'The girls go for them and ignore us.'

"I could see nothing for it but to take a firm line, so I told them. 'Who do you think is responsible for the difference between their pay and yours, them? No, of course they aren't. They are soldiers like you, and just do as they are told. Their government pays them a lot more than your government pays you. Any argument you have is with the people who run this country, not with these boys from America.' They saw the truth in it, and I never had any trouble between our lads and the Americans after that."

"Our reward will come," said the British soldier sipping half a pint while he watched a laughing American buy drinks for his two girl companions, "when this lot is over. We'll have a Labour government in power, and the scum who've made money out of this war will have to move out and make room for us."

"Shit," said an older, wiser looking soldier.

Some publicans and barmaids took advantage of the Americans. They pulled some unbelievable tricks to twist them of their money. "This sort of thing didn't appeal to me, thank goodness," says Mrs Ainge. "Whisky was very scarce, and more than once I was offered as much as £10 for a bottle. But I always said that to sell it like that would please only one person. By selling it behind the bar I brought pleasure to a lot of people."

That's what she did. Licensing hours were flexible, dictated by the amount of stock left. The doors of the Railway Arch Hotel would close, and the regular customers were shepherded into the Smoke Room where they would drink at bar prices. Like the owner of an American 'speakeasy' in prohibition days, Mrs Ainge would open the door only to the secret knock of a regular customer. But even this, in the circumstances, fair arrangement, was too selfish for Mrs Ainge. If she opened the door for a regular, and a strange serviceman was passing, she'd call out: "Would you like a drink?" The passing stranger would also be welcomed into the cosy warmth of the Railway Arch.

"Whisky! The lot I was with would give anything for whisky," recalls the man who, as a civilian vehicle owner, was attached with his lorry to a US Army unit in Dorchester. "I can remember running a lorry load of stuff into Dorchester — food, clothing, bedding, and coming back with a few bottles of whisky in exchange. Somebody local done well out of that deal. And he wasn't the only one, and that wasn't the only bit of black market I was involved in. Still, the food and that didn't cost the Yanks nothing, and they got the whisky they wanted so bad. Deserved it I suppose, because like I said, every bloody one of them was killed when they got over there."

Wood, like most other commodities, was either in short supply or non-existent. This was frustrating for people who had seen their property smashed by bombs, and were unable to find the materials to rebuild. A US Army lieutenant, who had become a close friend of the landlady of the Railway Arch, arrived one day accompanied by a truck load of empty wooden crates. "You might find a use for the wood," the American told her, in the usual half-apologetic manner used when things were given away.

"A use was soon found for it," remembers Mrs Ainge. "The wood was so good that a man living close to the pub was able to use it for floorboards. Then the same officer asked me if there was anything I was really short of. I could have given a list as long as my arm, but on the spur of the moment I said butter." Within seconds the officer had sent a driver hurrying from the pub, to return with four pounds of the precious stuff. This was before the days of fridges and freezers, so Mrs Ainge kept one pound and gave the rest to friends.

"They were incredibly generous at all times," another woman tells me. She listens to hear if her husband, a nightshift worker, is stirring in bed and possibly listening. "But in a pub they were really crazy the way they threw their cash around. I don't know whether it was just to be big, or if they thought that money wasn't going to be of use to them for much longer."

"I was engaged to one of them." Her eyes are wistful now, with thoughts of what might have been, and the husband upstairs forgotten. "He was killed on D-Day. I was told later that he hadn't even set foot in Normandy, but had been sliced to pieces in the water. Try as I may, I have never been able to connect the laughing lads in the pubs with the dead and injured soldiers on a beach. I know it sounds silly, but to me, who only saw the one side, it doesn't seem possible they were the same people."

American soldiers still had time to prepare for the evenings, this open air salon opening for business on the Chesil Beach at Burton Bradstock.   Photograph: Imperial War Museum.

Endings and beginnings

EACH DAY saw another illustration of differences between the Americans and British. An unexpected difference — that in hand signals given on the road — was tragically brought to light by the death of a young Dorset man. Cecil Gundry was around the same age as many of the GIs he passed on his motor cycle when travelling to and from his work at Dorchester. Eighteen, Cecil had not yet been caught up in the war, and was a bank clerk with Lloyd's. But he found danger in his journeys on Dorset roads that were alive with military vehicles. Often he would return to his home in North Row, Martinstown, and report a "near thing".

On a spring morning in 1944, Cecil rode his machine along the Bridport road into Dorchester. Coming towards him was a US Army lorry, and Cecil saw the driver's right arm out of the window, raised in the fashion for signalling a halt that was left over from the horse and carriage days in Britain. Cecil rode on.

Behind the wheel of the vehicle was GI Harry Kirkpatrick. Harry did not know anything about an olde English signal for coming to a halt. He wanted to turn right, gave a signal to say he was doing so, and he did not see the approaching motorbike. The impact of the motor cycle hitting the lorry was heard over a wide area. Everyone in Dorset learned that there was a difference between the hand signals of the Americans and the British, except Cecil Gundry — he had died instantly while proving the point.

On thinking back, most remember that the Americans were loungers. They never went unsupported when there was something to lean against. Two GIs, waiting in that awful void whilst military leaders decided just when to throw them to the lions, dangled over the railings that sided the pavement in Fortuneswell, Portland. Their eyes, like radar scanners, picked up sisters Sylvia and Mary Thomas, on their way home. The Yanks called a friendly greeting across the road. The two girls, full of fun, called back: "If you want to talk to us, you'd better come home to meet mum and dad."

Such a daunting invitation would have put most servicemen off, but it was a challenge to any worthy wartime GI. Mr and Mrs Thomas were sitting in their Hambro Road home when in walked their daughters — followed closely by two American soldiers. It might not be a conventional situation, but it caused no surprise in 1944. The mother, totally at ease, wisecracked: "A couple of fine daughters, you two are. You've got one each for yourselves — where's mine?"

"You want a Yank, Ma?" drawled one of the GIs, "you just leave it to me." After a pleasant evening at the Thomas home, the two polite young soldiers expressed their thanks and left. They were back a few nights later, accompanied by an extra Yank for Mrs Thomas. This was Joe. Quiet and shy, Mrs Thomas could not have asked for a better visitor. Joe gave her the address of his mother, and soon the two women were corresponding. Mrs Thomas, who had never had a son, became extremely fond of the modest, likeable Joe. The friendship grew over the weeks, to end when the American boys were first confined to base, and then left on that momentous voyage across the Channel.

The civic dignitaries at Dorchester decided to do something for their American guests. An invitation was extended for the GIs to attend an afternoon reception by the mayor at the Plaza Cinema. People lined the streets, gazing in wonder as the Americans, led by a band, marched to the cinema. Inside, it was the turn of the GIs to gape in wonder. It shook them to see the mayor and his ceremonial officers in their ancient regalia. The Yanks, always eager to do the right thing at the right time, wondered if this was a comedy show. Would it, they asked themselves, be polite or impolite to laugh. They had never seen anything like it.

The stern faces of the Dorchester officials discouraged laughter, and the guests from across the Atlantic realised that this was a part of British pomp and circumstance. One of the GIs, middle-aged now, recalls that he had remarked out of the side of his mouth, prison-fashion, to a comrade: "And they say we are full of bullshit!"

When the initial shock wore off, hosts and guests relaxed for what turned out to be a pleasant afternoon. The mayor stood to address the Americans, saying: "When you go on your great adventure the thoughts and good wishes of every man, woman and child in this town will go with you. And if in the march of events you find yourself back here to help us with our peace celebrations, boys, what a party we'll have."

The "great adventure" as far as the Yanks, who lived only for today, were concerned was the dance arranged in their honour at the Corn Exchange that evening. Dorchester did them proud, finding a surprising amount of food for them in the form of sandwiches, with soft drinks to wash them down. More importantly, many pretty girls had been rounded up and shepherded, without much difficulty, into the dance. It was a grand night, breaking forever the invisible barrier that had until then existed between the locals and the Yanks.

Sylvia Thomas had never been serious about any American. Like most of the girls at that time, she found them amusing and good company, but Sylvia left any possibility of courting an American to other girls; it just was not for her. That was until the night of a dance at the British Legion Hall where she met US sailor Ralph Williams from Florida. Ralph was a petty officer (3rd class) in the US Navy. Friendship quickly extended into love, and the couple planned their engagement. Like many an anticipation, this event did not stand up too well in realisation. There were no personal problems on the parts of Sylvia and Ralph, but it was the US Navy that spoiled the big day.

The couple were taking a stroll out towards the cliffs. Ralph had already told Sylvia of a panic on at the dockyard because one of the US Navy trucks was missing. As they strolled, talking of a future together, they reached the school that stands at the edge of the cliff. Outside, as prominent as a few thousand sore thumbs, stood the missing truck. After a quick look round the vehicle caused by curiosity, the couple hurried back to Sylvia's home. Her father, an old soldier, knew the score, and advised Ralph to say nothing about the truck. A still tongue, however, was no protection. With security at a premium, eyes were everywhere, and Ralph had been seen beside the rogue vehicle. The grand day of the engagement ended with him being locked up. Was this bad start an omen for the future? Perhaps so, but very many years of happiness were enjoyed by Sylvia and Ralph before tragic bad luck overtook him.

No enemy needed

"I SAW the three ships laying just off the beach as I came down the hill on my way to work," says the Portland man. "I could see that something or the other was being ferried ashore, and this was so unusual on that side of the island that I made a detour to take a look. I'm not soft, anyone here will tell you that, but I wish that I'd never gone onto the beach that morning. It was a real shambles. Wounded young American soldiers were being brought up the beach on stretchers. It was an awful sight, their bodies torn and mutilated. Other stretchers were fully covered and often oddly shaped by the bundles underneath. These were the dead, and there were many of them. A lot of the watching women were openly crying. Not because they knew any of the soldiers, but just generally grieving for the whole terrible tragedy."

To all but the top few, the date of D-Day was still a mystery. This was the night of 27 April 1944. The young Americans filing from the bone-chilling damp camps at Dorchester believed that this was the date that would go down in history. But it was to remain insignificant except for the families in the United States who were to be bereaved within the next few hours.

Landing craft loaded at Weymouth and Portland. Though apprehensive of what was to come, the Americans felt an odd sort of relief brought by being on the move after months of preparation. Those who planned the big move knew well that it was operations 'Tiger' and 'Fabius', in which the friendly shores of Slapton Sands, Devon, would be attacked in as close as possible a simulation of the projected Normandy landings.

Ships of the Royal and United States navies bombarded Slapton Sands in preparation for the landings by troops who were rounding Portland

Bill. Winter had stolen that night from spring, and the men huddled together for warmth as their craft headed into the ominous waters of Lyme Bay. Dark, with an unearthly silence, those waters rippled apart around the bows of each craft, welcoming the men to what had been an aquatic graveyard since ancient man had set to sea on a raft. The eerie silence didn't last. It was broken horrifically.

"It had been quiet in the Cove Inn that night," Mrs Doris Saunders remembers. "We had cleared up fairly early and gone to bed, then the gunfire woke us. Our home had a grandstand seat for some of the tragedies of war. We had stood on the steps of the pub early in the war and watched the terrible glow in the sky as Plymouth burned in the blitz. That night in 1944 I remember thinking that this was it. I didn't stop to think that a full-scale invasion couldn't have happened so quickly, there was too much to do. In the morning we found out it had been an exercise, and we stood outside again, watching the medical men scramble up over the pebbles carrying stretchers."

"They told the Yankee commanders not to risk it without escorts," says the local man who hints that he was close to Eisenhower during his stint in the Army. "They were warned that the German motor torpedo boats were out there waiting. But you know the Yanks — bigheaded sods, they just ignored the warning."

Wondering whether the commanders were warned cannot lessen the sorrow for the soldiers of that night. Unescorted, like sitting ducks, the landing craft were attacked by speedy Schnelleboots, German surface torpedo boats. Exploding torpedoes wrecked the peace of the night. Then came the grim barking of machine guns — the screams of the wounded and the never-to-be-forgotten shrieks of the dying. They had no defence, no escape, but just prayer and the hope that somehow, by some miracle, they would come out of this alive.

Men of the shore batteries, guns well stocked with ammunition and capable of scattering the German motor boats, watched the distant killing — fretting. They had orders not to fire, for their shells would cause as much damage to the Americans as the Nazis in such a close fight. Alerted of the incident, the British vessels HMS *Saladin* and HMS *Azalra* steamed to the rescue. They were later joined by HMS *Onslow,* and soon the gunfire of the German boats had shut off as if controlled by a switch. Under pressure from the British ships, the torpedo boats fled the scene. LSTs 507 and 531 were sunk and LST 289 damaged.

Help had come at last, but too late for the 441 US troops and 197 seamen who had died, and the twelve tanks that had been sent to the bottom of Lyme Bay. The men had travelled far from their homes, had trained to fight, then died without even seeing the attacking German 5th and 9th E-boat flotillas.

The following Saturday, in a church at Bridport, a bride turned to her US Army groom. There was no smile or real joy in this girl's big day. Not far from the church, lapping with deceptive innocence against the beach, was the sea that had claimed the bridegroom's younger brother a few nights previously.

Two cultures meet again. Rev. Arthur Dittmer points out the inscription on a table-tomb in the churchyard at Burton Bradstock. Before 1783 the two nations have a common history.   *Photograph: Imperial War Museum.*

On the move

"THE AMERICANS certainly moved when they put plans into operation", ex-Pc Chapple recalls. "They cleared and levelled a large section of Chesil Beach beside the road that leads from Weymouth to Portland, near Ferrybridge. This was used as a marshalling area. As you know, it's a car park for tourists now. Each time the air raid siren was sounded then, the coloured soldiers at Tophill would come tearing down in their trucks and rush out to the marshalling ground to let off a smoke screen. The way they used to hurtle down that hill was frightening. How someone wasn't killed during that mad rush I will never know."

"Chuck sat in his trench at Weymouth watching an air-raid over Portland," says Christine Jones, the Portland girl who swore never to go out with a Yank, and then became engaged to her US military policeman, Chuck Ward. "He wrote a letter to me saying what he'd seen. We still have that letter and get it out for a laugh quite often. The censor only left me the greeting at the beginning and a small section at the end. It seemed the authorities didn't want a girl who had been in an air raid to know what it had looked like from four miles away."

All of this activity brought fears to the local residents, as Bill Chapple well remembers: "We all thought that the hammering German bombers had given the area would be nothing compared with what would come now that all this was taking place. The authorities had the same thing in mind, and this was made obvious in respect of police reinforcements. At that time, police and firemen from other areas were being drafted in to cover the invasion preparations. In all other areas of Dorset these extra men were told where they had to go. Because Portland was expected to be hit hard from the air, volunteers were asked for duty on the island."

An attachment of police from Leeds arrived at Dorchester, and ample volunteers came from it to Portland. Oddly, though the whole county was packed tight with vehicles and equipment as well as munitions, the anticipated German air attacks did not materialise. It is a fact that is incredible.

"It's obvious, isn't it," spits out the cynic who says he saw it all. "The war was a complete set-up between the big boys of both sides. It was to their advantage that the invasion should go ahead, so no big attack was launched on the preparing D-Day forces." This, you tell yourself, is a stupid theory. Then you think, looking for another explanation. You begin to wonder if the cynic's version is any less incredulous than other theories in that crazy war.

Sam Polley, a Weymouth haulage contractor, became a legend because of his amazing capacity for hard work. Sam could load a lorry with bricks by hand almost as quickly as modern machines do the same task. His services were always in demand, for those hiring him knew they paid for one day's work and Sam managed to squeeze three day's results into it.

When the war began, Sam's efforts had really begun to pay off, and his business was on a firm footing. But, like other men of his age, his country said it needed him, and Sam was called up. Local dignitaries heard of it. They knew Polley, and were aware that call-up would make him just

American trailers and half-tracks along both sides of a grassy lane in south Dorset. Ordnance depots sprang up all over the countryside. US Army photograph.

another soldier. They felt Sam would serve the war effort better in his own field, and had his conscription put aside. Sam, together with his lorry, was attached to the Nothe Fort at Weymouth. After years of hard graft earning a living and building up his business, Sam found working for the government similar to a long stay in a Butlin camp. His war had been fairly uneventful — until the Americans arrived at Nothe Fort, and D-Day approached.

There was no doubting the size of this operation. Every available space in Dorset had been either turned into an arsenal, vehicle parking area, or a supply dump. There was overcrowding in the Weymouth and Portland area, with about ten thousand British sailors, US sailors and WRNs employed ashore. A tented camp was set up on the Royal Navy rifle range at Portland. The army relinquished East Weare battery, overlooking the harbour, which was then used as a naval barracks. Various hotels, the naval cinema, a sports pavilion, and even the Borstal institution provided quarters for personnel. The use of Borstal must have produced an occasion where the inmates were reluctant to leave.

Weymouth Bay saw its biggest-ever assembly of major warships, with HMS *Rodney,* plus two British and five American cruisers there in readiness for the bombardment of the French coast. In total, 6,488 merchant vessels were to support the greatest invasion in history. All the hardware was accumulating.

"Things seemingly happened overnight," recalls Bill Chapple. "I was sometimes on duty at the bridge in Castletown Road at Portland, checking the civilians in and out of the docks. On the Mere below us (now a helicopter base) a field hospital mushroomed up as if by magic."

A new cry was coming over the tannoy system at Nothe Fort: "Calling Sam Polley." Sam would hurry along to the office where a cigar-smoking, irate US Army officer would greet him with something like: "Polley, do you know where this goddammed place called Piddlehinton is?"

"Yes, sir."

"Well get on out there. One of our convoys heading for Portland is in trouble."

"Trouble," Sam quickly learned, meant that the drivers were lost in the meandering roads and lanes of Dorset. He would drive out, and as a 20th century facsimile of a red indian scout, he would lead the long line of vehicles through to Portland.

"People say they were braggers, but, my God, they had something to brag about. I met one hell of a lot of convoys, but, each time, the sight of so much power was a shock to me. I never got used to it. Like I say, it was a fine army, and I am proud to have known them.

"Mind you, they worried me. The orders were that, travelling at night, the lead truck could use lights but the others stayed blacked-out. I was glad of this, because, being in Weymouth when the German bombing was at its peak, I had a healthy respect for the Luftwaffe.

"But those American soldiers didn't seem to give a damn. I used to shiver when I looked behind me and saw the whole convoy lit up like a fairground. Conversely, if there was an enemy plane about, there was a great deal of panic among the Americans. When the danger had passed, blow me if they didn't get back in the cabs of the lorries and switch every damn light on again."

Was it bravado? Unlikely. The most reasonable explanation for the strange behaviour of the soldiers, understandable in view of their youth and the situation, was their fear of the dark.

Weymouth's medical officer during the war, Dr Gordon Wallace, did many arduous and important jobs. Even so, he found time to give valuable instruction in first aid to a US signals unit stationed at Sutton Poyntz. Though the course was never completed because the unit moved during the final preparations for embarkation, Dr Wallace was later commended for this work, which had proven to be of great value to the troops in Normandy.

"Sometimes I'd drive back with an American officer riding with me, as I led the convoys to Portland," Sam Polley reminisces. "That was always interesting. They liked a chat, and asked me a lot about England. I learned a lot about America in return. My job was to bring the convoys over Ferrybridge, on the road from Weymouth to Portland, then guide them into the marshalling ground that had been constructed. This worked well every trip but one. On that occasion, the convoy commander was the most arrogant man I have ever met. He caused me some trouble, but he caused himself far more. It went okay until I led the convoy over the bridge...."

About a week before the big day, on 28 May 1944, the air raid siren sounded at 01.03 hours, but the first bombs had already dropped on Weymouth two minutes before this. Most people leapt from their beds frightened that this was the mass attack feared since the build-up for the invasion had begun. It wasn't. It was the last German air attack of the war on Weymouth, and in comparison to previous raids it was small, but it was exceptionally vicious.

One of the first bombs hit Weymouth hospital, starting a fire in the outpatients' department and the nurses home. Blast caused widespread damage throughout the town, and the Christian Science Church was set on fire. Before the raid ended, a hundred houses had been severely damaged, and three hundred slightly damaged.

Liaison between the Americans and the Weymouth civil defence was good. On that bad night on 28 May, Colonel Knoblock of the US Army Medical Corps, helped with his men in rescue work. American ambulances transferred patients from the stricken hospital, and the rescue and first aid for others was assisted in by American troops. It was a night of both tragedy and incredible luck. The tragedy came with a bomb that killed three gallant civil defence rescue men on their way to the bombed areas. The luck was with a Dr Gallagher, who had been with the three men who had been killed, but had left them shortly before the bomb dropped to return to base for his forgotten torch.

The total casualties in the raid were the three dead rescue workers, and a junior commander in the ATS, who also lost her life. Ten men and three women were slightly injured, badly enough to be retained in hospital, and three more men were slightly injured and sent home after treatment. A fluke round from a German airgunner wounded a coloured soldier who had been operating a smoke generator. Hit by bullets, the GI was made comfortable by local rescue workers, then taken to hospital in an American ambulance.

"I'd got to where we had to turn right into the marshalling ground beside the beach," Sam Polley continues. "When the convoy commander came dashing up to my cab, and asked me what the hell I was doing. I explained to him that this was the drill. The convoys had to wait in the marshalling ground until a motor-cycle rider came out with orders to move into Portland. This would be when a landing craft was waiting at the jetty. When we'd come over the bridge I had seen there wasn't one

Melcombe Avenue, Weymouth, being cleared up the morning after the German air attack of 28 May 1944.

there, they were out in the harbour.

"This wasn't good enough for the officer. 'I don't want a goddam marshalling ground,' he yelled at me. 'I want the embarkation point.'

"It wasn't any good trying to reason with this bloke. In the end, he ordered me to lead him into the docks at Portland."

Sam travelled through Victoria Square and up Cadets Road, which led to the docks (this road was later renamed Victory Road in honour of the American troops who had passed along it). When he reached the embarkation point, now the Royal Navy's HMS *Osprey* helicopter base, Sam halted, and soon the convoy commander was at his side. "There's no goddam landing craft at the jetty," he yelled at Sam.

Sam told him, patiently, that he was aware of that, and that was why he tried to take the convoy into the marshalling area. Not answering, the officer angrily strode up and down the road, then suddenly dashed down to the shore, pushed a rowing boat into the sea, and rowed off in the direction of the craft at anchor in the harbour. There seemed nothing for Sam to do but sit in his lorry and wait. The giant convoy, now completely stationary, strung out behind him, all the way down Cadets Road, through Victoria Square, and partly out along the causeway. It was very quiet. Behind Sam, a GI sang a snatch of the Andrews Sisters' hit *Don't sit under the apple tree.* Then it was silent again, until the buzz of a distant motor-cycle engine could be heard.

The rider dismounted at the head of the convoy. Stretching his legs like a saddle-weary cowboy, he called out: "What's this convoy doing here?"

Sam waited in the hope that a GI would answer. But they were confused men in a confusing situation, and didn't want to get involved. So Sam stepped out of his lorry in an attempt to explain.

"It shouldn't be here," growled the newcomer who detailed how the vehicles should have waited in the marshalling area for orders to move in. Several times Sam made an unsuccessful attempt to interrupt and say he knew all about that. Eventually, he got through, and told the rider that the convoy commander had ordered the line of vehicles into Portland. The newcomer asked where the convoy commander was at that time.

Though he was telling the truth, Sam felt foolish as he pointed to a distant speck in the harbour, and said: "That's him out there in a boat."

"Shit," spat the motor-cycle man. For a few moments he stood in indecision, then strode down to the shore, took a rowing boat himself, and shoved his way out to sea. Realising that marshal law had come to the rowing boats of Portland, Sam climbed wearily back in his cab to await developments. Behind him there was an occasional raised voice, one or two short choruses of laughter from the Americans, then all was quiet until the buzzing-bee sound of motor-cycle engines approaching again.

This time it was two US military policemen that descended on Sam, impressive in regalia that approached the livery of circus commissionaires for gaudiness.

The old routine started again: "Who brought this convoy here? It shouldn't be here."

"Where's the goddam convoy commander now?" Sam stuck with it, and pointed out to where the convoy commander could no longer be seen: "Out there."

One of the military policemen pointed to the bike of their colleague: "And where's this guy?"

More embarrassed than ever, Sam pointed to what had also become a speck in the harbour: "Out there in a boat, chasing the convoy commander."

Cursing it all as a 'goddam mess', the two policemen made their way to

Portland embarkation: a fully loaded DUKW moves into the gaping jaws of a landing craft. This operation took place on a specially constructed jetty close to the naval oil tanks at Castletown. US Army photograph.

the shore, giving Sam fears that they, too, would soon be going to sea in a boat. But they didn't. They stood and waited, and a dot on the water approached and proved itself to be the returning convoy commander as it did so. As he shame-facedly stepped ashore, the two policemen descended on him in fury. Sam watched fingers jabbing his chest in emphasis, then pointing out to the marshalling ground, and the commander nodding. The ranting and raving went on. Sam looked at his watch. He was overdue at home now and his wife would be worrying. It looked like the dressing-down the convoy commander was getting would go on indefinitely. Sam walked cautiously over to the trio.

"Is it okay if I go. I've done my job bringing the convoy through, and I have to be..."

One of the policemen rounded on him in anger: "The goddam convoy shouldn't be here."

For what seemed to him the hundredth time, Sam began "I know that, but I told..." Cutting him short, the angry policeman shouted: "And you're a civilian, you shouldn't be here."

"Then can I go?"

"Can you hell. If this lot has to go straight to France, you'll have to go with it. We can't let a civilian get this far and then go back."

Ordered back to his lorry, Sam had gloomy thoughts of ending up in France, in the middle of a battle. His opinion of the Americans had slid down a sharp decline. He sat there watching an arrogant convoy commander who had caused the mess, and two noisy, tough-talking military policemen who seemed incapable of resolving the mix-up. Then he changed his mind, about the policemen, at least. With the minimum of fuss, the pair waved the convoy forwards.

At Castletown Pier they organised an invisible turntable, and the lead vehicles of the convoy were reversed and heading in the opposite direction. Under expert directions, the front of the convoy was passing the rear as it drove back in the direction from which it had come. If any German spy had been watching, this would confuse him.

Down past Victoria Gardens drove Sam. Sightseers stood watching now. The halted convoy had caused some traffic snarl-ups, even on the sparsely used roads of wartime. At last he drove past the final vehicle in the convoy, and led his string of vehicles back out to the marshalling ground. Pulling in, he watched the returning convoy line up, an impressive sight again now that the bumbling was over. Proud and haughty, the two policemen rode in on their machines. Annoyed by this time, Sam strode up to them. "Can I go now?"

The anger had subsided in them and there was a hint of a grin on the lips that answered him. "Yes, buddy, you can go now."

"I don't know what happened to that convoy commander. Whether he was ever again entrusted with command," Sam now muses. "But if he did get to Normandy, there couldn't have been much worse waiting for him there than he'd got when he came ashore from his rowing boat in Portland."

The final air attack on Weymouth had ended, but its effect went on. An unexploded bomb was discovered at the Weymouth & District Hospital, in Melcombe Avenue. When the hospital had been hit, the men under US Colonel Knoblock's command had evacuated the patients to the Weymouth College Emergency Hospital, so there was no problem there.

But the unexploded bomb always brought great worries with it, and this one was even worse, for it lay close to the main road carrying the convoys to the docks. Dorchester Road, the nearby main road, was rated as a second-class military road.

On the Dorset coast at the eve of D-Day — convoys, vehicles and trailers loaded with men and equipment travel the final few yards across friendly soil on their way to the waiting landing craft. US Army photograph.

251

Lieutenant R.A.J. Woods, of Dorchester, who had been Bomb Disposal Officer for Dorset since 1942, was called in, together with his squad.

There were further complications with the discovery that the bomb was fitted with an extension cap, which could well mean it was 'booby-trapped'. The bomb disposal team knew that speed was of the essence, but none knew that D-Day was just one week away. Caution was also essential, and the bomb was photographed and the prints studied.

Work began at around noon on Sunday. The bomb had penetrated 28 feet into the ground and it wasn't reached until 3 am the following Friday. After these long and anxious hours, gallons of sweat, and untold strain on the nerves of those involved, the bomb was made harmless.

In safety, the flow of military traffic to the docks continued along Dorchester Road.

A soldier's farewell

EVERYONE KNEW the time must be near. The training and preparation had steadily built up to hint of an imminent climax. It seemed to be here for Chuck Ward and his military police comrades one day. They were turned out, with particular attention paid to smartness of dress. This surprised no one, for those who have served in the army of any country know that shining buttons come before all else.

So a gleaming Chuck was out in the streets, ready to wave his gloved, disciplined hand in instruction to heavy vehicles on their way to the docks. What rolled towards him was no plodding convoy but motor-cycle outriders and impressive staff cars. General Eisenhower was on his way to Portland.

"Quick, Mum, Dad, come and look at this!"

Reg Gill heard the excited cry of his daughter, but didn't hurry to the front of his shop. The children could still be moved by something unusual, but this war was old now, and the adults were no longer credulous. Yet there was a special urgency in the girl's call, and the family stepped out into Castle Road. The splendour of fully-rigged US Military Police motor-cycle outriders dazzled them. A smart, in-line, impressive escort for a car that the startled Gills saw contained the King. Behind it came another vehicle carrying General Eisenhower, followed by another with the heavily-jowled face of Churchill peering through the glass, and then came a car occupied by the great British soldier of World War Two — General Montgomery.

This bit of pageantry, impressive at the time, has a pathos in retrospect. The VIPs inspected the United States Navy lined up on Castletown Pier. Those distinguished visitors must have fought to look

Men of an American Ranger unit file into landing craft at Weymouth Harbour on 1 June 1944.   *US Army photograph.*

RIGHT: Hands across the sea, in a manner of speaking. British sailors assist American Rangers from a lorry on the quayside at Weymouth. Minutes later the Rangers were sailing towards D-Day.   *US Army photograph.*

impassive as they walked slowly in the gaze of the eyes of men they would soon be sending to their deaths with just one stroke of a pen.

As the big day approached, the fun and frolic faded in the bars of the Railway Arch Hotel. An American sergeant sat in Mrs Ainge's backroom, arms stretched wide as he held wool her daughter wound in readiness to knit baby clothes. His face was slightly distorted by mental strain, as were the features of practically every GI at that time. Eyes softened by reminiscence, he spoke softly, more to himself than to Mrs Ainge and her daughter: "If I was at home right now, I'd be sitting there while my daughter was searching through the ice-box. She'd come back with something to eat for herself, and a can of beer for me. "Here you are, Dad," she'd say, then curl up beside me for the evening."

The sergeant's cheeks glistened with tears, and the two women, sharing his despair and sorrow, had to turn away so he would not see they too were crying.

"Five of the chaps we knew best," says the woman from Portland who had named her daughter after an American, "They came to say cheerio. Only two of that five came back alive."

Was that a fair average of casualties? I do not know the statistics, but the slaughter on Omaha Beach, where those GIs were headed, claimed a thousand lives on that first day, 6 June 1944.

He was very young, a Polish-American, and nice and friendly. It was his last visit to the Railway Arch Hotel. America's military might that had lain dormant in Dorset was on the move outside. More sober-faced than he had ever been, the young GI leaned over the bar to kiss Mrs Ainge. This was against the unspoken but strictly imposed rules of the Railway Arch, and Mrs Ainge drew back, sharply.

"I'm sorry," mumbled the youth, once always laughing and joking but now very sad. "I was thinking of my mother."

Regretting her instant rebuke, Mrs Ainge told him: "In that case, you may kiss me goodbye." A quick peck on the cheek, and the lad in uniform stumbled from the bar.

Long since gone was the novelty of having so many troops in Dorset. The uniforms of many countries, and the manoeuvres of troops, now blended into the background of the county. Then the tempo quickened on a wet Sunday in early June. A wilting daylight was succumbing to approaching dusk as sightseers lined the seafront at Weymouth. Across the road from them, on the Esplanade, an endless line of American soldiers did a soft-footed parade to the docks.

Local faces showed bewilderment. Accustomed to the crash of the British Tommy's boots, and his whistling and singing of marching tunes, they found the almost silent march of the Americans eerie. This was a new kind of soldier. Modern-minded young men, the GIs had no popular swing tune that would fit in with the plod of marching feet.

The fun-fair was at Dorchester. Close to the railway station, it was closed because it was midnight. "Everything seemed to happen at once," remembers the old lady of the fairground. "There were Americans everywhere and trains seemed to be arriving and leaving all the time. We lay awake, listening to the orders, the marching, and the lorries and tanks that shook our caravans as they passed. Perhaps I'm being clever in saying it now, but I truly believe that I knew it then, and whispered to myself that night: 'They've thrown their money away, now they are going to throw their lives away.' By one o'clock in the morning they had all gone. It was very, very quiet then."

People in Weymouth rushed to close their windows as thick smoke swirled around, knocking coughs out of many a chest. The Americans had laid a huge smoke screen to cover their embarkation activities. A massive convoy roared along the causeway leading into Portland.

Beside it rode the youthful Polish-American motorcyclist who had kissed a proxy mother in the Railway Arch Hotel. Movement had eased some of his homesickness. The machine felt powerful beneath him, like a part of the terrific power that he rode beside. Then the front wheel wobbled. He tried to hold the bike upright, but it turned towards the heavy vehicles. There was a crunch that was drowned by the noise of the convoy. Sparks flew as wheels and tracks chewed the motorcycle into scrap. In a horrifying manner, the life was crushed out of the boy from the United States.

"Dear God, we are in for it this time," Christine Jones, now engaged to her American, said to her mother on the night of 5 June 1944. The whole sky was resounding to the roar of aircraft, and even the house shuddered. But it was different this time. Neighbours stood on their doorsteps looking up. Christine realised that the planes were friendly. She describes the sight that met her eyes: "As far as the eye could see, and seemingly filling the vastness of the heavens, were tiny pin-pricks of lights like a myriad of miniature stars moving in unison. In the morning, the bombers and fighters had been replaced in the sky by tow-planes and gliders. These were so low that we could see the men inside waving to the people

GIs singing as they wait to embark on the USS Henrico *in Weymouth Harbour, 6 June 1944.*   *US Army photograph.*

257

in the streets."

"I could have been a security risk that night," muses the woman who befriended the Americans in Portland. "Security had the majority of US forces confined to base, but I had five engineers, bulldozer drivers, at home for their favourite supper, fish and chips. An officer called at the door asking for the men. I invited him in and he couldn't resist my invitation to supper but I knew it was the big night from the way he didn't let one of the five out of his sight for even a second.

"They must have sensed it, too, because when they left, one of them gave me his prize possession, a guitar. He asked me to look after it for him, and said I could keep it if he didn't come back. When they'd gone, the noise of the aircraft told me my hunch had been right."

At Tarrant Rushton airfield, near Blandford, it was all action and 36 planes took off, towing gliders behind them, for a destination close to Caen in Normandy. "That was a night I will always remember," says Bill Chapple. "I was on duty on the 5th, I'd seen it all build up, and had been closely involved with the US forces from the start, so I was aware of the size of the operation. Stevedores had been brought in to assist with loading in the docks. These had brought an extra security problem with them.

"As I say, I should have been prepared — but there was nothing to prepare a human mind for seeing so much power on the move at one time. Nor am I capable of accurately describing that memorable night." Restlessly, the people of Weymouth twisted and turned in their beds that night. The throbbing, ear-crushing sound of massed aircraft made sleep impossible. Then there was the memory of those smiling soldiers marching to the docks. The well-meant calls to them of "God speed and safe return," had withered at dusk. Where were they now — tossing about on a stormy sea. What were their thoughts as they awaited the terror of the unknown. No dead yet in the invasion, but their ghosts were haunting Weymouth in readiness.

High above the English Channel was Walter Farrar, who had served in England with the United States 8th Air Force since 1942, flying B17s and Flying Fortresses with the 92nd Group, consisting of nine bomber squadrons and three service squadrons. His group had attacked airfields, oil storage dumps, troop movements and convoys.

From his home in Florida, Walter wrote to me of that night: I looked down on that great and awesome sight of that mighty armada heading for the coast of Normandy to decide the destiny of us all. I often think of those brave men, so many of whom were to fall on the beaches, with only

The mass of men, equipment and supplies on the quayside at Weymouth Harbour on 1 June 1944. One man has spotted the cameraman, and points. Three or four others grin. The rest were too busy to notice. US Army photograph.

the lucky ones returning safely home."

"I couldn't sleep because of the noise," said a Weymouth woman who is a grandmother herself now. "My mother was getting on in years and not in good health, so I went to her room to see that she was all right. I panicked a bit because she wasn't there. I found her downstairs, kneeling and praying aloud. She didn't seem to notice me for a long time, then, when she'd finished praying, she turned to me and I realised she'd known that I was there. It wouldn't be true to say she'd been crying, but her eyes were very wet. She said to me: 'Pray, and pray hard, Mary. Don't just pray for those boys on their way across the sea, but pray hard for all of us, that we may by some miracle be worthy of what they are going to go through for us.'

"I didn't understand what she meant at the time. I do now, and I can only think that we didn't pray hard enough. We have never been worthy of the sacrifices made that night, and in the months that followed."

Also up in that sky which he shared with Walter Farrar and countless other men that night, was an airgunner from Swanage. Now living at Bovington Camp, Roland Hammersley had already flown on many dangerous missions before that night. He had lost comrades when his planes had been attacked in danger-filled skies. After D-Day had passed he was awarded the Distinguished Flying Medal.

At 01.36 hours that morning of 6 June he had taken off from his base with 57 squadron at East Kirkby, Lincolnshire. The target for the night was the coastal guns at La Pernelles. Out over the Channel it was fairly routine stuff for Roland, but the night sky, familiar but never friendly, started to tell him something new.

Part of his equipment was an airborne radar set for detecting other planes, working in conjunction with the navigator's H2S equipment. Roland's set, codenamed Fishpond, would show the movement and range of aircraft below his plane. These appeared as bright blips on the screen. These blips were suddenly in such profusion that Roland realised either thousands of German aircraft were below, or an invasion fleet was down there on the water.

This thought excited Roland, for it was truly a case of the 'Fighting Hammersleys' in this war. His father and two brothers were in the army, while a younger brother served in the Home Guard. His only sister was in the Land Army, and his mother, though at home, put plenty into the war effort. He reported his findings to the pilot, Ron Walker, who made searching sweeps until the joyful crew were all agreed that what they saw below was indeed an invasion fleet heading for France.

With more determination than ever, the Lancaster resumed course for its target. The records prove that the guns at La Pernelle were silenced in plenty of time for the arrival of the troops on the beaches. What Roland

The unprecedented scene on the Dorset coast as lines of US vehicles of all kinds converge into the landing crafts for the invasion of Europe.   US Army photograph.

did not know until later was that in one of those craft below was his brother — Walter.

On 6 June 1944 a new dawn came to Weymouth like an advertisement for a better world. It brought a sky full of Douglas twin-engined transport planes towing gliders, and confirmation of what was already known. This was D-Day. The harbour was like a giant watery dodgem track, with ships fussing in and out. Road military traffic was still heavy, and the rhythmic plod of boots along the Esplanade continued.

There was a distinct difference in today's marchers. Gone were the smiles and witticisms of yesterday's warriors. They had not known what lay ahead of them. The guessing game was over now. News of the beaches had come across the Channel by invisible telegraph. The men marching now knew of the carnage of Omaha Beach. They learned that many of those before them had been an hour in the water, while a huge number had never left the water at all.

This grim knowledge had the marching Americans stern of feature.

Signals Corps men of an assault unit 'Queue Up' beside Portland Harbour, awaiting orders to file on to the landing craft.   *US Army photograph.*

Each man carried his weapon and enough food to last him through that first fateful day. They marched on into the foggy destiny that this one day in their lives would reveal to them.

News came that Churchill needed to be restrained when he insisted that he accompany the invasion force.

"Bullshit," spat the young GI, who sat in a hospital train in Norfolk, nervously feeling the space where he once had an arm. "If he had come, he wouldn't have hit the beaches with us. It's all political bullshit."

The listeners felt sorry about his arm, but wished he would not talk about their Prime Minister that way. They put it down to shock. Today, when all politics have been disclosed as a giant game of words, hindsight makes it easy to agree with that American. It most probably was all bullshit.

Allied wounded were already arriving back in East Anglia. They rode to hospital on trains, peering out of the windows at a country they had not expected to see again soon — if ever. The newspapers said they were all 'cheerful'. And the wise ones read and wondered how a soldier tossed into hell, shot or blown to pieces, then dragged back for doctors to work on, could be described as cheerful. Visiting of the wounded was not allowed, except for those on the danger list. Their relatives were informed by telegram.

It was still D-Day, and Churchill, obviously recovered from any force

Lines of negro 'static' troops load rations for the D-Day invasion force in Weymouth Harbour at the beginning of June 1944. 	US Army photograph.

that had been used to restrain him from rushing to the beaches, was announcing the landing to the House of Commons, saying:

An immense armada of upwards of 4,000 ships, with several thousand smaller craft, has crossed the Channel.

Mass airborne landings have been successfully effected behind the enemy's lines. The landings on the beaches are proceeding at various points at the present time. The fire of shore batteries has largely been quelled.

The obstacles which were constructed in the sea have not proved so difficult as was first apprehended. The Anglo-American allies are sustained by about 11,000 first-line aircraft which can be drawn upon as may be needed for the purposes of battle.

There are already hopes that actual tactical surprise has been attained, and we hope to furnish the enemy with a succession of surprises during the course of the fighting.

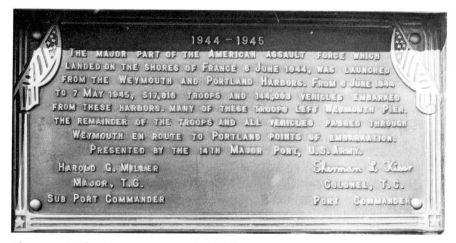

Plaque, at Portland, commemorates the logistics of victory. Photograph: Frederick G. Masters

The ardour and spirit of the troops as I saw for myself in these last few days were splendid.

GI Ernest Webster, like his comrades, had not wanted a war, and was not enjoying this one. Perhaps he thanked providence for bringing him to England and a meeting with his beautiful fiancée, Doris Mockridge, but even that faded from his mind as the ramp of his landing craft hit the beach at Normandy. The Americans leapt into the water, making for the shore, rifles at the ready. Ahead was a scene that no nightmare could have conjured up for them. Ernest saw it, then saw no more. His war ended there, as did a chapter of his life. Months of pain, years of adjustment, and a time for purposeful thinking lay ahead. Ernest Webster had stepped on a mine and he lost a leg.

On 8 June Churchill was adding a word of caution: "If this is the last time I speak to the House before the weekend, I earnestly hope that when members go to their constituencies they will not only maintain morale as far as it is necessary, but will also give strong warnings against over-optimism. Remember, although great dangers lie behind, enormous exertions lie before us."

The Allies had a footing in Europe, though hard-won and still tentative, and Hitler's morale was given a boost by his one remaining foreign friend, General Hideko Tojo, Prime Minister of Japan. In a telegram to Adolf, Hideko said: "We have full confidence in Germany's ability to score a crushing victory."

History supports a theory that this confidence was not entirely misplaced. Without detracting from the gallant and victorious efforts of the united nations, it was sheer weight of numbers that finally flattened the German Army, which fought with amazing skill and bravery until the last shot of the war was fired.

The waiting and the wondering were over. Most of the young men from America had gone from Dorset. News from the continent was top of the priorities list. Dorset's D-Day was over, but the effect lingers on, even to this day.

A bronze plaque inside Portland dockyard records the sheer scale of the logistics for the Normandy invasion. Carrying the names of Colonel Sherman L. Kiser, the port commander, and Major Harold G. Miller, the sub port commander, it was presented by the 14th Major Port, US Army and reads:

> The major part of the American assault force which landed on the shores of France 6 June 1944, was launched from the Weymouth and Portland Harbors. From 6 June 1944 to 7 May 1945, 517,816 troops and 144,093 vehicles embarked from these harbors. Many of these troops left Weymouth Pier. The remainder of the troops and all vehicles passed through Weymouth en route to Portland points of embarkation.

The unknown warriors

WITH THE media strangled by censorship, the heroes of D-Day performed their incredible acts of bravery without anything approaching individual recognition. But the public were wise in the ways of war. They read between the lines, wondering how men, made sick and weary by hours spent on a violently stormy sea, could find a reserve in energy and courage to storm up the beaches.

A journalist's report, written shortly after D-Day, provides the kind of reading that will be an epitaph into infinity for the brave men of 6 June 1944:

When the full story can be told of how our landing craft smashed their way through thousands of mines, iron stakes and girders, barbed wire and nets, and beached under shell and machine-gun fire, it will be an epic in sea warfare and in the history of the Royal Navy.

Many sank off the beaches, some were battered to pieces by enemy gunfire as they tried to discharge. Many were damaged but got their loads ashore and returned home to reload. Young crews who went into battle for the first time behaved like veteran fighters. Men continued to fire as their ships sank. Others, with their hands, their bare hands, warded off their craft from mine-rigged obstacles.

I have been on board craft that landed tanks. A young commanding officer, whose craft was mined, said to me: 'If the LCTs didn't take another tank or vehicle or gun to the beaches, they will have done their job. The surprising feature is that so few were damaged. Nearly all of us got back. Our craft seemed to be nearly unsinkable'.

That seems to be a fact. I have seen some remarkable examples of craft that survived mines and shells. Some have been patched up under fire on the beaches and are still ferrying vehicles across the Channel. Others, after a few hours in dock here, have left again for duty. Many of those very badly hit have been repaired in a few days.

Each of these ships has a story of adventure and heroism to tell, of how the landing was carried out against great odds. Three craft I was on board provide typical examples of what the LCTs did.

LCT 931 was commanded by Sub-Lieutenant D.A. McCaughley RNVR, who, in peacetime managed a hotel in Cardiff. With him on the bridge was Sub-Lieutenant Robert Loveless RNVR, of Torquay, formerly a schoolteacher, and Sub-Lieutenant D.H. Longden, of Sheffield, who was a railway clerk. Their craft was shelled on the beaches and nearly mined.

Though it looks like complete chaos, this is actually a well-planned shipment of an armoured unit. A few hours after this picture was taken, on 5 June 1944, this section of the invasion force was moved from Weymouth Harbour by the Navy and was on its way to Normandy.

US Army photograph.

267

LCT 931 had been three days on invasion duty. She was with the United States forces that landed near Cherbourg.

The next craft I went on board was LCT 519. Once she had her back broken but had been repaired. Even so, she was not supposed to carry a load of more than 40 tons. She carried over 150 tons to the landing.

We were mined, shelled, and spiked by sea defences, Sub-Lieutenant H.V. Heaseman RNVR, of Epsom, her commanding officer, told me with a grin. 'Our propeller was bent and that cut out speed down, and we had five shell holes in the engine room, so we had to cut our speed to keep the water from flooding us.'

This craft got all her load ashore although shell and bomb craters tended to bog down the tanks. They had to be hauled ashore by bulldozer, which the craft carried.

The first lieutenant of the craft, Sub-Lieutenant J.M. Phillips RNVR, of Lewes, was very young. He had received his promotion from mid-

Rations are loaded at Weymouth Harbour, early in June 1944. The majestic building in the background, the Ritz Theatre, survived the war but was burnt down accidentally during redecoration in the early 1950s.　　　　　　　　*US Army photograph*

shipman only a couple of days ago.

'There was a soldier in difficulties, trying to swim ashore,' he related. 'And we had on board a Catholic chaplain. He dived in and tried to rescue the man, but the sea was too rough. We had to haul him on board and the man was rescued from the shore.'

Discharging the load took place under enemy fire. Two craft alongside LCT 519 got stuck on the beach and were hauled off by her as she came away.

'Like almost all the LCTs, we ploughed through and over a lot of obstacles to get in,' remarked the commanding officer. 'There were mines everywhere — on cross girders, in the beach, attached to wires and nets. As we hauled in with the kedge anchor we detonated mines, and some of us brought them up, so we had to cut our wires to get free. Our craft was badly holed by obstacles.'

Another remarkable story was that of Sub-Lieutenant R.F. Offer

American tank crews load their shells in the final preparations for D-Day.

US Army photograph

269

RNVR, of Kingston. His craft, LCT 708, carried army guns and went in 40 minutes before the landing took place, to lay down covering fire. Describing the scene to me, he said: 'We dodged several mines as we closed on the beach. Shelling and bombing had covered the shoreline in dense smoke and dust. There were five other craft with us, and together we fired a very large number of shells into the shore defences.

'We then lay off until it was time to go in and land our load. Three mines missed our bows, scraping by. Another mine exploded at our bow and seriously injured the army officer in charge of the troops. We got our loads off except for the doctor's van. The doctor stayed behind to tend the wounded officer and didn't dash off until the last minute. As his van went ashore it hit a mine and I am afraid the doctor was killed.

'His driver came up and was in difficulties, so our coxswain, Leading Seaman H. Walford, of Stoke-on-Trent, put on a lifeline and dived overboard. He struggled for twenty minutes to reach the driver. He got over the barbed wire and over mines, but the sea was too rough and we hauled him on board. A mine went off when he was in the water and that nearly knocked him out. The driver was saved from the shore.

'We had to get away quickly as we were coming under heavy fire. As we edged off two shells hit us. One left a whacking great hole in the starboard side and the other went straight through the craft to the port side. We are particularly annoyed with that shell because it destroyed our month's supply of cigarettes and other stores.'

This craft transferred the wounded man to a destroyer so that he could be rushed to hospital, and then made her way back to England under her own power.

Anyone who may think that the landing was easy should take a look at the battered and torn LCTs that have come back to this invasion port.

There is another point to remember. Many of the commanding officers are no more than 21, and most of the crews are youngsters of 18 and a little older. I do not think any tribute could be too generous for their magnificent work. Had it not been for their audacious handling of the craft, their courage and determination, the invasion could not have been a success.

Business as usual

THOUGH MUTED, and tinged with a sadness brought by knowledge of what was happening on the continent, the social life of Dorset went on much as usual after the Normandy landings. The Weymouth branch of the Old Contemptibles held what was their most successful dance, with members of the US forces, eager to join in any gathering of the sexes, swelling the numbers. It was a four-hour non-stop event in the Regent Dance Hall. Valuable spot prizes were awarded, creating an extra interest for the six hundred dancers present. The prizes were presented by L.B. White, of the USAAF, and a much coveted award in those days — a bottle of whisky, was won by Pete Pandaff of the US Navy.

On the quays where the might of America's war machine was still flexing its muscles, a pitiful stream of sorrowful human rejects became a regular sight. As the Allies gained ground in Normandy, the displaced people of war shuffled, starved-looking and terrified, into Weymouth.

Four miles away, in Portland's Castletown Road, there was no shuffling feet to the newcomers there. Proud and arrogant, the smart soldiers of Hitler marched under American guard to the stockade that had been built on the naval recreation ground. They made eyes at the watching English women, and spat their contempt on to the ground as they saw men viewing them. At the stockade they were documented, deloused, then marched to trains standing at the nearby station, and were transported from the island.

As the film neared its end at the Regent cinema, salesgirl Doris Mockridge stood in the darkness waiting for the interval when she would take her tray of cigarettes and confectionery to the audience. Her mind was with GI Ernest Webster, whose purchase of matches from her had started a romance. Among a chorus of wolf-whistles, Doris stepped out into the limelight. A striking girl of just 20 years, she was used to this attention. With her hair piled high in the style of the day, she had been told a thousand times how attractive she was. But the men around her were like ghosts that night. Doris could think only of Ernie, fighting across the Channel on the hell the world now knew the beaches to be. She was grateful to the auditorium's darkness, which hid her sorrow.

Bad news came with the police constable who knocked on the door of 7 Kempstone Road, Weymouth. He was there to tell the parents of 20-years-old Robert Nairder that the German radio had announced their son had been wounded and was a prisoner of war. The whereabouts of another Weymouth man were unknown, but it was thought he could be in a hospital in this country. The parents of 21-years-old Wireless Operator Leslie Cheeseman, at Lower Lennox Street, received a telegram saying he was suffering from blast injuries, shock and shrapnel wounds.

With the serious war games all across the Channel, sport still went on in Dorset, though the playing fields had lost their monopoly. The British-loved game of cricket was no longer supreme. In keeping with the times, a Dorset newspaper reporter used a Damon Runyon style to report on the game of the day — baseball. The game was suggested by Rev. G. Clare Morrow, of Holy Trinity, Dorchester, officiating chaplain to the forces, and organised by the American authorities under the aegis of the Brighter Dorchester Campaign committee. The game raised £25 for war charities.

The writer added that if any "GI Joe" should take exception to the report, he was welcome to try his hand at reporting a cricket match:

This is the report of a ball game which I saw together with some 700 other citizens the other day.

I knew nothing about ball games before the play and I know even less now that it is over, but this is to the good as I do not consider it is the sort of game which makes the British Empire what it was.

Furthermore, the game is so noisy that I cannot get a wink of sleep the whole afternoon as I can during a cricket match, which is much more dignified and English.

First there is a band which plays very loudly to get the citizens used to noise, and it seems that this is very much liked by the younger citizens, particularly young dames who like dancing to this sort of music, and they think it is a great pity that this music should be interrupted by the ball game.

Secondly, there is a guy named Redelmann, who is a Lieutenant, and he is trying to tell one and all what the game is all about, and he has a

Tightly packed for a ride into hell. An American assault unit waits to begin a nightmare voyage from Weymouth Harbour to the beaches of Normandy.　　　　*US Army photograph*

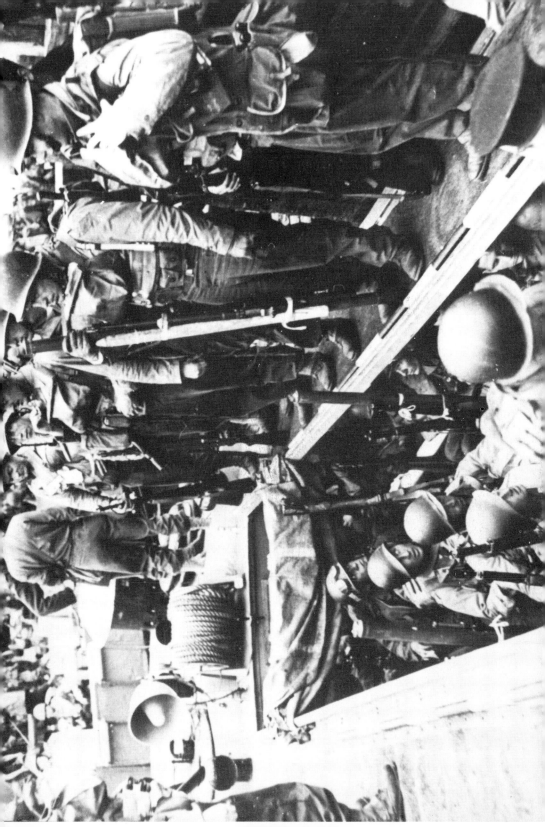

voice which is liable to crack the microphone at any minute, if this is not an American microphone and used to such a voice.

Moreover, there are many GI Joes among the citizens who consider it their duty to pepper up the play by making very loud comments on the ability of the players.

It seems that such goings-on are encouraged as it would not be a ball game at all if these things did not go on, except there is one GI Joe who sits near me saying there should be a guy with a tray of peanuts wandering up and down the bleachers to make it a *real* game.

And if you do not know what bleachers are — they are seats in the sun. The report continues with detail of the game between the Brooklyn Dodgers and the New York Giants, won by the Giants.

Brooklyn Dodgers: Lieutenant C. Redelman, New York; R.Whittaker, Princeton, W. Virginia; B. Benson, Long Island, New York; M. Lum, Bastrap, Louisiana; C. Shields, Clarence, Missouri; R. Orlando, Philadelphia, Pennsylvania; Sergeant Gruskin, Marlboro, New Jersey; M. DuPuis, Lafayette, Louisiana; W. Wallace, Jacksonville, Illinois; S. Ignoffo, Chicago, Illinois; F. Wellborn, Mobile, Alabama.

New York Giants: (all from New York) F. Janke, Flushing, Long Island; B. Summers, Baldwin, Long Island; The Rev. G. Clare Morrow — lending moral support; R. Sweeney, Elmhurst; Steinacker, East Rockaway; D. Cappolo, Shenectady; B. Reinhardt, Troy; H.A. Hoffman, Rockville Center, Long Island; J.J.Bressan, Bellerose, Long Island; P.J. Tagliento, Renessoer; R.E. Maynard, Brooklyn; M. Silverfarb, Bronx; P. Pirini, Corona; R.R. Russo, Flushing.

By now the daring padres of Dorset were in the news. In Normandy with the 7th Armoured Division, was Rev. Wingfield Digby SCF, an old Desert Rat who was formerly vicar of St George's, Oakdale, Poole. In Normandy, he was bishop of a flexible and often almost indefinable 'parish'. With him was the Rev. M.W. Wilson, formerly padre of Tripoli church, and who was at Salerno with the County of London Yeomanry. Before the war he had been vicar at the church of Holy Angels, Parkstone.

Even as the first landing craft ramp dropped on a Normandy beach, the Army Postal Service had the first batch of mail steaming across the Channel. The authorities, aware of the importance of mail from home to fighting men, kept a regular flow of letters to France, and there was much praise for the Army department handling this essential side of things. In return came the heartbreak.

More casualty news from Normandy included the tragic death of Lieutenant Colonel J.W. Atherton. A solicitor, Atherton had been a partner in the Weymouth firm of Jex and Atherton. Prior to the outbreak of war he had joined the Territorial Army as a subaltern, and

Weymouth GI bride Doris Mockridge and her US Army husband Ernest Webster. She had sold him matches at the Regent cinema. Photograph: S.J. Herbert.

commanded a company at Bridport. Mobilised at the start of hostilities, he quickly gained promotion and was an officer popular with all ranks.

With only ten months army service behind him, Private Pomeroy, whose wife and two children lived at 2 St Andrew's Annexe, Radipole, Weymouth, took part in heavy fighting on the beaches, and was slightly wounded by shrapnel before the Longest Day had ended. Eight days later, his wounds healed, Pomeroy rejoined his unit, but must have felt that the army was not for him, as he was immediately wounded again. This time it was serious, and he was in hospital on the danger list. Before going into the army he had worked seven years service on the staff of the Weymouth telephone exchange, and had reached the position of night supervisor.

With things going well in Europe, summer came to Dorset. A dose of sunshine turned Weymouth's wartime Dr Jekyll image back into Mr Hyde. Holidaymakers lay on a beach that had shortly before trembled in dread of the tread of jackboots. Children and adults leapt about happily in the sea. Delight made their screams as loud as those of dying soldiers across the Channel. The war had moved far enough away to be forgotten. American men and vehicles still moved about in the county, but the assault forces had long gone. The Yank had fought with valour. He had taken the unkind jibes and criticisms, turned them around, and rammed them into the mouths of those who decried him. He had won his place on the wartime roll of honour, but fewer places in the hearts of the British he had met along the way.

Mrs Bailey walked the quayside of Weymouth, which was still bustling with American military activity. She was on her way to visit her mother, at 12 Trinity Road, when she saw her youngest sister, Doris, rushing in her direction. The 'baby' of the family was distraught, and it was some time before Mrs Bailey could make sense of the sob-interspersed words. Then Doris managed to blurt the message out: "It's Ernie, he's been badly wounded in Normandy."

Hands across the Sea

ONE BRITISH man had no doubts about the courage and ability of the GI, for he had experienced it first-hand. Bill Eason, from Harlow in Essex, wrote to American ex-flier Walter Farrar, following a letter Walter had written in remembrance of D-Day, which had appeared in English newspapers. Walter Farrar sent me a copy of the letter, saying: "Surely this man deserves a mention in your account of Dorset's D-Day."

It does, and gives a roundness to the book by concisely illustrating where all the preparations and embarkations led. I attempted to contact Bill Eason, unsuccessfully, in an attempt to enlarge upon his interesting reminiscences. However, this is the letter he wrote:

Dear Walter

May I say thank you for your letter on the anniversary of D-Day, printed in the columns of the London *Evening News* on 6th June 1975.

I do not know whether this will reach you, but the postal services have a way of finding people, and I am sure the US Mail is not second to our own GPO, in ensuring mail is delivered.

I was especially delighted and proud to read your letter of greetings, for I am perhaps one of the very few British ex-servicemen who had the honour to be attached, during the fighting in Normandy, to a number of US headquarters in turn — including Bradley's and the HQ of the US 9th Air Force — although I initially landed at Sword Beach with Montgomery's Advanced HQ of 21st Army Group, being a radio mechanic of General Montgomery's personal radio link with London.

As a member of the Royal Signals Special Communications Units I was one of those whose task was to maintain a network of radio stations, mobile — a mobile radio station at each of the Allied Headquarters —

all of which were in continuous radio communication direct with London from the Normandy beachheads. Thus information from each headquarters, of German positions, could be sent back in code to London, and relayed back to allied commanders along with information from Resistance groups.

These small radio units, modelled on amateur radio principles, using low-powered radio transmitters, worked with the forward combat units — sometimes landing up behind enemy lines!

My unit at 21st Army Group TAC HQ pushed on with the 2nd British Army through the Falaise Gap after breakthrough, with the destruction of Caen, and entered Brussels with the forward British armour. It was at the HQ of Montgomery at Brussels that I received a posting to Bradley's HQ at Verdun, and thereafter I became, with a small group of Royal Signals, an honorary member of the US Army. I was in Luxembourg City, at the UD HQ, at the time of the attempted thrust through the Ardennes by the SS Panzers — having, unwittingly, on a return trip from Brussels to Luxembourg, passed through a column of Panzers in a jeep. It was snowing hard: the SS thought we were Germans in American uniforms: we thought the tanks belonged to the Americans until we looked back and saw the insignia on them. We got the hell out of it and did the rest of the trip at record speed. Back in Luxembourg we did a foxhole stint on the outskirts of the city, with US combat troops, until the advance was halted.

I remember that, in Luxembourg that Christmas, I had a remarkable experience in the canteen of the railway station, by talking to a group of US buddies about the history of the war from 1939, and ended up by giving a full-scale lecture on the canteen stage to some hundred GIs about the war from 1939 — including the Dunkirk evacuation, the RAF Battle of Britain and the Desert Campaign against Rommel.

I was astonished that my American friends should be surprised that I had been fighting since 1940, and that I had been a kilted Seaforth Highlander fighting in Norway, that I had been one of the first radar mechanics on anti-aircraft gunsights during the Battle of Britain, before being transferred to the Royal Signals special communications units linked with the radio network of the Resistance Forces in France from 1941 to 1944.

I learnt from my lecture that many of my GI buddies knew little of the things they were fighting for — that perhaps they hadn't had time to learn. It was on advance to the Rhine and that crossing that I made so many friends among combat GIs — two of whom I saw shot in the back as they crossed a square in Wiesbaden — by a twelve-years-old boy in Hitler Youth uniform, firing from behind a garden wall. I remember seeing a huge top sergeant advance on the boy, pick him up by the scruff of the neck and lather the hide off him before the MPs moved in to stop him strangling the German lad. And so on to Berlin, and a glorious link-up with Russian soldiers, during which celebrations I was out cold from libations of real Russian vodka.

As non-commissioned officer, I brought my unit back from Germany, along the Moselle, across Luxembourg, across France to Paris, and then back to England.

After leave, I was on a troopship through the Med., Suez to India, New Delhi and across India to Calcutta — and so into the Burmese Jungles — thanking God for the Atom Bomb, for none of us relished a long campaign against the Japs.

So you see, I have a special regard for my American comrades — the GI combat troops. I recall astonishment at seeing a US General sporting a pair of pearl-handled revolvers, and then there is the memory of nights in the foxholes in the Ardennes — and the time when I cried to see the bodies of the GIs massacred by the SS — and the time when my jeep drove into Bastogne after the SS had been driven back.

Last summer, I returned for the first time to Normandy — although, of course, visits to my friends of the Resistance in Brussels and Paris have been a yearly reunion.

But standing again on the beaches where I landed thirty years before brought back all those memories. I drove inland to Caen and to St Mere Eglise, to pay homage to the paratroopers who died there. I went to Omaha and Utah beaches, and to Pointe du Hoc where I marvelled at the courage of the American Ranger battalion that scaled those cliffs, and where the scene of the battle remains just as it was in 1944.

For my own side I paid homage to the British airborne who landed to take the Pegasus Bridge, as it is now known, and held it as the first part of France to be liberated during the night of 6 June until relieved by Lord Lovatt's Commandos, who marched straight from the beaches with the battalion piper playing his pipes, to link with the airborne glider boys.

Strangely enough, Normandy has changed very little: the countryside is as green as it was then, and the birds sing above the hedgerows. The beaches are very quiet, with just the lap of waves against the shore, sections of the Mulberry Harbour still remain, and there are the museums of the landings. Despite the quiet of the beaches there is a strange feeling of clamour and battle remaining, that can only be sensed by those who saw a ramp go down and scrambled to the beach. This is the sort of feeling that many people say grips them when they visit places where the bloody battles of the English Civil War took place between Cromwell's troops and Royalists, so long ago.

The most sad experience of all was to visit the great US cemeteries and read the names of American boys.

So you see, Walter, there are those of us in Britain who will never forget the Longest Day. My pride is that I served not only with the British 2nd Army, with 21st Army Group, close to Montgomery, but that I served with the American Army and the American Air Force, and got to know and love my American buddies — even though they first called me a 'Goddam Limey'.

Bill Eason, Royal Signals.

In Weymouth, an excited Doris Mockridge packed her bags and journeyed to Kidderminster. There, at St Ambrose's Roman Catholic church, she made the headlines of the national daily newspapers by marrying Private Ernest Webster, US Army. The soldier, in a Midlands hospital following a leg amputation, reached the altar on crutches.

The lovely Doris wore a gown of white silk, with veil and headdress of white roses, and carried a bouquet of red roses. Her matron of honour was Mrs Doris Brewer, and her bridesmaids were Hazel and Pat Thompson. With the bride was her mother, daughter of Weymouth's well-loved 'Grannie' Wallis, who lived to be a centenarian. Mrs Mockridge, wearing a green silk dress with a spray of red carnations, was determined to be present at the wedding of the youngest of her fourteen children.

As the weeks passed, America was losing its physical grip on Dorset. Old soldiers now, the GIs that were left began to fade away. There were enough of them left to join the locals in the celebrations of VE Day. Then they slipped, often sorrowfully, away. They had been made important by war. Comparatively rich men, they had made the most of their affluence. Now they faced a sea journey which, for many of them, was a voyage back into poverty. What was possibly Dorset's most traumatic era had ended. Perhaps another generation or so, completely replacing the people who lived through the period, will finally rid the county of the Yankee spiritual presence. Until then, the GI Joes will continue to haunt the area.

Epilogue

THOUGH THE original intentions were good, all efforts to commemorate the American presence in Dorset were as ill-fated as the landings on Omaha Beach. It was not for the want of trying on the part of Portland urban district council. They renamed the road travelled by the Yanks as Victory Road, and selected a nearby spot in Victoria Gardens for a Portland stone memorial.

On the wet Wednesday afternoon of 22 August 1945, large crowds gathered in Victoria Square. British and American servicemen were on parade, and the chairman of Portland council, A.N. Tattersall, greeted US Ambassador John G. Winant.

The stone, draped with the Stars and Stripes and Union Jack was unveiled in a moving ceremony. The people stood in silent respect, the servicemen saluted, and the cameras clicked — all undaunted by the rain. A special committee was set up by the Portland council, when the bands had stopped playing and the crowds had gone home, to look after the D-Day memorial stone. The first task of the committee was to widen the park gates to allow access to the stone.

Then, like a rapid erosion of D-Day glory, the tragic John G. Winant shot himself when back in his homeland. As if influenced by this suicide, the local authority became apathetic. The corrosive sea air of Portland chewed hungrily at the memorial plaque. Words, once sincerely grateful, could not be read. No one seemed to care, except the late Councillor Albert Page, who fought a successful campaign to restore the memorial.

Worse was to come. The eager planners of the 1960s cast their eyes on Victoria Square. The road was widened, a gigantic and ugly roundabout built, the park gates removed and the entrance blocked off — leaving the

D-Day memorial only capable of a pathetic rearguard action. It can now only be approached from behind, after a devious and confusing journey through the park. Many visitors to Portland start out on a search for the stone but the majority leave the island disappointed at not having found it.

Weymouth constructed a worthy memorial to D-Day on the Promenade. But, grand as it is, it early lost a battle with the plastic gaudiness of money-spinners dangled from shops to bait the holidaymaker. They walk in the security of sunshine where the GIs marched in the shadow of death. No doubt a survey of tourists in Weymouth, to discover how many notice the memorial, would provide no sad evidence of this forgotten army.

"If only I'd known their addresses," murmurs a thoughtful Mrs Ainge. "then I could have written and told a wife that her husband's last thoughts were of her, or a mother, that her son had longed to kiss her before he had died. None of this would alter the fact that the men were dead, but, at the time, it would have surely brought comfort to many a broken heart if I could have written."

Characteristic thoughts, from a woman whose kindness to the wartime GIs was acknowledged in United States newspapers after the war. In the ensuing years she corresponded regularly with her favourite lodger, Dan Ewton, and his wife, Rose. When Dan died, the friendship between Isobel Ainge and Rose Ewton stayed strong. Mrs Ainge visited the Ewton home in the USA, and this long-surviving link across the Atlantic eventually brought about a sequel that no writer of fiction would dare to include in a novel.

They have been back to the Cove Inn at Portland. Feet that once unerringly guided their owner to his favourite tavern in the blackout of wartime, have stumbled along the wrong roads, the wrong streets, the wrong lanes. Then, at last, middle-aged and sweating, the Yank, who as a youngster sprang into the bar each night, staggers into the Cove Inn complaining: "Gee! Did I have a job finding this place."

Ex-Pc Bill Chapple is retired now, and relaxes at his Portland home with memories of his long career in the police. "The D-Day period is very prominent in my recollections," says Bill. "It was a lively time, and Portland had certainly not seen anything like it before or since. There is, of course, much to be said for the community spirit and comradeship that existed in those days. But we mustn't overlook the price that was paid for the enjoyment of those two things. In many ways they were good times, but belong in the past and I wouldn't want them back, with all the attendant horror and misery." "I never forget," says another serious-faced man, "but I'd say I was one of a tiny minority. At the time I was a boy on a baker's delivery van. We were delivering bread in the Castletown area

The unveiling ceremony for the D-Day memorial at Portland on 22 August 1944. It was a dismal, wet afternoon and had a miserable sequel. The United States Ambassador, who performed the ceremony, returned to America and shot himself.

just after D-Day, when they had started bringing the wounded back. There were stretchers on the roads and pavements, and every bit of space seemed to be taken up by torn, twisted and bloody bodies. You'd have to be something less than human to forget it. I most certainly couldn't."

Two worlds existed for Mary Ewton ever since she could remember. There was the tangible excitement of growing up in Hometown, Illinois, USA, and the fairy tale world of England, tantalisingly weaved by the reminiscences of her father, Dan Ewton. Mary always thrilled when letters and photographs arrived from Mrs Ainge.

Learning came easy to the intelligent girl. After graduating at a local Roman Catholic school, she attended the University of Colorado, in Colorado Springs. An innate desire to travel included an urge to visit Europe. Perhaps subconsciously, this urge was strongly motivated by a need to visit Weymouth, where her late father had spent a significant year of his life. So she arranged this, and Mrs Ainge, then approaching eighty years of age, found the excitement of meeting Dan's daughter was shadowed by dread of an old lady hoping to entertain a young girl.

Isobel Ainge saw her salvation in her grandson, Michael. He had been just a boy when the Americans were in Weymouth, and though he did not relish the idea of wasting his holiday on some girl from America, Michael agreed out of loyalty. Mary, too, had misgivings about the arrangement.

On her first morning of meeting Michael for a day out, she faced him with a suggestion that he went his way, and she hers, and they would meet that evening for a return to Mrs Ainge. But they decided to give the day together a try.

They both found the holiday went well, and were sorrowful when it ended. Some several holidays later, after Michael had travelled to America to visit Mary, she flew back across the ocean her father had sailed over 32 years before — with the same destination, Weymouth, and married Michael at St Joseph's Roman Catholic church in the town. Guest of honour at the wedding was 84-years-old Mrs Ainge, who looked at the happy couple and said: "I knew this would happen."

Christine Jones, now Mrs Chuck Ward, remarked to herself how good life was. She had married the man she loved and was booked to return to his homeland with him. The other important person in her life, her widowed mother, was going with her. Today, Chuck, Christine, and Mrs Jones live in Ohio. The Wards have a son, who is a policeman, and a daughter, with grandchildren making up four generations of Jones in the new land.

Like most GI brides, Doris Mockridge, now Mrs Webster, found it to be a frustrating and confusing time just after the war. With a son now, waiting to join her husband in the States, she was back living with her mother at 12 Trinity Road. Eventually she made her voyage across the Atlantic, to join her husband in New Berlin, New York. Her family grew to five children, but her health was on the decline. In fact, Doris's weak chest prompted a big move for the whole family — from New York to Daytona Beach, Florida. Nothing, however, could save her. At the age of 42, the girl whose loveliness had turned heads in her native Weymouth, died many miles away from home.

It was an almost frantic time for Sylvia Thomas, of Portland, then Mrs Williams. Living with her mother at Portland, and her two-years-old daughter, Susan, Sylvia managed to get aboard the final "GI bride boat" bound for America. Had she missed that voyage she would have had to pay her fare across.

More worry and frustration was waiting when she landed in America. Her ship had been used as a gigantic drug container, and the US authorities stripped the illegally used ship down, finding drugs in the oddest places. When every hiding place had been discovered on the vessel, the authorities turned their attention to the passengers. Sylvia, eager to rejoin the husband she had not seen for two years, fretted as she was detained. Her infant daughter had a tightly-bandaged crippled foot, and even these bandages were removed in the search for drugs.

At this time, her husband was meeting every train arriving in his home town. Fraught with worry, he got in touch with the Red Cross. They located Sylvia and, not without a lot of opposition, Ralph travelled to collect his wife. Homesickness was something Sylvia found to be very real. Particularly at Christmas, having a picnic out of doors in the warmth of Florida was no substitute for a cosy English yuletide.

Soon Ralph had rejoined the navy and Sylvia was travelling the world with him, spending four years in Spain. Out of the navy, Ralph was managing a park. In 1968, he was due to work at Christmas, but a colleague offered to do the Christmas stint if Ralph would work over the new year. Christmas with the family was what he wanted, so Ralph agreed.

On new year's day, there was trouble with the monorail at the park. It fell while Ralph was working on it, catapulting him out then landing to crush him to death. Another trans-Atlantic romance, happy and enduring, had ended. "I kissed him goodbye in the morning, and never saw him alive again," says a still bewildered Sylvia.

How does the Portland woman who gave a "last supper" for five Americans on the eve of D-Day look back on the period? Old now, she hopelessly longs for the carefree friendliness of those days, but her voice is still strangled with tears as she recalls: "The boys I knew were bulldozer drivers. They weren't over there for long, just to clear any obstacles and pull armoured stuff ashore. They were soon back, those who survived, and then on their way out to the Pacific to assist in landings on the islands there. But whenever I look back on those days with fondness, I see again the face of one of the boys who did come back. When he'd left my house he had been young and handsome. Just a few days on the beaches of Normandy brought a terrible change in him. He came back with his dark hair absolutely white, and his face was that of a lined and haggard old man."

Sad as their end was, those lying in the endlessly stretching rows of graves in the Normandy American cemetery might not always have been the really unlucky ones. Mrs Thomas has been dead some years, but she had continued to write to her young GI friend's mother right up to the time of her death. A sensitive, motherly woman, Mrs Thomas was badly hurt after the war, when the American's mother replied to her eager query about Joe's homecoming. Mrs Thomas knew that he had lived through the landings and subsequent battles, and wanted to share in his mother's joy.

"Sometimes it is called battle fatigue, sometimes shell shock," wrote Joe's mother. "All I know is that Joe's mind has been completely unhinged by his experiences in Europe. He is in an institution now and the doctors have told me there is no hope — he will spend his life there — driven mad by war."

A fitting ending for this book can be found in the naval cemetery at

Portland. New houses now edge an intrusion into the almost eerie peace of the place. If you walk among the bright-white, austere headstones of the war graves you can find the tombstone of the ATS Junior Commander B.M. Dickie, who died in the final German air attack on Weymouth, at the age of 33, on 28 May 1944, just days before D-Day.

Turn to read the inscription on the tombstone beside her. It is that of Clemens Rudolf, a 22-years-old German flier who died on an air attack on 11 May 1944. Yesterday's hatreds mean nothing to these two who lie side by side. Find a fitting epitaph to bridge those two tombstones and you will also discover the futility of it all.

Index

Index